THE RELATE GUIDE
TO STAYING TOGETHER

THE
RELATE GUIDE
TO STAYING TOGETHER

From crisis to deeper commitment

Susan Quilliam

VERMILION
London

First published 1995

5 7 9 10 8 6 4

Text copyright © Transformation Management and Relate, 1995

First published in the United Kingdom in 1995 by Ebury Press
Random House, 20 Vauxhall Bridge Road, London SW1V 2SA

Random House Australia (Pty) Limited
20 Alfred Street, Milsons Point, Sydney, New South Wales, 2061, Australia

Random House New Zealand Limited
18 Poland Road, Glenfield, Auckland 10, New Zealand

Random House South Africa (Pty) Limited
PO Box 337, Bergvlei, South Africa

Random House UK Limited Reg. No. 954009

A catalogue record for this book is available from the British Library

ISBN: 0 09 179007 7

Editor: Margot Richardson
Design: Bob Vickers
Printed and bound in Great Britain by Mackays

Papers used by Ebury Press are natural recyclable products made from wood grown in sustainable forests.

CONTENTS

Acknowledgements

I wish to thank everyone who has made this book possible. First, Marj Thoburn, Head of Psychosexual Therapy, Relate, who linked idea, author and organisation and initiated the whole project; Peter McCabe, former Director of Fundraising, Relate, who negotiated us skilfully to contract stage; Ingrid Thomas, Head of Corporate Development, Relate, who helpfully took the book through its first post-contract months; Derek Hill, Head of Counselling, Relate, who provided a map to guide me through the theoretical maze and then checked that I had followed the map; Suzy Powling, Head of Publications, Relate, who with endless and professional supportiveness finally saw the project to fruition.

Next, my gratitude to all the Relate sex therapists and counsellors who gave of their invaluable time and expertise to talk to me about their work, and to help me understand the process of how couples can revitalise their relationships: Pam Bailey, Barry Bezodis, Maura Bourdon, Rosalie Bourne, Kay Brand, John Brazier, Karen Bullough, Gill Carr, Marguerita Downing, Judith Foreman, Maureen Gatner, Catherine Goode, Jo Goodwin, Val Gough, Jenny Green, Vicky de Groot, Kathryn Hammond, Elizabeth Hargreaves, Rosie Hitchins, Sue Hollins, Chris Holmes, Edna Impey, Janet Jones, Jenny Kelly, Juliette Khan, Denise Knowles, Peter Lawson, Gill Lockhart, Wendy Lovell, Sarah Maddocks, Patricia Morton, Sue Norris, Maggie Noskean, Julia Parsons, Wendy Postlethwaite, Elsie Riley, Sue Shaw, Francesca Skelton, Paddy Stewart, Joanna Vials, Janet Ward, Hermione Ward, Kay Watson, Colin White and Mary Whitehead.

Thanks also to the following for their valuable help and support: Barbara Levy; Lisa Eveleigh of A P Watt; Sarah Sutton and Riona McNamara of Vermilion.

As ever, to June Bulley for her administrative excellence; and to Ian Grove-Stephensen, my husband, who as always makes all things possible.

Finally, a special thank you to Sarah Litvinoff for her generosity in allowing me to learn from her experiences when writing the first three books in this series of Relate guides.

All the case histories in this book are based on those of real people. Names and details have been changed so that the couples are unrecognisable.

FOREWORD
How to use this book

This book is for people whose relationship is in difficulty. You may feel unsure of how serious things are, but you do know that there are problems in your partnership. If you are in this position, this book can help you by offering you a reflection of the kind of counselling that is offered by Relate.

The book's text, case histories, tasks and talking points can take you through the Relate process of first understanding your partner; then communicating that understanding; re-negotiating an improved relationship; and developing the skills to make that improvement last. The book can take you through this process before you enter counselling, preparing you for the experience. It can also do this alongside counselling, helping you to understand what is happening and supporting you as you both work together. It can act as a follow-up to counselling, to remind you of what you have learned, and help you keep up the good work. If you decide that counselling is not for you, then you can still learn a great deal from this book, things which will help you rebuild your relationship and replace the old pain with new hope and happiness.

What the book won't do is to replace counselling, if that is what you really need. If your relationship is at the point where you just can't feel positive about each other at all, then counselling is what you need. In this case, only an 'outsider' can provide the safety and support that is necessary in order to re-build your relationship, the external point of reference that you may need in order to be able to step back and see your partnership as it really is. If you don't ever feel good about each other; if you aren't talking to your partner; or if when you do talk, you do nothing but row, you may do better to set this book aside and look up the phone number of your local Relate centre. (Equally, this book isn't sufficient in a situation where your relationship difficulties go hand in hand with a drug, alcohol or violence problem. Although the guidelines offered here will help, you also need specialist support.)

Alternatively, if you both have some good feeling for each other; if you can still think about and talk to each other without constant blame; if you are both determined to find a solution to the problem, this book can offer you some help, whether or not counselling is part of that solution.

Can you use this book if your partner won't? The fact is that if both of you read the book, it shows that you are both committed to the relationship and that you can work together to build it. You will also be learning the same things, at roughly the same time, doing the exercises together and sharing what you have learned. The benefit you get will be more than doubled. If only one of you uses the book, you can both still gain from it. Having said that, the very fact that only one of you is learning what this book has to teach means that you may be approaching the solution to your problems in very different ways. As well, there may be a temptation, if you are the one reading the book when your partner isn't, to use that fact as a weapon; to prove that you are working to make things better, while he or she is doing nothing at all.

A final point to consider, before starting to work on your relationship, is that as a couple you are never alone. You will always be surrounded by other people: your children, family, friends and colleagues. Even though these people are not part of your relationship in a very direct sense, they are part of it indirectly. They all have their own opinions, about you, your partner and your relationship. They will all, however well meaning, have their effect on your problems and how you are trying to resolve them. Whether they want to or not, they will always influence what is happening by their actions, their words or even their resolute silence, and whether they intend to or not, they may actually make things worse. So, while it's usually impossible and often unwise to cut yourselves off from your family or social network while you are working to improve your relationship, nevertheless it is always useful to be wary of that network's influence. Try to tackle your problems together, as a united couple, rather than talking about them with everyone except your partner. Beware confiding or criticising behind your partner's back, when the most helpful thing is to learn to be direct with each other. And never expect family or friends to give you unbiased advice; when you need that, turn to someone who has been professionally trained for it: in other words, a counsellor.

So how should you use this book? You will notice that it offers you several ways of improving your relationship. The four sections of text guide you through a process to rebuild what you have lost.

Part 1, Realisation, examines what happens when you realise that there are problems, helps you see just what those problems are, and guides you through a process of deciding what to do about them.

Part 2, Understanding, explores the distant past and how it influences your relationship, then looks at your mutual past and how it has created your present problems. This section begins the work of appreciating what has gone wrong and what you need to do to put it right.

Part 3, Change, shows how, once you have understood what is happening for you, you can change things: by communicating more fully; handling your emotions more skilfully; meeting each other's needs more effectively; making love more pleasurably; and enjoying the time you spend together more completely.

Part 4, Maintenance, helps you to check how well you are doing, to trouble-shoot the problems, and to prevent further difficulties. It particularly explains the impact that other people can have on you as you work to maintain the progress in your relationship.

The case histories in the book help you to understand just how Relate counselling works. In particular, they help you to see what happens for the people who improve their relationships by going to a counsellor; you can compare your own experiences of exploring your relationship with the experiences of the clients described in the book, and apply the lessons they learned to your own situation. Clients come from a wide variety of backgrounds. For the sake of client anonymity, many of the personal details of couples' ages, professions and backgrounds have been changed, but be reassured that Relate does offer support to people from every ethnic, religious and cultural group.

Equally, it is one of the strengths of Relate that its counsellors also represent a range of approaches and individual strengths. As one of them put it, 'We are a very mixed bunch'! Hence, not only is your counsellor unlikely to be the same as the ones described here, but your experience would never be exactly the same as that of the clients you read about, and your sessions would never follow the exact course of any of the sessions presented here. Every counsellor has his or her own style, so don't accuse yours of 'not being the same' as the ones in the book.

There are many key ways in which Relate counsellors support their clients to work through their problems. At the core is the process of helping partners explore the past and the meaning this has for each of them. Counsellors may also use their own interactions with clients as a kind of reflection of what is going on, for each individual and within the couple; a living example to highlight things that clients may not be aware of. Counsellors may also help by suggesting exercises for clients to do: ways that they can actively improve their relationships.

The book often describes these exercises, or suggests similar ones you can use. These are marked in the text as Tasks, Talking Points and Quizzes.

Tasks are things to think about or to do. As you may want to do these tasks with your partner or separately, many have two parts: one to use if you are working alone, the other to use if you feel able to swap notes with each other.

Talking points are specifically aimed at encouraging you to talk with your partner about issues that the book raises.

Quizzes ask questions that allow you to overview your relationship. You may want to complete them on paper so that you and your partner can do them separately.

Relate clients do their exercises within the safe context of counselling. If a task stirs up strong emotion or disagreement, the counsellor is there to trouble-shoot. This book – simply because it is a book and not a human being – can't offer that sort of safety net. So here are some guidelines.

● It's wise not to try any exercises if you are feeling unhappy, particularly if you have just had an upsetting interaction with your partner. That's the time to get support, not to attempt the kind of serious thinking that the exercises demand.

● If a particular exercise seems to stir up strong, painful feelings for you, then it's best not to continue with it. It's obviously the kind of exercise that you need to do in the safety of a counselling session rather than on your own.

● It isn't wise to insist that your partner does any of these tasks with you if he or she doesn't want to. A partner's resentment will stop the exercises from being useful.

● Some exercises, particularly towards the end of the book, are for couples who are making progress, are feeling good about each other, and are building on that good feeling rather than still being in difficulty. A note within each exercise points this out; it is best not to attempt these tasks if there is still conflict between you and your partner.

A final warning. This book is not a guaranteed manual for relationship success. First, one or both of you may come to the definite conclusion that you need to part, and if you do, a book is not what you need to help you stay together. Second, reading this book is not enough on its own; you need to work to improve your relationship in order to get the results.

Even so, *The Relate Guide to Staying Together* is based on many decades of wisdom taken from Relate's work with couples who have suffered just as much as you are suffering now. If you can learn from this wisdom – through receiving counselling from Relate, through reading this book, or through a combination of the two – then you will have a much better chance of moving your relationship on, from crisis to deeper commitment.

PART 1
REALISATION

1

FIRST DOUBTS

Realising that you have doubts about your relationship can be a sudden and spontaneous thing. It may be that something your partner has done for years, something which has irritated you for years, simply tips you over the edge on one particular occasion. Even a few minutes before, you felt good about the relationship. Then once too often, he snaps, or once too often she sulks, and 'I looked at him and realised that I just didn't like him' or 'I thought, I'm not putting up with this from her any longer.'

Alternatively, the realisation can come gradually, over years. For example, the first time you both disagree about money, you laugh about it. Gradually, however, it dawns on you that not only do you feel that his ideas are misguided, and that he thinks the same of yours, but that this rift is never going to get any smaller. Your conversations about the topic become more tight-lipped, then bitter, then stop altogether. Your bitterness spreads into other areas of your relationship, until eventually it's hardly worth while talking at all. You realise guiltily that you now think of your partner not as someone you love, not even as someone who thinks differently from you, but as someone with a basic weakness of character that you now feel you can't live with.

You may learn with horror that other people have noticed problems. Your best friend comments – almost but not quite jokingly – that she 'doesn't know how you put up with him'. Your nine-year-old son says, in passing, that 'you and Mum never have a laugh together like Sam's parents do'. And your stomach turns at the realisation that you've been too close to see what's really happening, that actually, things are not good between you both and they haven't been for a very long time.

The realisation may, of course, come out of a clear blue sky,

triggered by something that seems completely unlinked to your relationship. The two of you are fine. You have what you want out of life
together: companionship, good sex, a common future. Then suddenly, he gets made redundant; she changes her job; your mother is ill
and may not recover; your son is excluded from school. Suddenly,
you aren't coping. One or both of you start behaving in ways that
previously you wouldn't have thought possible. Whatever bombshell
life has dropped on you, your loving relationship seems to have
exploded along with it.

Sometimes, shatteringly, that bombshell is dropped by your
partner. They say or do something that, quite simply, cuts across
everything you've ever agreed between you, ever believed in, ever
promised. They announce one day that they're unhappy with what's
happening, and have been for a while. Maybe this unhappiness has
led your partner to have an affair, or to plan to move out. You try to
convince yourself that there isn't really a problem. But you find yourself trembling with rage and shaking with fear as you realise that
nothing will ever be the same again.

This is what happened for Jill, who rang her local Relate centre
early one morning. She had spent the night huddled in a chair crying;
at one point she had phoned the Samaritans. The previous evening,
the night of his birthday, her husband Peter had announced that he
was leaving. He had had enough of their relationship, and was moving out that weekend. As far as he was concerned, it was over.

By the time Jill came for her first counselling session in fact,
Peter had decided to come with her. Though he was still unsure that
their relationship could ever work, given time to think things over,
he now at least wanted to try.

Jill was an attractive redhead in her early thirties, and Peter a
tall, rather thoughtful man a few years older. They had been together
for nine years, married for seven, and had two small children. For the
last eighteen months, Peter had been unwilling to have sex with Jill.
At first, she'd been sympathetic, thinking that he was tired, and he
let her believe this. But eventually, he explained that he didn't want
to make love with her. Tempers had flown, and for the first time in
their marriage, they hadn't kissed each other good night.

According to Peter, things had gone downhill from then on. He
had felt pressured by Jill to make love; she'd back off for a while, but

then would nag again. On one occasion she had even made a joke about his lack of performance in front of their friends. Quite soon, he had felt he didn't even want to hug her in case she expected more, and after that they became tense with each other almost all the time. On his birthday, they had had a terrible row, which had made Peter realise that things were over. He wanted a supportive loving family life; what he was getting was unhappiness all the time.

For Jill, the experience had been completely different. She had been very hurt by the fact that Peter wouldn't have sex with her, nor even give her pleasure any other way. He had completely cut off from her sexually. She had spent a lot of time worrying that it was all her fault, but every time she had mentioned it to Peter, he had said he didn't want to talk. Then, on his birthday, they had had a lovely supper, had something to drink, settled in front of the fire and begun to kiss. The evening had been wonderful, and for the first time in eighteen months, Jill had started to really hope things were getting better. Then, once again, Peter had pulled away and said that he had to be up early in the morning. Jill had completely lost her temper, throwing things, shouting and screaming. Peter had simply said that in the morning he was going to pack and leave. Then he had locked himself in the spare bedroom.

By the time they came to counselling, both Jill and Peter were able to admit that there was something seriously wrong. Their problems had to be faced, or sooner or later they would split up. Their counsellor explained to them that by exploring their relationship, they might well uncover things that worried them. In the end, they might find that separation was inevitable; but there was also a strong chance that, if they did work to improve their relationship, they would eventually develop a deeper commitment. Both Jill and Peter agreed that it was worth the risk.

Over the weeks of counselling that followed, they explored not only their own personalities, but also how their relationship had developed, with its own weaknesses and vulnerabilities. They began to realise why they were reacting to each other the way they did.

When they first met, Jill had been very much the stronger character. She was a successful secretary; Peter, a computer engineer, had been completely overawed by her when she had visited the company where he worked. He had tried to impress by showing off about his knowledge of computers, and had succeeded: their professional relationship had grown into love.

However, Peter had always been a thinker rather than a doer, and in the long term, this irritated Jill because projects he started never got finished. So over the years, she had developed a habit of 'organising' Peter, making lists of things that he had to do, reminding him every day of what his jobs were, over-riding him when he made other suggestions. Peter had felt very controlled. In the end, his original admiration for Jill had become resentment against someone who tried to organise him all the time.

As the counselling continued, and Jill and Peter began to realise these things about themselves, their counsellor also encouraged them to learn again how to talk to each other. Certainly, they had lost the knack: for a long time, their conversations had just been an opportunity to hurt each other. The counsellor set them exercises in communication, where they took turns to talk, listened carefully to each other, learned not to interrupt but to really accept what the other person said. Over the weeks, Peter began to feel less criticised; Jill started to believe that he did pay attention to what she said after all.

Peter and Jill also had to work to meet each other's needs within their relationship. They were much more relaxed by this time. The counsellor asked them to list out what they really wanted from each other. They described several day-to-day things. They arranged, for example, that Peter would spend two hours at the weekend helping Jill look at a new programme for her word processor. In return, Peter simply wanted Jill to go for a walk with him. At first, Jill said that she wasn't sure that would help the relationship, but the counsellor explained that wasn't the point; the exercise was about Jill giving Peter what he asked for, as far as she could.

The following week, both were pleased with the result. Peter had kept his promise to help Jill think things through, and she had started to remember just how much she liked his ideas. Jill had enjoyed the walk, and Peter had felt that he was able to suggest something that wasn't part of Jill's plans, and have her take him seriously.

Underneath all this, they were both realising just what Peter's unwillingness to make love was all about. Saying no to Jill sexually was the only way that he felt he could still be in control in the relationship. This was, at least, one area where he was in charge.

This interpretation of what had happened was difficult for both of them to accept. Jill took a while to agree that she threatened Peter so much that he had lost his desire. Peter found it hard to come to terms with the fact that his way of behaving was frustrating Jill so much. Both of them slowly learned to admire each other's real strengths – creativity on Peter's part, organisation on Jill's – rather than concentrating on their weaknesses. They also learned to change the ways they were interacting with each other: Jill so that she stopped nagging and blaming, Peter so that he genuinely tried to take an equal part in the work that had to be done.

The counsellor wondered whether, after so long without making love, Jill and Peter would perhaps need some specific exercises on sexuality to help them 'get back into it' again, but one week, they came to their counselling session reporting that they had made love that weekend. They had taken things slowly and very lovingly; they both knew that they had a long way to go. But they also felt sure that they had understood enough, and had changed enough, to be certain that they would stay together.

What is encouraging about Jill and Peter's story is that they began with a relationship that was in crisis, and turned it into a relationship that was more deeply committed than ever. They actually improved their relationship by facing up to its problems. Jill and Peter's story is hopeful in that it is completely typical of many couples who come to Relate. Most arrive at their first session confused, unhappy and convinced that their partnership is at an end. Some separate, and some stay together but are still dissatisfied, but many couples understand their problems and change their relationships. They leave counselling, weeks or months later, with a partnership that is not only better than the one they came with, but is also more fulfilling than the one they began with many years ago.

All this may seem far too optimistic. If you are reading this book because you suspect that your relationship is in difficulty, you may not yet be able to imagine there being any improvement possible. You may, in fact, be unable to imagine yourself having a relationship at all by this time next year. But, as Jill and Peter's story shows, the reality is more hopeful than that.

By exploring whether there are difficulties, by acknowledging that there might be and facing up to them, and by starting to take action through reading this book, you have actually taken your first few positive steps.

! ————————————————— *Task* —————————————————

Dress rehearsal

Does your partner know that you are having doubts about the relationship? If you haven't yet told your partner what you are feeling, then you need to start deciding how to do so.

If you don't, you may well let the news slip in a way you may regret.

Think about your partner, what you know about his or her vulnerabilities and strengths. Now imagine telling your partner of your doubts. Think of three occasions when you could do this, in three different settings, with three different ways of raising the subject. Can you, for example, imagine telling your partner quickly, slowly, lovingly, angrily? How do you imagine your partner reacting in each scene?

Breaking bad news is never easy, but what have you learned from your mental 'rehearsal'? Which is the way – that will help rather than harm – to tell your partner about your relationship doubts? Which way will be positive for your relationship rather than creating more problems?   !

! ————————————————— *Task* —————————————————

Help line

If you have accepted that your relationship is in difficulty, then either individually, or as a couple, you may want to plan how to cope. A relationship problem can have just the same effect on your body and mind as a physical emergency does, and you may need the same kind of practical support.

Using the check-list below to guide you, try jotting down what your needs are. After that, work out how you can meet those needs. You may want to ask family or friends for child-care help, or your boss for time off work. (As mentioned in the Foreword, it may be wise, at this stage, not to say that there are real difficulties. Once they know that there is a problem, people can 'move in' on you and not give you the space to sort things out between you.)

Checklist of needs

	One of you needs...	*both of you needs...*	*where to supply this need*
Time together?			
Time alone?			
Time with other people?			
Support to run the house?			
Childcare support?			
A place to go to think or talk?			
Good food?			
A short holiday?			
A listening ear?			

NB If you need immediate support at odd hours of the day or night, ring your local branch of the Samaritans. This is a strategy suggested by several Relate counsellors, including one who said that she had done so when her own marriage hit problems. A call to the Samaritans offers the opportunity to put thoughts and feelings into words and to have them accepted as real. With that support, many find that they gain a clearer view about what they must do next.

2
TAKING STOCK

Once you have started to doubt your relationship, you may feel a number of things. You may try to deny your doubt; may panic that your doubts are correct; may feel guilty that you have ever doubted.

When you tell your partner what you feel, another set of emotions may take over as his or her reactions mix with yours. Your partner may refuse to believe what you are saying and insist that there are no difficulties; may get angry with you or even violent; may plead with you; may go to the other extreme and suggest an immediate parting, as if to force you to say that you were mistaken. Your partner may panic: one Relate client said that she was unable to really talk about her relationship doubts for over a year because every time she even approached the subject, her husband had an asthma attack. Or, your partner may feel relieved, because for a long time he or she has been thinking the same as you have; at least now it is all out in the open.

At some point, whether before or after you break the news to your partner, you will almost certainly want to take stock. You'll need to find out whether your first doubt was appropriate, or whether you were just overtired, over-stressed or exaggerating the problem. Many relationships that are in difficulty still contain a great deal of love, warmth, cuddles, sympathy and sexuality. If yours still does, you may wonder whether you have any need to worry. And so, sooner or later, briefly or over several months, alone or with your partner, you will take a long hard look at your relationship. Are you really unhappy, and if so, for what proportion of the time? How long have the problems been going on? Can you change? Do you have to live with things the way they are? Do you have to part?

You may not want to consider these questions. You may be afraid that doing so could mean your relationship will end when you don't want it to. Or you may, if you are unhappy enough, be afraid that considering these questions would make you stay when you really want to leave. The bad news here is that if either of you remain certain that you want a separation, then that will probably happen; but the process of reviewing your situation won't, by itself, cause a split. You never have to part, however unhappy you both are, if you want to stay together; and you never have to continue your relationship if you are sure you want it to be over.

Relate clients are taken through a process of taking stock of their relationship by working with their counsellor in a whole variety of ways: discussing issues, recalling the past, sometimes drawing or writing the ways in which they see their relationship. This stock-take is an essential part of the counselling: clients use the realisations they have come to during their stock-taking to guide them as to what to do next.

If you need specific guidelines to help you take stock, then the next few pages contain a brief 'Relationship Survey'. This is designed to support you in thinking alone or talking with your partner, to help you realise what is happening, to help you begin to think

!━━━━━━━━━━━━━ *Task* ━━━━━━━━━━━

Worst fears

The best way to get rid of fear is by facing up to it. Saint George didn't beat the dragon by riding up to it with his hands over his eyes! Write out these sentences on a piece of paper and complete them.

My three worst fears about taking stock of my relationship are

1 _____

2 _____

3 _____

For each of your fears, think about ways you could cope if the worst happened. What could you do? Where could you get support? Who would help?

!

about what you want to do next. Take your time. Do the survey over several days if necessary, and once you have completed it, take a few more days to think before taking any action. Of course, you can use the rest of this book without doing the survey. Quite simply, once you have thought through your situation, move to the next section of this book, Reactions (page 29) and continue reading from there.

THE RELATIONSHIP SURVEY

You can do this exercise alone or with your partner. In either case, complete the sections on your own at first. If relevant, swap notes later.

1: What are the problems?

The first thing to think about when taking stock is what's happening in your relationship now, particularly the issues that have made you have doubts in the first place. What does your partner do that annoys you? What do you do that annoys your partner?

Write down the things that are a problem for you. How much of a problem are they? The list on page 23 may help to get you thinking, although your particular problems may be very different from the ones mentioned there.

If you are able to swap notes with your partner, you may find that you agree about what the problems are, though you may disagree about the causes of each problem, and particularly whose fault each problem is. Don't get drawn into argument here; at this stage, the thing to explore is what the problems are, not the causes of them.

Once you've listed your problems, take stock. How many problems are there? How serious is each one for you? Think about whether, if these problems continue, you would want to stay in your relationship. Do all these problems have to be resolved, or could you settle for a reduction in just one or two?

(Remember, as you think through these points, that many couples come to Relate thinking that their whole relationship is ruined, but often they discover that what seemed like a dozen problems actually boils down to a single, solvable issue.)

?_____**Quiz**_____

Common problems

Here is a list of some of the most common problems that people have in relationships. Use this list to help you think through what you and your partner are doing.

Having too close a friendship with someone
Spending too much or too little time together
Wanting more or less personal space
Disagreeing about bringing up the children
Disagreeing about friends or family
Feeling that a partner doesn't take responsibility
Having an affair
Disagreeing about money
Not showing enough affection
Making unreasonable demands in bed
Not being romantic with each other any more
Getting moody or depressed
Being critical or angry with each other
Not feeling much sexual desire any more
Having a specific sexual problem such as erectile difficulty or a lack
   of orgasm
Getting bored with each other, or with the relationship
Not respecting each other
Not having fun when you are with each other.

_____**?**

2: How are you handling the problems?

Next, think about how you are handling the problems you've identified. All couples have difficulties; but the difference between those who succeed and those who don't is how they cope with those difficulties.

Note down the ways you react to problems. The list on page 24 may help to get you thinking.

If you are able to swap notes with your partner, you may differ dramatically in your answers. What one of you sees as 'I help her by reminding her' or 'I keep a tactful silence' the other may note down as 'He nags', 'She sulks'. Don't start defending yourself here; the interesting thing is to look at the ways of handling problems that you've both listed.

Now take stock. How much of what you do is negative or painful? How much is positive and hopeful? How much helps you cope and solve problems, and how much actually causes further difficulties? (Remember that all the helpful ways of handling problems are relationship skills. There is nothing magic about these skills and you can easily learn them; in fact, a large part of the work that Relate counsellors do is to teach them to clients.)

?———————Quiz———————

Handling the problems

Here is a list of some of the helpful and unhelpful things that people do in relationships. You can use this list to help you think through how you and your partner handle problems.

Accepts and acts on suggestions
Asks questions to find out more
Checks out what the other person means
Encourages the other person to talk
Explains clearly what he or she means
Is really honest about what's going on
Is willing to negotiate
Keeps calm
Keeps interacting until sure that the other person has understood
Keeps perspective and a sense of humour
Likes to touch or be close when talking
Listens with interest
Looks at the person who is talking
Makes helpful suggestions
Seeks out contact with the other person
Remembers what's been said
Takes the time to talk
Talks about feelings
Thinks about what's been said

Avoids contact with the other person
Blames
Can't bear to be close or have physical contact when talking
Can't look directly at the other person when talking
Changes the subject
Demands too much
Doesn't act on what's being said
Doesn't listen to what's said
Doesn't make time for touching down or talking
Gets violent
Has no sense of fun in the relationship
Hides or fudges what's going on
Keeps 'dragging up' previous disagreements
Nags
Shouts
Sulks
Talks far too much, hogs the attention
Assumes knowledge of what the other person means
Won't talk about things.

_____**?**

3: How do you feel?

The way you feel about your relationship is a key way of estimating just what is going on. Because you are having problems at the moment, you will probably be feeling a whole mixture of emotions; but which emotions are they?

List out all the feelings you have had about your relationship recently. You may want to add a note about how strong these emotions are and how often you feel them. The list of emotions on pages 26–7 may help to get you thinking.

If you are able to swap notes with your partner, it is possible that you feel the same as each other. More often, however, in relationships that are undergoing difficulties, you will find that you feel differently; one of you may feel very negative or pessimistic, the other more positive or optimistic

Now take stock. What are your feelings? How strong are they? Are all your feelings painful ones, or is there a sprinkling of happier emotions? Are you just not feeling at all, because things have been so hurtful that you have had to shut off? Which emotions do you feel most often, which hardly at all? What does this tell you about your relationship? (Remember, as you think things through, that you can expect to have painful feelings at a time like this. If you do continue your relationship and find ways to improve it, these emotions will be easier to understand and control.)

?_____Quiz_____

The feelings

Here are some ways you might feel about your relationship. You can use the quiz to help you think about which emotions you have, how strongly you feel them, how often you feel them. Tick the relevant column.

	Strongly	*Moderately*	*Not at all*	*All the time*	*Most of the time*	*Occasionally*
Accepting						
Afraid						
Alive						
Angry						
Annoyed						
Anxious						
Aroused						
Bitter						
Bored						
Confident						
Content						
Defensive						
Depressed						
Disappointed						
Disgusted						

	Strongly	Moderately	Not at all	All the time	Most of the time	Occasionally
Disillusioned						
Excited						
Fascinated						
Forgiving						
Fulfilled						
Happy						
Heard						
Hopeful						
Hopeless						
In charge						
Jealous						
No feeling						
Over-ruled						
Overwhelmed						
Pessimistic						
Powerless						
Protected						
Reassured						
Relaxed						
Resentful						
Sad						
Safe						
Satisfied						
Stable						
Tense						
Threatened						
Trusting						

?

4: What can the past tell you?

However bad or good things are, most couples who are taking stock of their relationship look not only at what's happening now, but also at what has happened before. If the relationship has been generally good up to now, then they are far more willing to try again than if it has been generally bad. So it's worthwhile looking back at your time together.

If you are able to swap notes with your partner, you may well find that each of you remembers things slightly differently. Don't worry about this; concentrate on finding out whether your overall picture of the relationship since it began is positive or negative.

Attraction

Most couples are drawn towards each other because they seem to make each other happy, seem to meet each other's needs.

Take stock. Think back to when you first met your partner. Was there real attraction? Did you both seem to meet each other's needs? If you actually didn't feel satisfied with your partner then, do you now feel that there is any chance of being happy with him or her in the future? If you were satisfied then, do you still feel that the relationship is worth fighting for? (Remember that if you think there never was a time when things were good, working on the relationship can help you discover new reasons for being together, even if you just imagined the old ones.)

Disappointment

Most couples hit problems once they have been together for some time, usually when they discover an irritating failure to meet each other's expectations.

Take stock. Think back to times when your partner irritated you because he or she didn't do what you expected or wanted. How serious and long term have these disappointments been? Have they been there from the start, or only recently? Have they got worse over time, or have many of your disappointments simply faded away? Despite your panic now, have your disappointments actually got fewer since you met, or are you actually coping with them better now than you did? (Remember that many couples who doubt their relationship feel that the disappointment has got worse over the years, and that much of the work that Relate counsellors do involves trying to reduce this disappointment. If you feel that your problems have been sudden and recent, then it could be that some particular event in your life has triggered them. If so, by exploring that event, you may be able to start rebuilding trust and love.)

Disillusionment

Many couples whose relationships are troubled identify an event or series of events that finally tipped them over the edge into admitting their problems.

Take stock. Remember what finally convinced you that there was a real difficulty. Was it a sudden thing that you now realise could be easily put right? Or has it been a slowly-developing disillusionment that is so long term that it seems to have been going on for ever? Is it something that you think that you could get over? Is it something that you know has finally killed all love?

Remember as you take stock that it's only once you realise that there are problems that you can start improving things.

REACTIONS

Taking stock, whether or not you did it through the Relationship Survey, and whether or not you did it with your partner, isn't like doing a 'tick box' quiz in a magazine. There are no right answers and no wrong answers. Any one person or couple who stands back and takes a long hard look at their relationship will be left with a mixture of reactions. So at this point, you may be starting to become aware of what your reactions are.

You may feel that your relationship is beyond repair and that the love has gone. Perhaps you are horrified at how awful things have become, how bad they have been for some time, and how terrible the future looks. Remember, though, that if you can see past the painful emotion, this isn't necessarily the end. There are things you can do to rescue even the most painful relationship, if you are prepared to work at it.

Alternatively, you may feel very disillusioned at what has happened, but still very involved with your partner. Most of your feelings may be painful – you may be in a constant state of war with each other, and you may have given up hope of any real change in the relationship – but for any number of reasons, you may still want to stay together, despite all the pain.

You may feel that, even though there are problems, your love alone will make everything all right. Perhaps you've both been panicked by how bad things were, and at how near you have been to splitting up. You may have had several reconciliations already where you have promised each other that this time everything will work. So now, though you know things are bad, you keep hoping.

You may, having thought it through, come to the conclusion that in fact you were panicking. Things are good and you feel fine; you are lucky to be in your relationship. If you feel like this, do take care. Make sure you are not just refusing to see the hole in the ground because you are frightened of falling into it. Every partnership, even the best, has its bad times, but if you have suffered enough to begin to doubt your relationship, then there may well be something wrong.

Perhaps the most hopeful reaction to the process of taking stock is the one that seems the least romantic. If you can admit that there are problems, and are determined to take real action to solve those problems, you may well have a good chance of a happy future. You might not feel secure at the moment; you may be less than sure that your relationship will survive. But if you're neither giving up on the relationship, nor hanging on for grim death, nor being over-optimistic, you can often see clearly what needs doing – and then do it.

MAKING THE DECISION

When you have taken a long hard look at your relationship, whatever conclusions you have come to, your must decide what to do next. You could end your relationship now because you feel that it is over; you could stay with your partner, even though you can't change the relationship, because for various reasons you don't want to live apart; or, you could aim to stay together, change your relationship, and find a deeper commitment.

If you both agree on a course of action, it is very likely that you will go ahead with it, whatever it is. But if you disagree – whether to go or stay, whether to let things ride or to try to improve things – there can be battles. And here, the one who wants to leave or who doesn't want to change will often hold the casting vote. It takes two to tango, but only one to walk off the dance floor.

Having said that, when a relationship has problems, a 'balance of doubt' – where one partner feels that everything is at an end and the other wants to carry on – is very typical. Many couples who come to Relate are like this. The partner who wants the relationship to work feels panicky and abandoned, angry at the pessimistic partner, hopeful that there'll be a happy ending. The partner who feels that things are over may well feel pressured to stay, guilty that he or she wants to go, or sad that what started out so well now seems to be over. If you and your partner are suffering a balance of doubt, then why not explore what is happening, not making any hasty decisions, but taking your time to find out what you both really want? If you are willing to accept the support of a counsellor, you can often come to a decision that feels right, not just for one of you but for both of you.

This part of the book explores the various things you could decide to do. You will almost certainly need time and space, much thought and many discussions before you can make your decision.

ENDING YOUR RELATIONSHIP

There are many reasons why you might want to end your relationship now. If the day-to-day horror of living with your partner is too much for you to bear, then everything else will seem unimportant and you will probably choose to leave. Alternatively, you may feel that your unhappy relationship is having a bad effect on your children, and that it would be best for them if you parted. Or, by now, both of you may be so uninterested in each other, or feel so bad about each other, you are clear that nothing can happen to stop you splitting up.

As well, you may feel your life will be better if you leave. This is more likely for women, who usually have more friends to support them; research has shown that women are more able to survive happily and healthily on their own. It is also more likely that your life will be better if you are already having another relationship elsewhere and are sure that if you leave, you will be able to develop a fulfilling partnership there. In fact, you probably began your new relationship, without realising it, in order to ease you out of the old one. It may be that what you need to do now is to break the news and go.

Even so, people who choose to end their relationship rarely find it pain-free in the short term. There is always a pull between wanting to break away and wanting to keep your relationship together, even if you separate as friends and even if you have another partnership to go to. Relate clients who have ended relationships say they suffer a terrible sense of loss; that they hate themselves and their partners; that they feel guilty and humiliated because they think they've failed; that they are afraid of never being able to form another relationship again. Partners may be defensive and angry; families may pressure you to get back together; children may misbehave, become depressed or even get physically ill because of the strain.

In the long term, though, things are more optimistic. You may have regrets, but there is a good chance you will work through them and find a good life, alone or with a new partner. If you are certain that you want the relationship to end, then eventually there is a very high chance that you will look back and say that you did the right thing.

An example of this is the story of Charmain and Lee, who came to counselling because they couldn't seem to be together in the same room without feeling tense and rowing. In many ways they looked remarkably alike: both tall, sports-mad, both in their mid-twenties. They had been living together for about a year.

They told the counsellor how they had met. When Charmain started to work for the same firm as Lee it had been, for both of them, 'love at first sight'. At the end of the first week, they drove back to Lee's flat together 'and I never really went home,' said Charmain. They slept together almost immediately, moved in together very quickly, and then were hardly ever apart.

By their third counselling session, they seemed to have made progress. Both of them realised that they had started a relationship very suddenly, without knowing much about each other. Charmain had only recently moved into the area when she started her job, and she admitted that she was happy to have the security of a relationship to help her settle. Lee had just ended a relationship with a married woman, and was looking for 'someone of my own'. They both accepted that, because they hardly knew each other when they met, it wasn't surprising that they were now, a year along the road, feeling like strangers.

The counsellor suggested that Charmain and Lee spend a regular time each week communicating about 'who they actually were'. She asked them to concentrate on really listening to each other, really sharing what they thought and felt. Together, they drew up a list of areas they wanted to explore: their different childhoods, their likes and dislikes, their future hopes and dreams.

Two sessions later, they came to counselling in a very bad way. Lee said that he was convinced that Charmain was falling out of love with him. Charmain insisted that she wasn't, but said that she felt uneasy with the communication exercises and wanted to take things more slowly. The counsellor suggested that each of them see her separately, to explore what they really wanted.

In her first individual session, Charmain admitted that over the past few weeks, she had realised that Lee wasn't the person for her. At first, she'd been flattered and reassured by the fact that he needed her so much; but now, it just felt more and more trapping. She realised that she wasn't ready for a committed relationship, and certainly not with Lee.

Charmain agreed to go away and think about what she wanted to do now. She said she would report back to the counsellor the following week, but Lee turned up to his session, two days later, with the news that Charmain had already packed and left. Lee was very upset by this, and arranged with the counsellor to come for regular sessions 'to see if Charmain and I can get back together'.

Over the weeks, Lee explored his own past, and the reasons that he had been so attracted to Charmain. His parents had had a whirlwind romance when his father was on leave from the army. Despite long periods apart, his mother and father had built a solid relationship which Lee always saw as a perfectly happy one. Part of the attraction of Charmain was that theirs had been a sudden romance, just as his parents' relationship had been; he had expected it to last, and even when it was failing, had clung on to it regardless. Lee slowly realised that he didn't have to have a relationship that was like his parents' in order to be a success, but that he had been trying to do just that.

When Lee started to come to terms with the fact that his partnership with Charmain was over, he also started to look at her more realistically, not as the perfect partner he'd imagined her to be. He discovered to his surprise that there was a lot about Charmain's outlook on life and her personality that he actually disliked, but he'd been afraid to admit this dislike in case he spoilt his fantasy romance. By the time counselling came to an end, Lee admitted, without bitterness, that they had both had a 'lucky escape'.

In this case, Charmain realised very clearly that for her the relationship was over; she had no doubts. If one or both of you are completely sure that your relationship is finished, then it may well be. One Relate client, who had come to counselling to help him through a very amicable divorce, spoke of the 'look across the restaurant table, and the sad smile that said it was over between us'.

It can be that both of you actually want the relationship to end, but you don't dare admit it. Perhaps you are each holding back, partly because you're afraid of being alone and partly because you don't want to hurt the other. It's quite common in counselling for a couple to work for weeks on rebuilding their relationship, but then at exactly the same moment, almost 'look across at me' as one counsellor put it, 'and say "Please miss, can we split up now?"' If you and your partner are in this situation, then complete honesty is the best way, and as soon as possible.

But as mentioned before, if in doubt, keep your options open. A small problem can often seem to spoil everything, but if you fix it, everything is solved. A big problem can seem too huge to tackle, but like eating an elephant, everything is possible if you do it in small chunks!

!————————————— *Task* —————————————

Take it to the limit

How would it be if you did split up from your partner? Whether or not you feel you want to, it is a useful exercise to think, in as great detail as you can, what life would be like. Think as specifically as possible about where you would be in two years' time, once separated. Where would you be living? What would you be doing? How would you be dressing? What relationship would you have with your former partner, your children, your family, any new friends or partners in your life?

The point of this task is not to plan ahead, nor is it to make you split up. The aim is to put you in touch with how you feel when you imagine separating. Does the thought fill you with horror, confusion, relief or delight? Whatever you feel, by doing this task you can learn a lot about whether you ought to end your relationship or not.

!

STAYING TOGETHER WITHOUT CHANGE

If you stay with your partner without changing your relationship or trying to improve it, you are probably doing so for many reasons. Perhaps you have made a formal or religious vow that you believe in, and which is binding for you. Perhaps you feel that your children will suffer if you separate. Perhaps you are nervous about life without your partner and want to stay together for the company. If any of these ring true for you, then however unhappy you are, you may well choose not to part.

Nevertheless, the forecast of your life together is very uncertain. If your first reaction to your Relationship Survey (page 22) showed that you both feel very bad about each other, then you have some hard times ahead. Couples who stay together when they have lost all goodwill and who don't change their relationship end up 'tearing each other to bits' as one Relate counsellor put it. Bitter comments, endless rows or week-long silences make their lives a misery. There is no place as lonely as a partnership based on hatred.

If your reaction to your Relationship Survey was to feel that your love alone will make everything all right, then you will probably be just as disappointed. To quote one Relate counsellor, 'If you carry on doing what you've always done, then you will get what you have always got'. If you don't change the way you behave to each other, things will go from bad to worse, however much of the emotion of love you actually feel. You may celebrate 'getting back together' on Friday night, and then be on the point of splitting up again by Sunday evening. In the end, one of you may simply take drastic action, such as having an affair, in order to bring things to a head and force you both to face the real facts.

Perhaps the only workable option of staying together without improving your relationship is, curiously, when you believe that 'the relationship is over' and have stopped feeling much about it at all. Though you are essentially in a dead partnership, if you are committed to staying together regardless, for your own reasons, then it is sometimes possible, if not probable, that you can settle to a 'marriage of convenience'. This may, if only for a very limited period of time, work because you choose it to.

This was the choice that Geraldine made when her relationship with her husband Steve seemed to have come to an end. When they had met, thirty-two years ago, Geraldine had been a slim, long-haired teenager who enjoyed wearing the latest fashions and listening to the music of an up-and-coming group called the Beatles. Steve had worked in a record shop; she had spent most Saturdays with her friends buying records, and they had got talking.

Steve was a quiet man, the youngest of a family of five. He had always been the protected baby of the family, and so he felt at ease with the way that Geraldine mothered and looked after him. She in turn liked building a home, making him happy by making life comfortable. With him, she felt really needed. They had been married only a year when their first child was born; three others followed over the next ten years.

When they came to counselling, thirty-two years later, Geraldine said that she thought she didn't love Steve any more. She desperately wanted to love him, because he had always been so important to her; she cried as she admitted that all her feelings for him had just drained away. Steve sat quietly watching, and simply repeated that he was sure he still loved Geraldine, and that he wanted the marriage to last.

The counsellor helped Geraldine and Steve explore what had happened. At first, their partnership had worked well: she had looked after him, he had enjoyed being babied as he had been when he had lived at home. But Steve was a very passive man, and had rarely taken the lead or really done anything to support Geraldine. When the children had come along, she had expected things to change, for Steve to help her to bring up the children. When he hadn't, she had at first complained, then got angry – then realised that it was pointless. She said that she had learned over the years that 'this is the way things are . . . he does his best'.

Recently, Geraldine's mother had died. This had hit her very hard, and one of the things she had realised was that she too was going to die. She was frightened of what lay ahead; a few more decades of life where she did everything and he did nothing. More than that, over the years, Steve's total lack of initiative had made him very stay-at-home, and he always needed Geraldine to stay with him. Only last summer, she had wanted to go away for the weekend with a friend, but Steve had been so upset at the thought of being left alone that, in the end, she had cancelled the holiday.

The counsellor felt that if they were to stay together, Geraldine and Steve had to make many changes, such as learning to give and take on a more equal level. He suggested that they try to share the responsibilities of daily life, starting with very simple things, such as making tea in the morning. He felt that if they could do this, Geraldine would start to regain her confidence in a more positive future; maybe then she could support Steve to do more with his life. Steve agreed, but at the following session said that he had overslept on one of the mornings he had agreed to make the tea, and on the next occasion had felt too ill to get up early. Two more similar exercises over the next few weeks met with similar failure, until Geraldine finally looked at Steve during a session and said: 'You're never going to change. I realise that now.' She left, followed by Steve, who looked stunned and upset.

To the counsellor's surprise, Geraldine came to the next session alone. She announced that she had decided to stay in the relationship and end the counselling. She was calmer and more sure of herself.

She now knew, completely and certainly, that Steve would never change; she wasn't hoping for some fantasy happy ending. At the same time, neither was she bitter. She had realised that, in a strange way, she too was dependent, and just as afraid of being alone as Steve was. They had spent several nights simply holding each other and, as Geraldine put it: 'We've decided to stay together. I know it's a cop-out, but it's the best I can do. Now I know that he'll never be any different, it's up to me to live with the consequences and try to make us both as happy as we can be.'

The counsellor commented that to him this was an unexpected outcome, but it was one that Geraldine and Steve had chosen. Steve didn't want Geraldine to leave, and she had taken the decision not to. Perhaps in the future, Geraldine would get more confidence and change her mind but, for the moment, she was realistically accepting that her relationship was dead. Given that she was facing facts, perhaps she could, on some level, make it successful.

If, like Geraldine and Steve, you stay with your partner without changing your unhappy relationship, then certain things have to happen for it to work. First, you both have to want to stay together and honestly agree to that; if one of you doesn't, then he or she will capsize the boat sooner rather than later. Second, you need to set aside any critical emotions you may feel about your partner, for things they have done in the past or for things that irritate you now. You need to act towards your partner as you would to a respected acquaintance, avoiding conflict, making sure that you are courteous and amicable.

You also have to be prepared for both of you to meet some of your needs outside the relationship. Couples in a 'marriage of convenience' will often, for example, get financial and practical support from their partnership, but look elsewhere for their friendships. They may share bank accounts, but wouldn't dream of going to the pub together. So you both need to negotiate carefully, in advance, for what you expect, and make it clear to each other what is 'out of bounds'.

Finally, expect that, once your reason for being together is no longer relevant, the relationship may end anyway. Couples who stay together because of the children, for example, often separate within a few years once the youngest is off their hands. When the reason for staying disappears, then they simply up and go.

____TOWARDS DEEPER COMMITMENT____

The third option for your partnership, and the one that the rest of this book explores, is to stay together and change. In short, you choose to work at the relationship in order to achieve a deeper commitment.

If you do this, you're not necessarily choosing the easy option. Working to improve your relationship is a brave thing to do. There are no cast-iron guarantees that things will actually improve, nor that you won't, in the end, split up anyway. And second, you will need to give up a great deal in order to get an improvement and to keep that improvement going. In order to make it work, you will have to be prepared to compromise, to give up things that are important to you because they hurt your partner; to say no to relationships that may threaten your partnership. In this day and age, it sometimes isn't fashionable to ask people to say 'no' but that is, in fact, what forming a relationship is about: saying 'no' to 'me' and 'yes' to 'us'.

If you're willing to take the risk, you can very often win through. Time after time, as I spoke to Relate counsellors in the course of writing this book, they told me of relationships that had completely re-formed themselves, of couples who had come to counselling ready to part, and left counselling more deeply in love than ever. If you are prepared to admit your problems and work on them, then you may end up not with the relationship you had when you first met – 'Relationship Mark One' as a counsellor called it – but an entirely new relationship, one that in fact is better than before: 'Relationship Mark 2'.

An example of someone who, by opting to stay and work at his partnership, completely turned things around, was David. He came to counselling convinced that his relationship was completely at an end; he had in fact already started an affair with another woman.

David was a very good-looking man whose work was installing office furniture. He had married Penny six years ago; she was the sister of a colleague, and from the start he had liked the fact that she was warm and affectionate, and simply 'felt right'. They had gone out for just a few months before he had asked her to marry him and she had accepted.

Very soon David had started to stray: his first affair had actually been a month to the day from the day they had married. His job involved meeting lots of people, mostly women, in various offices where he worked. It was all too much of a temptation, he said. Over the years, he had tried to hide his affairs; sometimes Penny had found out, sometimes not. Over his latest affair, she had seemed to lose her temper completely, and cut off from him. Now, they hardly ever talked.

He said he thought that maybe he shouldn't have got married; he was too attracted to other women. He was now sure that his marriage was over. He felt, looking back, that this had been inevitable; he had actually given very little to the relationship and Penny had just kept giving and giving. Now she was angry and had cut off from him. He was sure that she would both accept and welcome it if he left. He didn't want to, but he supposed he ought to go.

David's counsellor suggested otherwise. He was here in counselling to explore his thoughts and feelings. Why not take the time to do that? It was a big move David was thinking of making; why not make it carefully?

With the counsellor, David first explored what exactly in his upbringing had caused the situation. He realised, through the various ways of looking at the past that the counsellor suggested, that he came from a family who didn't show their feelings; as a boy he had felt unloved in general. That was one reason why Penny's warm nature had made him so happy. But that very sense of being unloved was also driving him on to form relationships with other women, so that he always felt reassured that someone wanted him. At the same time, his family's wariness about feelings had made him very anxious about showing his own emotions. He simply wasn't able to show Penny how much he loved her, and had spent years wanting her affection but giving nothing back.

By this time, David was really beginning to understand just how and why his problems had begun. The encouragement he was receiving from the counsellor to explore his feelings was beginning to make him realise that his family's attitude to emotion was not typical, and that there was nothing wrong with feeling strongly and expressing that.

Having begun to realise his problems, how could David bring them to an end? He felt sure that he had lost Penny for good. He decided to ask her to join him in some counselling sessions, to explore what could happen next.

When Penny arrived at the session, the counsellor was surprised. In place of the angry, ready-to-divorce woman that David had described, Penny seemed sad and anxious. She looked at David with deep concern and affection. David explained to Penny what he had discovered about himself and how he felt. He also said that he felt it was unavoidable now that he had to move out and leave their relationship.

To David's amazement, Penny broke down. In the safety of the counselling room, she poured out what she felt. She had always been in love with him, she said, and she still was. She had known he was having affairs, but had kept trying to build a close relationship with him. The more he had strayed, the more she had tried to understand, but he had kept shutting her off. In the end, she had lost her temper and withdrawn emotionally from him for her own protection, but that didn't mean that she didn't still want the relationship to work.

David was completely taken aback. He explained that in his family, where emotions were not usually expressed, anger such as Penny had shown when they argued meant the end of everything. His father, for example, had had a row with his boss one day, walked out of his job, and never gone back. David had assumed that Penny's anger was terminal in the same way, that she had given up on him and that that was the end.

The counsellor remembers what followed as one of the most moving sessions she had ever experienced. Both David and Penny were in tears, holding on to each other, and when they left, they went back home and talked throughout the night. When they returned to counselling the following week, they both knew that there was still a lot of difficult work for them to do. but they knew that they wanted to do it.

Their original partnership had been based on so many misunderstandings of each other, and of what partnership meant, that they first had to go back and find out what each of them needed and what each could give. David had to work through a great deal of past hurt about his family before he was able to open up to Penny. She had to really understand why he had had affairs, and both forgive him and forget. Penny also had to learn to show her needs more; part of the difficulty between them had been that she was doing all the giving, but none of the taking.

They worked for many months, re-learning how to talk to each other; how to negotiate for what they wanted; how to plan for a future which both of them had at one time thought was impossible. At the end of the counselling, however, the counsellor commented that she had never seen a couple so much in love: 'it was as if they had completely rediscovered each other and their relationship, and were starting again from new'.

What David and Penny had to do was what every couple must do if they want to move to deeper commitment. First, you need to make a conscious decision to try to understand what is really happening in your relationship and how it has come to this point. Second, you need to change your partnership actively rather than just hoping that it will get better by itself. If you are prepared to do both these things, then although there are never any guarantees, there is a good chance that you will be able to make things better than before, even if at present it seems as if everything is over.

If you have decided that rebuilding your relationship is the right decision for you, you now need to take action. As a basis for moving forward, you may want to think about doing the following things, whether or not your partner has currently agreed to work with you on your relationship improvement.

Drawing up an action plan
You will need to decide whether to go to counselling, whether to continue reading this book, or whether to do both. If counselling is an option for you, then the exercise on page 45 will help you to think through the issues involved. The Further Help section at the back of the book gives you the details of how to contact your local Relate centre.

If you plan to use this book in your work, although reading all of it is vital if you are to make progress, the following guidelines may help you to see which chapters will help you in particular ways.

Chapters 4, 5 and 6 will help you to understand the deeper reasons why your problems may be happening,

Chapters 7, 8 and 9 will help you focus on difficulties that may have begun from the very start of your relationship. Read these carefully if your answers to the fourth section of the Relationship Survey (page 28) highlighted this as a problem.

Chapter 10 helps you to explore any particular events in your life that may have triggered your doubts. Read this chapter in particular if your answers to the fourth section of the Relationship Survey (page 28) suggested that this is happening in your case.

Chapter 11 will help you understand more about how you can change your relationship before you move on to taking specific action.

Chapter 12 will help you communicate more effectively. Use this chapter in particular if, from the second section of the Relationship Survey (page 23), you realised that the way you are actually handling your problems is causing you difficulty.

Chapter 13 will help you to make your actions towards each other more positive. Read this chapter if, in the first section of the Relationship Survey (page 22), you pinpointed a number of specific issues that are a problem between you.

Chapter 14 will help you cope with your own and your partner's emotions. Turn to this chapter if the third section of the Relationship Survey (page 25) made you realise that your feelings are painful.

Chapter 15 highlights ways of improving your love-making; read this chapter if in the first section of the Relationship Survey, you pinpointed sexual difficulties as an issue between you.

Chapter 14 will help you enjoy your relationship more fully as you begin to solve its problems.

As you become more certain that you are over the worst, Part 4 of the book will help you maintain your progress both in the short and in the long term.

Getting practical support

Rebuilding your relationship is a time-consuming and energy-draining task which will take several months rather than weeks. So whether or not you have put into place immediate coping strategies, as suggested on pages 18–19, you now need to set up long-term practical support. This may do some or all of the following, as appropriate to you: it may allow you both more time with each other; give you regular opportunities for private conversations and love-making; support you with child care during the hour a week you may be spending at counselling. You may want to begin to think of ways in which you can organise all this.

Setting some basic ground rules

To cover you both for the time you are working on your relationship, you may need to agree some very down-to-earth things that you think should be done or not done. These might include: who to tell that there is a problem; whether to sleep in the same bed together; whether to stay in the same house together. Discuss these things so that you know what is acceptable and what isn't.

Calling a truce

Rows, blaming, nagging or other signs that you are in conflict won't help you rebuild your relationship. If you can, avoid them. Try not to start a conflict, and if your partner tries to start one, avoid it where you can. Be reassured: if you understand more about how your relationship works and build the skills to avoid disagreement, things will get better.

Putting the heavy artillery away

If something is an issue between you – he keeps spending, she keeps shouting at the children – agree, if you possibly can, that this behaviour will stop, for perhaps a week or a month at a time. This allows the partner who feels bad about the issue to have a break from it; but the other partner won't be made to feel that he or she has to 'be good' for ever. It may be particularly important, if one of you has had an affair, to end it or at the very least call a halt: you each need to know that you are both concentrating on the partnership alone and not being distracted.

If you offer to 'give' on an issue, and your partner doesn't, try not to withdraw your offer in revenge. For the moment, keep giving as every little helps. If things work out, then in the end your partner will give in return.

Finally, remember that moving to a deeper commitment is not a once-and-for-all thing. From now on, you will have to work on rebuilding that commitment every day of your life; sometimes twice a day if you are hitting problems. On the other hand, most couples who survive relationship difficulties say that their turning point was actually admitting the problems and then deciding to do something about them. So if now, as you read this book, you have already made that admission and taken that decision, then in fact, you may have already passed the real crisis point. The worst may already be over.

'════════════════ Talking Point ════════

Should we go to counselling?

Relate counsellors work in a structured way, with one or both of you. After a first appointment to explore your situation, you attend for a series of regular hour-long sessions with the same counsellor each time. The main activity in counselling will be to explore your relationship and, with the counsellor's help, try to understand it. You'll also sometimes be asked to do 'tasks' during and in between the sessions. Relate will expect you to pay for counselling, according to your means, but a sliding scale of charges is often available.

Counsellors will:

- offer you something different from what you can do on your own
- ask you to explore the present and the past through talking about it
- teach you practical skills to make your relationship work
- through their relationship with you, help you understand your relationship with your partner
- through their relationship with you, show you other, better ways of relating to your partner
- encourage you to aim for a solution that suits you both.

Counsellors won't:

- tell you to split up
- tell you to stay together
- push you into being more emotional than you want to be
- defend your views or behaviour against those of your partner
- make you feel better immediately.

If you can talk things through with your partner, discuss together the points above. How do you feel about seeking counselling? What would make each of you happy to go?

,

!——————————— *Task* ———————————

Best hope

Think of your best hope for your relationship. It could be 'I want us to be together and happy in ten years' time' or 'I want to create a wonderful home with you'.

Make your best hope positive, one that doesn't sneakily put either of you down; so don't put 'I wish we didn't row' or 'I want you not to be so selfish'.

Take a blank piece of paper, and write your best hope down. Then keep it in a safe place, to come back to in a few months' time.

If you can share things with your partner, then you could also leave your 'best hope' somewhere where he or she will find it, as a nice surprise.   !

!——————————— *Task* ———————————

Decision time

Imagine that a friend has just written to you. He or she is in exactly the same situation as you are, having to make a vital decision about which direction to take in his or her relationship.

What would be the best advice you could offer? What choice would you advise your friend not to make? Why?

Either imagine talking to your friend, or write him or her a letter in return. What do you learn from what you have 'advised' your friend?   !

PART 2
UNDERSTANDING

4

THE CHALLENGE OF UNDERSTANDING

The first step to deeper commitment is understanding. You need to begin to understand why your problems have happened at all. This understanding is vital and makes an immediate difference. In fact, one of the things Relate counsellors said made them happiest was seeing clients begin to understand what had gone wrong and what they could do about it. 'The sense of confusion is replaced by understanding,' commented one counsellor, describing how a couple she worked with had changed their panicked decision to split up to a clear determination to stay together.

Stephanie and Barry entered counselling when their baby son was just six months old. Stephanie was a tiny woman, but emotionally very strong; she spoke proudly of how she and Barry had survived the early years of their marriage, when money had been short.

Now once again, they were under pressure. Barry was a carpenter, and because of the slump in the building trade, had been made redundant just before their baby was born. He had also started drinking quite heavily. Stephanie was upset about this and didn't really understand it. Barry felt that she was being unfair on him. He said that he did drink a bit, always had done, and now that work was short, he felt that he deserved a bit of sympathy. Stephanie saw everything they had worked for sliding away, and over the months since the baby was born, she had become more and more angry.

Now Barry had started coming home from the pub later than before, and bringing drink home with him. The counsellor said 'There was a sense of blind panic about them when I first saw them.

They both knew that things were out of control; neither of them knew what to do about it.' Stephanie kept repeating that Barry would have to leave. Barry, who was very angry and aggressive, kept saying that if that was the way she felt, he would go right away.

The counsellor's first job was to offer Stephanie and Barry some hope. She couldn't promise that things would work out, but she did explain to them that crises like this, that come out of the blue in the middle of a solid marriage, can often be resolved. They both were reassured by this, and even by the end of the first session, were talking about giving their relationship a chance rather than just giving up.

Next, the counsellor talked Stephanie and Barry through their individual backgrounds. Stephanie's mother had also been a forceful woman who had supported her family single-handedly, after her husband had left, shortly before Stephanie's third birthday. Barry's parents, on the other hand, had both been strong characters; they had had a very close marriage and had just celebrated their thirty-fifth anniversary.

The counsellor asked Stephanie and Barry each to draw a diagram showing how they saw their families as they were growing up. (Relate clients are helped to use the means which will best increase understanding of their situation.) Stephanie drew a large circle to represent her mother, with smaller circles within it, for the children; her father was nowhere in the picture. Barry's diagram, on the other hand, showed two large circles at the top of the page for his father and mother, with a row of smaller circles underneath.

Over the weeks, the counsellor suggested ways of discussing things that helped Stephanie and Barry to understand what had been happening in their families, as shown by the drawings. More importantly, the counsellor encouraged them to link their memories of the past with what was happening now, and interpret those memories. Stephanie realised that she was, in many ways, replaying in her own life the role her mother played: the strong woman who took charge. 'My mother didn't need a weak man around, and neither do I,' she said during one session.

Stephanie also realised that her anger and frustration was driving Barry away. Particularly since the baby was born, she had become more and more irritable with Barry's lack of energy, annoyed that he was out of work. When he did get a part-time job, she had told him to go for a full-time one, giving him the message that what he was doing wasn't good enough. As well, she had locked him out from looking after their baby, almost as if he didn't deserve to be a father.

Barry, in the meantime, found it hard, at first, to understand what he was feeling. For several sessions, he only talked about how unfair it was that he was unemployed, and how this was causing all the problems. But as counselling continued, and he and Stephanie were able to look more deeply into what they really felt, he started to get in touch with something quite unexpected – fear. He was afraid of having a child. He had worried that, as he wasn't as strong as his father had been, he wouldn't be able to handle it. And losing his job, which had happened just before the birth of the baby, had convinced him that he was right. Stephanie's worry added to his fears, and her anger at him drove him away. He had tried to stand up to her, but every time he did, she seemed to shout him down. He wasn't even able to have with her the kind of equal and solid relationship that his parents had had with each other.

Alongside the discussions within the counselling session that helped them to appreciate what was going on, Stephanie and Barry were talking regularly at home about their feelings. They increasingly understood each other and started to feel close again. During the week after Barry had acknowledged his fear, he didn't drink at all. The happiness on Stephanie's face when he reported this back to the counsellor said it all, and there was no more talk about their separating.

The change in Stephanie and Barry, through their understanding, had been dramatic. When they left counselling, they knew that there was more to understand, but they had made a start. Of course, the issues that were at the heart of their problems were not obvious ones. They couldn't just have 'decided to act differently' and kept on doing that for the rest of their lives. They had to know what was going on underneath to even begin to be able to rebuild their partnership. This is why, at the heart of Relate counselling, and often taking a large amount of the counselling time, lies the process of exploring what is happening in your situation, how things have developed like this, and what that means.

The most basic thing involved in improving your relationship is understanding yourself. This means realising more fully what makes you tick: identifying your ideas, your beliefs, your expectations. Particularly, it means exploring your past and how that's made you who you are today. Only then will you see how you are adding to the problems in your relationship, and so realise just which of your attitudes and actions you need to alter.

The second step is understanding your partner. Real love, above and beyond first romance, is about stepping into your partner's shoes, and exploring the particular past that makes him or her unique. Above all, it is about realising that your partner's thoughts and feelings are just as important as yours.

Finally, rebuilding involves understanding of how, and why, your relationship works. If you look back, you can see what brought you both together and what has happened since then, and you can begin to realise why things went wrong. Once you do that, you can begin to see how to put it right.

THE PAST

When exploring all these elements – yourself, your partner, your relationship – it's particularly important to understand their past history.

Why is the past so important? The reason is that from the moment we're born, or even before, we start building up our personal idea of the world. Our mind is like a little 'life hoover' that gathers up everything it experiences – sees, hears, feels, tastes, smells – and stores it away for future reference. We store all those things we experience directly: wanting milk, having our nappy changed, kissing Mum, being cuddled. And in later life we store what other people tell us, or even what they themselves experience: our mother's scoldings give us the message that we mustn't play with matches, and our little sister getting burned teaches us the lesson that we shouldn't play with fire.

Then we generalise from what we have learned, and start to imagine that everything happens in just the way we have seen personally. So if at three years old, we howl our eyes out because Dad yet again broke his promise to spend time with us on Sunday, we may grow up believing that everyone in the world is hurt by broken promises – which may well be true. But we may also start to believe that everyone in the world breaks promises and can't be trusted – which simply isn't true – or that everyone 'should' keep every promise they ever make, which is something to hope for, but certainly isn't a cast iron law of the universe.

Yet we believe these things as true; we act on them as if they were true. We base our thoughts, our actions and our needs on them. Unless events tell us otherwise, we use these personal 'life rules' as the basis for all our future relationships, particularly that very special relationship we call love.

You may already be starting to see the problems we can meet if we run our relationships according to our life rules. Life rules can be mistaken or simply incorrect. If they are, they can lead to our being unable to form happy relationships, because we just don't know how. If, for example, we believe that everyone breaks promises, then we'll find it difficult to trust a partner in any situation, which will be very hurtful to him or her. Or if we believe that everyone, all the time, 'should' keep promises, and we can't keep a promise we make to a partner, we may feel overwhelmingly guilty – with a negative spin-off to the way we act in our relationship.

Our life rules all too often just don't help us to run our lives. They may not teach us to trust ourselves or other people; they may make us feel unconfident or lacking; they may give us unhelpful expectations about being male or female, being in love, having sex. They may make us unable to communicate, make us unable to meet our own needs or other people's, or leave us helpless to handle our painful emotions.

Realising in this way that who you are is rooted in the past can be very helpful. If you are able to spot your mistaken life rules and re-think them, you can start to see things in a new way, behave in a new way, run your relationship in a new way. And if you understand that it is these life rules that are leading to your painful feelings about yourself or your partner, and that these rules were formed many years ago, then you can often set aside those feelings. Once you realise that your panic or anger about the relationship isn't particularly about what your partner is doing, but is much more to do with things that happened in the past, it is much easier to stand back and act more calmly. You can realise that you are no longer a child but an adult, and that therefore what was true for you then doesn't need to be true for you now.

THE DIFFERENCES

Understanding what is really happening also allows you to begin to understand some of the reasons why conflicts arise between you and your partner. Each person's life rules are different. Your childhood experiences give you your life rules; your partner's experiences give him or her a different set of life rules. Unfortunately, everyone tends to believe that theirs are the only 'true' or 'right' ones, particularly when they find their life rules are clashing with those of others.

Therefore, particularly if we are suffering difficulties in our relationship, we tend to expect and want our partner to behave as if he or she had our life rules. This isn't possible, simply because a partner won't have had our past experiences. When they can't behave like we do, we don't just feel misunderstood, we feel betrayed. We don't just think they are mistaken; we think they don't love us. We can get very hurt if our partner does something that, by our personal rulebook, is hurtful, even if they, acting by their rulebook, actually meant no harm. If our relationship is falling apart, and our partner promises to be home at six o'clock but hasn't arrived by a quarter past six, we may feel that they are out to hurt us when in actual fact, they just missed the bus. It is treason to us, and 'absent-mindedness' to them. All too often, convinced that our life rules are the only ones to play by, we are too busy being hurt to check out our partner's real intentions.

If you understand how your partner's past has created life rules, then you are often much more able to feel better about him or her. With more understanding of 'why', you can both appreciate each other more fully. There is often a key moment in counselling work where one partner looks at the other and says 'Oh, that's why you do that. I didn't know. How come you didn't tell me?' We make so many assumptions about each other; often, after years of problems, assuming the worst. When we really understand, our anger and bitterness disappears.

This part of the book is aimed at helping you understand your situation more deeply. Of course, text can never replicate the core process by which Relate counselling brings clients to a greater understanding: by leading them to remember their own individual past experiences, to talk about these experiences, compare their particular meanings. Nor can words replicate the particular role the counsellor plays in all this, reflecting meanings back to clients, helping them interpret what is happening, sometimes even using the working relationship between counsellor and clients to shed light on the relationship between the two partners.

Nevertheless, this part of the book will begin the process of helping you to recognise the life rules that you and your partner work by; which people and events have helped to form these rules; which rules make you feel or behave in a particular way; how these rules have created difficulties in your relationship.

Not all the topics in this part of the book will be useful to you: you will have to recognise those that are, and interpret them for yourself. As you do, and you begin to recognise why your current problems are happening, you can start to become aware of how you can act differently, and how you can change things.

!————————— *Task* —————————

I do understand

Try to remember a time when you felt you really understood your partner. Maybe it was during a long, in-depth conversation about something very serious, or maybe it was a moment's insight into something very ordinary.

Remember this time as a proof that it is possible for you to understand what your partner feels and thinks.

!

5

THE LEGACY OF THE PAST – THE MESSAGES

 The first place to start in understanding is the distant past, your early childhood and adolescence, and the years up to the point where your relationship began.

WHOM CAN YOU TRUST?

The earliest message you get in your life is probably the one that affects your relationship most. It is about whether you can trust the world and whether you can trust yourself. For how much you trust lies at the heart of how successfully you can love.

When you are a tiny baby, you're totally dependent on everyone else. The hard fact is that you can't look after yourself; if other people don't give you what you need, then you die. But if you are hungry, cold or wet, then in a normal world, after a short wait, an adult appears, feeds you, warms you, cuddles you and makes you feel good again. You learn the basic lesson that, in time, most of the time, someone will be there to help. You believe that you can trust the world, and the people in it, to give things to you when you need them.

As you grow up, a second basic lesson is added to the first. As you learn to feed, warm, calm and comfort yourself, you also learn that, to one extent or another, you can meet your own needs. You can trust yourself.

Because you trust both yourself and the world, you are able to interact with it happily. Then you start to explore what happens if you stand on your own two feet (in more ways than one); you know that you can get so far on your own, and that if you hit a problem, you can always go back and get help. You become first a confident child, then an independent adult. In the end, you become happy to receive from the world and relaxed about giving to it. This giving and receiving lies at the heart of what we call love.

Unfortunately, these lessons – these life rules – often go wrong. We don't completely learn that the world is to be trusted, or we never quite believe that we can look after ourselves. In some ways, this is wise. There are some people who can't be trusted, and even as adults, we do need others to support and help us. But most of our relationships with others would develop in a much better way if we weren't wary of them or lacking confidence in ourselves; and our love relationships, which are the ones most important to us, are the ones most affected.

So a child whose needs were seldom met, was kept waiting too long, was often disappointed (or even actively denied or ill-treated) may never learn to trust other people. As an adult, particularly when things go wrong, he may feel unsure of his partner, tend to suspect that he isn't loved or that his partner actually has bad intentions towards him.

While it might seem that a child whose needs were always met, and who always had support and attention, would grow up to be a happy and loving adult, in fact, she may not have fully learned to trust himself. In relationships, especially when she feels under stress, she may put herself down, feel guilty or helpless, lean heavily on her partner for love and affection.

As well, if a child was, when ready to stand on its own two feet, restricted by a worried dad or a clingy mum, the little one may believe that it's not safe to strike out on his own. He may lose trust in his own ability to cope in the world. As an adult, when faced with problems, he'll hold back from taking the lead or making important decisions; or, fight against all that and become fiercely independent, running away from relationships so as not to be 'tied down'.

In fact, because life isn't perfect, all human beings lack trust in themselves or others to some extent, and so all of us behave in some of the ways described above, particularly when we are under stress. For example, your partner comes home in a bad mood. If things are already going wrong in your relationship, you can tend to mistrust this, and interpret it pessimistically. So you may see your partner's mood as meaning that she is angry with you; you may think 'After all I've done for her, the least she could do is be pleasant to me . . . This must mean she doesn't love me.' Given a basic trust in other people in general, you might have been able to stand back and see her as a person who has had a tiring journey home, or to check out what happened for her at work today and then offer a cuddle for comfort. Instead, you assume the worst; and then, assuming the worst, you react negatively, and wind your partner up even more.

Or you may tend to lose trust in yourself. Just as when you don't trust your partner you tend to think negative thoughts about him or her, so when you don't trust yourself, you tend to see what you are doing as wrong. Faced with your partner's bad mood, you think, 'I'm weak . . . I can't do anything here. Well, I'm off out.' Rather than reminding yourself of times you have helped, or finding the confidence and energy to be kind to your partner, you tumble into a hole of doubt and fear. Needless to say, this doesn't help to rescue what, by this time, is probably doomed to be an unhappy evening together.

In the long term, this basic mistrust of the world and yourself, formed when very young and 'reactivated' by your relationship, underlies much of the pain you feel when you try to relate to your partner. If you can stand back from it and realise what is creating the problem, then you may well be able to react much more calmly, much more helpfully, much more lovingly.

BEING GOOD ENOUGH

As you grow from baby to child, you add extra life rules to the basic ones. You learn who you are, and also who you ought to be. For everyone around you – parents, brothers, sisters, friends, teachers – tell you not only what sort of person they see you as, but also the sort of person they regard as 'the best'. So you may learn that it is good that you are a boy, but that you should be more active, not quite so good looking, less emotional. You may learn that it's good that you are a girl, but that your parents would really have liked you to be more beautiful, more intelligent, less rebellious.

If the gap between what a person thinks is the ideal and how they see themselves is very small, they will grow up as an adult who likes themself. Now, a person who genuinely likes themself (as opposed to one who pretends they're completely wonderful because they secretly believe they are terrible) typically finds it easy to like others – and easy to love their partner. But the larger the gap between the ideal a person has and the way she sees herself, the less at ease they will be around other people. They may feel that they are not the way they should be, and try to make up for that. They may try to defend themselves against the problems that they think will happen because they're not good enough. Particularly when they hit difficulties, they'll start to think even more critically of themselves, which will make things worse. And of course, because love relationships are particularly important, they will feel these feelings even more strongly, and try to defend themselves even more actively, in their partnerships than in any other relationship they have.

Here are some of the types of 'defending' that people do in partnerships. You may want to notice how many of them happen in yours.

Because we believe we're not the way we should be, we . . .

● fear that our partners will see through us and one day leave. We get very possessive, guarding against others who might tempt our partner away.

● feel angry at ourselves because we're not perfect. We turn this anger on to our partners, with words or even actions, particularly if he or she seems to criticise us.

● feel so bad about ourselves that it hurts. We pull back to avoid the pain, and cut ourselves off emotionally from our partners.

● expect people to reject or ignore us. So we reject them first.

● expect people to criticise or attack us. So we constantly defend ourselves verbally, or leap to the attack so as to get in first.

● want reassurance from as many people as possible. So we have more than one love relationship at a time.

● expect that we will get it wrong. We reckon that if we choose to make mistakes it at least leaves us in control; we tend to rebel, be awkward and undermine our own success.

● imagine that the best way to make sure no one threatens us is to be in total charge of our world. We attempt to control all our partner's actions and emotions by what we say and do.

! ———————————— *Task* ————————————

Where you are, where you want to be

These pairs of words list some of the judgements you may make about yourself. Place a cross according to where you think you come on each scale: for example, if you feel you are very easy-going, place a cross under the figure 1; if you feel you are very demanding, place a cross under the figure 5.

	1	2	3	4	5
boring – exciting					
easy-going – demanding					
hardworking – lazy					
honest – dishonest					
lovable – unlovable					
pushy – unassertive					
relaxed – tense					
satisfied – dissatisfied					
sociable – withdrawn					
undependable – dependable					
unhelpful – helpful					
untidy – tidy					

Now go back, and, with a different coloured pen, place a cross on each scale according to what you believe the ideal to be. If, for example, you feel that an ideal person is balanced between easy-going and demanding, then put your cross under the figure 3.

Then look at the difference between where you see yourself and what your life rules say is the ideal. The bigger the differences between your two sets of crosses on each line, the more likely it is that you tend to be dissatisfied with yourself, and the more likely it is that you sometimes behave in some of the ways listed on page 57.

If you can swap notes with your partner, check his or her dissatisfaction level. Can you help? Can you encourage your partner to believe in him or herself – particularly in areas where he or she feels a failure?

!

The problem with defensive actions like anger and rejection is that all too often, they don't just defend but also attack. All of them are ways of behaving that will hurt or frustrate a partner. Then he or she starts to defend in return, to protect against what is seen as an attack by being even more angry, or more rejecting. In a neat but vicious circle, each partner's defences encourage the other to lash out more.

Do you recognise your situation here? If so, it may help to remember that both of you are reacting defensively. If your partner seems to be on the attack, it is more than likely a way of behaving that he or she has learned when very young, a protection against 'not being good enough', a defence against criticism from all the people who, over the years, have managed to make your partner feel small. If you can remember this, as problems arise, then each of you may feel less threatened by each other. Over time, it is possible, in this way, to replace anger, emotional coldness or rejection by calmness, emotional warmth and acceptance.

GENDER MESSAGES

You learn that you are a boy or a girl when you're very young, but learning exactly what that means takes a lot longer. As with so many life rules, you get most of your early messages from your family, who may simply tell you what is expected of you: 'be a good girl' or 'act like a man'. Or they may actually show you, by what they do, that men 'in this family' work hard or that women 'in this family' are often depressed. When you get older, your friends will also give you messages about what boys and girls do, based on what they've learned from their families. When you watch television, read books or go to a film, you add on even more messages to your idea of how you ought to behave, as a man or a woman yourself, and in your relationships with men and women.

The problem is that many of these messages aren't actually true. They don't describe what individual people feel, think, do or want to do. They are 'myths': generalised ideas that are handed on, like Chinese whispers, from person to person, getting a little more inaccurate every time they are repeated. Many stereotypes of what each gender should and can do – such as 'a woman's place is in the home' – are now being challenged. That particular phrase is already seen as irrelevant and out-of-date, but the idea behind it still clings on, influencing what people do and the way they behave. In spite of the fact that each man and woman is different, and has different strengths and weaknesses, there are many myths like that one which creep into our relationships and cause problems. Here are some examples.

'The man's the boss'

If as a boy you were brought up to believe this, you may expect to make the major decisions in a heterosexual relationship, such as how money will be spent or where you will live. You may then resent all the responsibility, or feel unhappy if your partner challenges you about what you decide.

If as a girl you were brought up to believe this myth, you may expect a male partner to take the lead in things, and then feel let down if he doesn't.

In fact, there are no laws that say a man must make the decisions or take the lead. A loving relationship builds on the talents of both people, and lets each of them specialise in what they do best.

'A woman who gets angry is a real bitch; she should keep smiling'

If as a girl you were brought up to believe this, you may be unable to feel comfortable with being angry, particularly in partnerships. Instead, you may push your feelings down and get very depressed.

If as a boy you were brought up to believe this, you may get very upset or threatened if a female partner is even slightly irritated or angry with you.

In fact, both men and women may feel angry when they believe that they are being attacked. Though both genders need to handle their anger positively, there's nothing 'worse' about an angry woman than there is about an angry man.

'Boys don't cry'

If as a boy you were brought up to believe this, you may stifle your 'weaker' emotions and only let them out in the form of 'stronger' feelings such as anger. This may mean that you get angry a lot, or that if you do cry you feel guilty.

If as a girl you were brought up to believe this myth, then you may find it difficult if a male partner expresses one of the gentler emotions such as sadness or anxiety, and will feel disappointed in him if he does.

In fact, boys do cry; more and more people nowadays are realising that being able to feel a wide range of emotions is part of being completely human, whether you are a man or a woman.

'It's OK for a man to have lots of partners, but a woman who does is cheap'

If as a girl you were brought up to believe this, you may feel guilty if you've had sex with more than one or two people – and be unable to be honest with your partner about your past.

If as a boy you were brought up to believe this particular myth, you may feel threatened if it turns out that a female partner has slept with lots of people, particularly if she has slept with more than you have.

In fact, both men and women nowadays are likely to have had several partners by the time they find the person they want to stay with. As long as they feel happy about that (and have used safer sex methods to stay healthy), then that is their choice. Experience may well have made them more knowledgeable about sex and so more able to please and enjoy themselves.

'A man should be the provider'

If as a boy you were brought up to believe this, you may feel it is really important to be working for a living; be unhappy if a female partner works; become depressed or violent if you lose your job.

If as a girl you were brought up to believe this myth, you may feel betrayed and resentful if a male partner can't provide for you for some reason.

In fact, most homes now rely on both partners' earnings, and many rely on the woman's wages alone. Nowadays, when the economy is so unstable, a man who is not the main provider isn't inadequate, but just may have had some bad luck.

'A woman's place is in the home'

If as a girl you were brought up to believe this, you may feel under pressure if your partner wants you to go out to work, or less than perfect if you aren't very domestic.

If as a boy you were brought up to believe this myth, you may expect a female partner to stay at home and feel let down or threatened if she doesn't.

In fact, men's and women's roles are changing very quickly at present. Many women prefer to put most of their energy into their job, just as many men do, and to find ways to avoid doing the cleaning and cooking. There are no laws that say that this isn't a perfectly good way to run a household!

Problems caused by gender messages

Gender myths can cause you problems because they give you ideas about men and women which simply aren't true, or which you simply can't live up to. Eric and Felicity came to Relate because Eric had had a series of affairs with much younger women and one of them had demanded that he marry her. When he refused, his lover stormed up to his house and confronted his wife, Felicity.

Eric defended what he was doing by saying that Felicity 'never made any attempt to look good'. When they started to examine what they really believed about life, it turned out that, as Felicity had reached her fifties, she had simply assumed that she wasn't attractive any more. 'I looked round at all these young beauties and thought, I just can't compete.' Eric, too, was buying into exactly the same myth: believing that a woman who didn't stay young and beautiful wasn't worth desiring. Together, they'd pushed their relationship into a situation where they weren't having sex; then they'd both silently agreed that in fact, Eric had a right to look elsewhere for his pleasure.

Gender messages also cause problems if they clash. As explained on page 52, much of the deepest unhappiness in relationships comes when a life rule that one partner believes clashes with a life rule that another partner believes. A woman whose father was always kind and supportive may grow up believing that all men are like that or should be like that. Then, if she falls in love with a man who sometimes needs support himself, she can hit problems almost immediately. She may regard him as 'moody', 'weak', 'impossible to live with'; he may feel that 'she just doesn't let me be myself'. Both views are simply personal opinions, but each can think that the other is not only incorrect but somehow essentially 'bad'.

If, as a couple, you can accept that you believe something that is simply different, then you can step back from thinking that there is something harmful in the other's ideas. You can set aside the myths and the generalisations, and start to decide for yourselves just what a man and a woman are able to do in your particular relationship, at this particular time.

!————————————*Task*————————————

Challenge your personal stereotypes

What are your ideas about the way men and women behave or should behave? Complete these sentences.

Men usually . . .
Women usually . . .
I expect a man to . . .
I expect a woman to . . .
I'm wary of men because they . . .
I'm wary of women because they . . .
I like men because they . . .
I like women because they . . .

When you have completed the sentences, read what you have written. Do all men and all women behave in the ways you've described? Do you know men or women who behave differently? What problems do you think your ideas, expectations and fears about men and women might have created in your relationship?

If you can talk things through with your partner, swap ideas. Each of you can comment on the other's completed sentences, saying whether you agree or disagree. What difficulties do you think the differences between you might have caused in your relationship?

!

WHAT LOVE MEANS

You learn the life rules of love from your parents. Their relationship literally 'acts out', in front of your eyes, what it means to have a one-to-one partnership. So if your parents (or key adult couples in your childhood) chatted a lot, then you will believe that love means talking to each other; if they rowed a lot, you'll think that love involves disagreement; and if they hardly ever showed their affection, then you may end up believing that love is about keeping your distance.

When you get together with your partner, you will then tend to run your relationship just as your parents ran theirs: talkatively, aggressively, distantly. This will be true even if you didn't much like what you saw in your parent's partnership, if in fact it was full of deep depression, constant infidelity, or physical violence.

Human beings tend to repeat what they are familiar with, whether it makes them happy or not, simply because it is what they are used to, whether that is seeing one parent hug another, or seeing one parent hit another. So time and again, Relate counsellors spoke about clients who reported their partnerships as being unusually miserable until, by exploring the past, they realised that they were just repeating the particular kind of misery that their parents suffered thirty years ago.

Interestingly, the best sort of relationship to copy is not a perfect one. A relationship where both partners communicate well, never have power struggles and rarely fight doesn't show you what difficulties can crop up and how to cope with them. Later in life, you may feel panicked if you hit problems. You may simply give in if you meet conflict. The best sort of relationship to copy is one where, because both partners work to overcome their difficulties, you learn useful skills of the sort that Relate teaches.

Ideas about love may also be causing you both difficulties if you are each from a very different background and are trying to run your relationship in very different ways. You want a relationship where you always chat about things; your partner is used to cosy silence. You love a row to clear the air; your partner is more used to 'letting things go'. The secret is to see where you are different and realise that there is no blame. Neither of you are wrong for having the ideas of love that you do.

You don't only get your messages about love from real life. You watch soaps on television; you read romantic novels or raunchy magazines; you get hooked into the latest newspaper scandal. The problem, however, with these media messages about love is that they give a completely false idea about what it means to have a working relationship. In the media, particularly films and romantic fiction, love is all too often perfect, so we worry if our love isn't one long romantic dream. Love in these contexts is immediately successful, and so we don't realise that we have to develop skill to make love work. Love is often confused with sex, so we believe that if we simply desire someone, we'll naturally be able to build a good relationship. Above all, love is seen as problem-free, so when we have difficulties, we tend to panic and feel a failure, to fall back on emotion rather than put in the effort to make love work.

This is what happened for Ned and Lucy, two Relate clients who came for counselling after only a year and a half of marriage. Both in their early twenties, after a short but very intense courtship they had settled down to married life, really expecting that they would live 'happily ever after'.

By the time they came to Relate, they were at their wits' end. They kept arguing over tiny things: the way a picture should hang, how much milk one of them had put in the other's coffee. It seemed that every time one of them spoke, the other would disagree. In the counselling room, they could hardly look at one another because they were so angry.

Their difficulties became clear when the counsellor asked them to talk about how they thought a loving relationship should be. Ned's ideals were very philosophical; he had chosen Lucy, and would stay with her whatever problems they met. Love was about the closeness he felt when they had sex, and the strong emotion he had experienced when they first met. He just wanted that to come back, naturally, in its own way. He wasn't interested in talking or in exploring the past. If they loved each other, it would feel right here and now. Lucy had a romantic ideal of marriage. If Ned loved her, he would make everything all right, as the heroes in the romantic novels did. She was unwilling to discuss what their real needs were; if they really loved each other, they would just know.

The counsellor suggested that Ned and Lucy try some of the basic communication exercises that Relate recommends, to share the ways they saw things; but the first time, they couldn't agree on which exercise to do, and the second time they returned saying that the tasks were useless. They both felt that what they were being asked to do was false and unspontaneous, and that true love was about feeling good without trying. After this meeting, they started missing counselling sessions, and very soon stopped attending. Their counsellor was very pessimistic about their future: he felt that they still admired each other a lot, and could have made things work if they had been willing to improve their relationship skills. However, their airy-fairy view of love was literally blocking them from having the real thing.

Many couples hit problems, as Ned and Lucy did, because they think that love is a positive emotion that makes people feel good all the time. They believe that if that emotion dies, you either have to get it back or part. In fact, the feeling of 'in love', which is based largely on novelty, will automatically fade as you both get to know each other better. The shift that you have to make when moving towards a deeper commitment is to realise that real love is a practical thing. It is less about feeling, and much more about doing. It involves, day by day, on a very down-to-earth level, finding out just what each other needs and then providing it, with generosity and kindness.

That idea is explored more fully on pages 106–7; the challenge at this point in the book is to begin to understand exactly where your ideas of love have undermined your relationship. Are your ideas so idealistic that you can never fulfil them? Are your ideas tied in so much with your feelings that if you ever feel bad about each other, your love disappears? Are your ideas so based on what you saw of your families' painful relationships that you both spend most of the time hurting each other? If you can start to let go of these false ideas of love, and get a clear image of it as a way to meet each other's needs, then you will have won a huge battle.

! ───────────── *Task* ─────────────

Love is . . .

Write down as many ways to complete this sentence as you can think of. 'Love is . . .'

If you can talk things through with your partner, swap ideas. What differences do you notice? What problems might these differences have been causing you?   !

! ————————————— *Task* —————————————

Reflections

What memories do you have of your parents' relationship? Choose three vivid memories, ones that are typical of the way you saw your parents relate when you were a child.

Now, be honest. How similar is your relationship now to your parents' partnership?

If you can talk things through with your partner, compare memories. Did each set of parents have a very different relationship?

How could both of you stop reflecting the unhappy parts of your parents' relationship in your own?

!

THE RULES OF SEX

Your first messages about sex came, to start with, from the physical affection you received when you were very young. The way Mum holds you, the way Dad cuddles you, even the way you rough and tumble with your big sister or your little brother; all these teach you whether to be comfortable with your body. If your family is relaxed about touching, then you'll develop a sense of your body as good and pleasurable. If people around you hold back, touch you when you don't want it, or even abuse you (see page 78) then you'll grow up anxious and unsure.

Later, when it comes to touching yourself – which most children do, even in their cots – you'll get more messages. Does Mum shriek when she walks in and finds you with your hand between your legs? Does your big brother scare you by saying you'll go blind if you pleasure yourself? Later still, how well you are prepared for puberty may give you further lessons about how good or bad it is to be a mature, sexual person, and this will also affect the way you think about sex. If you do grow up guilty or anxious, the problem is that, when you fall in love and start being sexual with your partner, the guilt and fear may not simply switch themselves off; the pleasure and emotion may not simply switch themselves back on again.

These very early lessons give you the basics of what you feel about sex. On top of them, later in life, you get more indirect lessons. For while you learn about love mostly by seeing what your parents do in their relationship, you can't learn about sex the same way. The taboos on sexuality mean that you usually don't 'see' sex as observers, but second hand, through the eyes of parents and teachers, religious leaders, friends and classmates, books and films. You get told the facts of life; and you get told the life rules of sex: what men and women are each 'supposed' to do in bed.

Often, these generalised rules are just as untrue as the gender myths explored earlier. They don't tell you anything about what people really want or like; all they tell you are inaccurate myths. You may be told that men need sex and women don't; that men enjoy sex and women don't; that women are allowed to say no to sex but that if a man does he's not a real man; that sex is about getting it up and getting it in and everything else is irrelevant; that the only real sex is between a man and a woman and that anything else is weird. On top of all this, you may also learn that sex is not only exciting, delicious and a status symbol, but also that it is dirty, naughty and just plain wrong.

It's not surprising then, that by the time we form our first sexual relationship, most of us are quite confused, believe a number of things that contradict each other, or feel guilty about enjoying ourselves. Early sexual experiences can add to this unhappiness because, particularly at first, they're all too often based on mutual ignorance: we don't quite know what we're doing, and very often, neither does the girl or boy we're trying to get close to.

The result is that when, a little later, we form a long-term and loving intimate partnership, most of us are generally able to enjoy sex, but maybe have a few blind spots along the way. Perhaps we could enjoy things more; perhaps we could hold back emotionally a little less. Understanding why we have these blind spots, building our self-confidence and improving our relationship will all help us enjoy love-making more fully, and often this is all we need to sort out the difficulties. Sadly, however, some of the lessons our lives teach us about sex lead to deeper problems. Chapter 15 explores these further and describes some possible solutions.

6

THE LEGACY OF THE PAST – THE INFLUENCES

Looking at the messages that you get from the past is one way in to understanding just who each of you are and what you have added to the problems within your relationship. Another way in is to look at where messages come from: the people and events that have most affected you, and most created the life rules that you live by.

Relate counsellors look particularly at these influences, encouraging clients to explore them in many different ways. Often, there are some amazingly clear patterns. You may discover a particular event in your life which, even now, affects your relationship in an unhelpful way. You may realise that one particular relationship you had twenty years ago is creating problems right now. If you can track these patterns down, you can begin to come to terms with them, resolve them and start to reduce their effect on your relationship.

YOUR RELATIONSHIP WITH YOUR MOTHER

When you are in your mother's womb, you are as close to another human being as you will ever be. In the early days of your life, you are absolutely dependent on her for that life. So it's not surprising that you are likely to feel a very close link with your mother, or whoever acted as a mother to you when you were very young. As well, you are far more likely to believe as true her ideas and feelings about things, than those of anyone else, particularly her feelings about you.

Most of our mothers, most of the time, feel good about us. From this, we get the idea that we are lovable, and this creates a kind of 'knock-on effect', allowing us to be loving and warm in our relationships with other people. But what happens when your mother feels bad about you in some way? What if she gets frustrated that you aren't getting potty trained quickly, or angry that you've left your toys out on the floor again? In these situations, most of what your mother is feeling is fear and guilt because she believes that she's a bad mother, but you won't realise this. You will think that if your Mum is angry or unhappy, then you should feel bad about yourself, and you may do just that, all through your life and particularly in your closest relationships.

Re-creating the relationship

It may be hard to believe, but whether you are male or female, you will be looking for Mummy in every relationship you have. You won't be looking for a mummy who actually suckles you and changes your nappies, but you will be looking for someone who supports you, listens to you, cuddles you, loves you. You may also be looking for someone who in more specific ways reminds you of your mother: perhaps because he or she is very calm as your mother was, or perhaps because he or she is very intelligent, as your mother was. Choosing a partner who reminds you of your mother feels familiar, and so it feels safe. To some extent, if the two of you form a loving bond and so your partner succeeds in meeting your needs, you can rediscover your mummy, all over again – and that feels wonderful.

Even so, it can also feel very bad, because first, you may choose a partner because he or she reminds you of your mother in negative ways as well as in positive ways. While this feels familiar and therefore comfortable, you can still get just as hurt by your partner as you did originally by your mother: such as when she tended to criticise you, overprotect you, or make you feel small.

Second, you can tend to expect from your partner what you expected from your mother, and to react to your partner as you did to your mother; but he or she is not the same person. So you may expect everything from a partner, just as you expected total attention from your mother when you were only a few months old. You can feel betrayed if your partner doesn't fulfil all your needs, just as you hated your mum when you were four and she refused to let you eat all the cakes. As well, if your partner is angry with you, you may feel just as confused and hurt as you did when your mum screamed at you for playing with the carving knife. This can be as disappointing for you as it is unfair on your partner.

It's not only that you expect your partner to act like your mum. Very often, you react to your partner as you would have liked to have reacted to your mother.

Laura and Bill came to counselling because Laura had nearly had an affair. It had been a one-night stand, at a conference she'd attended due to her job as a sales rep. She had regretted her 'near affair' immediately, told Bill, and asked him to wipe the slate clean.

Bill wouldn't. Laura sat in the counselling room crying quietly as Bill told the counsellor that he felt completely betrayed, and that he could never forgive her. He said he was there at counselling really to 'make her see what trouble she's caused'. (Of course, the counsellor said that doing this was not what she was there to do.)

When Laura and Bill looked back at their relationship, they both felt that they had had a very stable and happy marriage up to this point. In fact, they had been thinking about starting a family. When asked why she had had the affair, Laura's only explanation was that her lover had made her feel important, but as soon as she got into bed with him, she realised that it was a mistake and had left.

Laura repeated over and over to Bill, in front of the counsellor, how sorry she was for what had happened but, in the counsellor's words, Bill 'seemed almost to enjoy not forgiving her'. At the same time, it seemed that the last thing he wanted was for the relationship to end. He continued coming to counselling, and the counsellor felt that, underneath the anger, he was still very involved with Laura.

They both began to track back to what had happened in their childhoods. The counsellor had some pebbles in a bowl in the counselling room, and Laura was asked to place them in a way that reflected what she remembered from being a child. She took two or three pebbles of a similar size and scattered them over the table in a jumbled way. When the counsellor asked which pebble represented her, Laura smiled and said 'I don't know . . '. She realised that in her childhood, she had never felt 'special'; and her only complaint about Bill was that he often took her for granted. She wanted to be told she was the centre of his world, but instead had accepted that Bill 'treats me as he would treat himself, as if I'll always be there'. She began to realise just why she had been tempted by the affair.

The breakthrough came during the sixth session. Bill had been exploring his feelings about his family. He realised that when he thought about Laura's affair, he felt the same sense of complete rage and panic he had experienced when, the year he went to secondary school, his mother had gone back to her job as a nurse. She had loved the reward of helping sick people, but Bill had, for the first time in his life, felt that he was less important to his mother than other people were. The counsellor asked, 'Did your mother know how you felt?' and Bill replied: 'I tried to tell her, but I couldn't.'

The counsellor then suggested that Bill imagine his mother as if she was sitting across the room from him, and say to her what he had always wanted to say. After a brief pause, Bill started to talk. He spoke of how jealous he had been of the people his mother had visited, how betrayed he had felt when she started work again and enjoyed it so much. But he had felt he could never tell her: his mother might have been angry; she might have rejected him even more; he had secretly been afraid that she might even leave. In the end, with the counsellor's support, Bill said how much he loved his mother, and how much he regretted never having said how he had really felt.

Bill realised that how he was reacting to Laura was linked with how he had felt about his mother all those years ago. When Laura also had found someone else more important than Bill, even for just a few hours, he had at last got the chance to express his anger and panic. This time, he had actually made a real impact; he had made Laura feel bad, and had carried on making her feel bad by still refusing to forgive her.

Once Bill had been able to face up to his feelings about his mother and express them in counselling, he was able to feel better about Laura. He was also able to see how he had added to the possibility that she might have an affair by not showing her how how special she was to him. This made a big difference to their relationship. Both of them were able, in the weeks that followed, to re-contact the love they had for each other. The work they were doing in counselling very soon turned into exploring what would happen when Laura became pregnant, and how they could really make a success of starting a family.

Ideas about women

There is another way in which your mother influences you. It is from her that you learn what being a woman is all about. You learn that women do the cooking, or that they hate housework and much prefer studying. You learn that women are moody, or calm and even-tempered even when life falls apart. You learn that women allow other people to insult or even abuse them, or that women have a great deal of personal power and get what they want when they want it. Although during your life you take on board many other ideas of what a woman is like, that first idea you got from your mother is likely to last longest and strike deepest.

Later, if you are a man, you will expect other women to behave like that. If you are a woman, you will see your mother's version of womanhood as an option either to admire and aim for, or to resent and rebel against. You may or may not like what your mother is; in fact you may hate and try to avoid it; but you will have a deep belief that this is what women are like and that will deeply affect how you behave within your partnership.

! ———————————— *Task* ————————————

Your mother's legacy

What did your mother, or the person who was nearest to a mother to you, believe about the following?

- How good is it to be a woman?
- How should women handle anger; their own and others?
- What part do women play in making decisions?
- How emotional are women allowed to be?
- What was women's role in the family?
- Were women allowed to take a job, and in what way?

How many of these things do you now believe about yourself as a woman, or have you rebelled against? If you are a man, how many of these things do you believe about women?

If you can talk things through with your partner, swap notes. Where do you differ in your views about women and how they are? Do you think your differences have caused any problems between you?

!

YOUR RELATIONSHIP WITH
YOUR FATHER

Your relationship with your father may be less close than your relationship with your mother. Your father – or whoever was a father to you when you were a child – may not have been around during the day, and when he was there, have been the kind of person who finds it hard to show emotion, to give you attention, to hug and cuddle you. But in fact, because of that, you may actually need your father's approval more than you need your mother's. He may be important to you because of his rarity value.

Your father influences you in all the ways your mother influences you. You may end up, as an adult, judging yourself as he judged you. You may learn from him what it means to be a man in the same way as you learned from your mother what it means to be a woman, and you may identify with that or rebel against it.

Re-creating the relationship

As you did with your mother, you may also seek out a partner who reminds you of your father. You may expect that partner, male or female, to re-create for you the relationship you had with your father. If that relationship is one that made you happy – because your father seemed kind, wise or cuddly – then you'll want your partner to be like that all the time. But if your father disappointed you when you were small – by being violent, ineffectual, never there – then you may still choose a partner who's like that because it feels familiar. Of course, you may try, this time round, to re-create your relationship with your father just as you would have liked it to be, in the same way as Bill tried to replay his relationship with his mother through Laura (page 72).

Another possibility is that you run your relationship in the way your father would want you to, particularly if your father was the one who gave out the discipline in your family, the one who controlled what you did and set standards for you. You may well choose a partner to suit what he wanted rather than what you actually want.

This is what happened for Davinder, who came to counselling because she was on the point of finishing a relationship with a partner – yet again. She was in her early thirties and very timid in manner. She had had many relationships with men, all of whom she described as somehow 'unsuitable'. When the counsellor asked why these men weren't suitable, Davinder seemed unsure, though she described them as being in unreliable jobs: actors, artists, students. Her pattern had been to become very involved with such men, fall in love, find herself enjoying life and being very contented. Then after six or eight months, she would start to 'wake up', as she put it, and feel unsure about the long-term future. Despite the fact that she 'fitted' with her partner on a personal level, she would end the relationship, often suddenly and painfully.

When the counsellor asked Davinder to talk about her family, she spoke about her father a great deal, though never with much affection. He seemed to be an unapproachable man, with very high standards that Davinder had always tried to meet and failed. On the day she had gained her university degree, with good marks, he had spoken to her with pride about one of his colleague's daughters who had gained an even higher degree.

Through talking about her father, Davinder began to realise that she had spent the last thirty years letting her parents run her life for her. She had checked out all her partners through her father's eyes, and found they just didn't meet his standards. So whether or not she was happy with these men, as each relationship developed to the point where she was ready to commit herself, Davinder had always ended it. She had a fantasy, she told the counsellor, that if she told her father that she was moving in with or marrying any of these men, he would be so shocked that he would die. She slowly came to terms with the fact that she had to begin to choose her partner for her own sake, not for her father's.

During the course of counselling, Davinder's father, who was now in his eighties, did become ill. She travelled up to see him, having decided during counselling that she would tell him she was moving in with her current partner. At the next session, she said that she still hadn't been able to do so, though she had been more direct with both her parents about what she thought and felt. Two months later, on another visit, she did break the news. In fact, her father was so ill and old that he was been unable to fight her, and quite simply wished her well. She came back down to her home town, and moved

!——————————————— *Task* ===============

Your father's legacy

What did your father, or the person who was nearest to a father to you, believe about the following?

● How good is it to be a man?
● How should men handle love and affection?
● What part should men play in bringing up children?
● What role have men in a family?

How many of these things do you now believe about yourself as a man, or have you rebelled against? If you are a woman, how many of these things do you believe about men?

   If you can talk things through with your partner, swap notes. Where do you differ in your views about men and what sort of people they are? Do you think your differences have caused any problems between you?   !

in with her partner the same week. She told the counsellor that her relationship would probably not last for ever, but she had made a commitment to it. And, in doing so, she had grown up.

—————YOUR BROTHERS AND SISTERS—————

Brothers and sisters influence you in your relationship in many ways. For example, the size of your family is important. If you're an only child, you may find it easy to fit in with your partner's needs because you like the fact of having company; or you may find it hard because early in life you just weren't used to sharing. If you are part of a large family, you may find it easy to give, or you may always feel threatened by your partner because you are so used to having to fight for the attention, the love or the pocket money.

   If you're the eldest child, and used to managing all the others, you may be happy to take responsibility in your relationship, but expect your partner to toe the line, just as your younger brothers and sisters did. If you were the youngest, you may expect to be looked after or babied; you may also expect to follow someone else's lead and feel insecure if you are with an unassertive partner who can't give you that lead.

Your brothers and sisters also teach you just how to manage relationships, giving you lessons in the sheer nitty-gritty of getting your needs met when you are with an equal. From them you learn how to share, to fight, to come to terms with the unfairness of not getting the toys or the sweets you wanted. If you sometimes won and sometimes lost in these battles, you'll probably be able to give and take in your relationship. But if you always lost, you may well lack the self-confidence to ask for what you want in your partnership.

If you always won, the problems may be different. One Relate client, a successful and charming man in his twenties, was at his wits' end because his wife insisted on making all the decisions in

! ——————————— *Task* ———————————

Family album

If you have photos of yourself as a child with your family, take them out one day and look through them. How do you feel about each family member; what sort of relationship did you have with each one?

Think too about similarities between your partner and each of your family members: in appearance, way of behaving, strengths and weaknesses. How do you behave towards your partner in a way that's just the same as the way you behaved towards this person? How might this be causing problems between you and your partner?

Jot down a list of all the similarities you're aware of between your partner and the family member. Now make a list of all the differences you know of between your partner and the family member. Keep listing differences until you have more differences than similarities. Next time you are tempted to react to your partner as if he or she were someone else, think of this list of differences. Remember who you're talking to.

!

their lives. When they explored the issue, she shrugged 'He lets me'. It turned out that she, from a family of six, had learned very well how to fight for her rights; he, an only child, never had. He needed to learn the skill of winning, she needed to learn how to lose sometimes.

SEXUAL UNHAPPINESS

Being sexually abused is deeply hurtful for anyone, particularly for a child. It can also create deep rifts in a person's ability to form loving relationships. For while willing sex with a loving and equal partner can be the most wonderful experience on earth, the experience of sexual abuse is quite simply the complete opposite of this. It is not willing, it is not loving, it is unequal; and it creates a whole mixture of feelings. The child will certainly feel out of control, because they are being controlled; but they may also feel that they should be in control, and very guilty that they didn't say no. The whole event may be full of fear because the child has been hurt, or made to keep a secret through threats. And if the child has felt some sexual pleasure, then this will pile guilt on guilt.

Later in life, a person who has been abused may feel bad about themselves and their body. They may see themselves as ugly, be unable to feel physical pleasure or really be good to themselves. They may feel disgusted by sexual contact, because they've never had any that didn't feel disgusting. They may also find it difficult to work out whether sex is a sign of love or not; the adult who abused them may have called what was happening love, the child felt otherwise but is now unclear about what to believe.

One very dramatic example of how past events can explode within a relationship was the case of Bernadette and Andrew, a couple in their early twenties. They arrived at counselling looking fit and tanned, but obviously in a state of shock. They explained with embarrassment that they had been married only three weeks, and had just come back from their honeymoon, which had been a complete disaster.

They had met two years ago and had immediately fallen for each other. Both were from religious backgrounds, and though they were not now practising churchgoers, Andrew had had just two previous sexual partners, and Bernadette had been a virgin. Before their marriage, they had enjoyed passionate kissing and cuddling, but had decided that, as they were so sure that theirs was going to be a lifelong partnership, they would wait until after the wedding to enjoy full sex.

On their first night, Bernadette had become extremely upset. Andrew was happy to go slowly, but as one day of the honeymoon followed the next, it became obvious that she was unable to let him touch her intimately or to penetrate her.

There was no question that Bernadette and Andrew were deeply in love with each other. Both were clear that they were not about to give up on the relationship easily, but they were both very concerned. Bernadette was upset that she was reacting so violently to something that she wanted to do and believed was part of a loving relationship. Andrew was anxious he was in some way turning her off or being insensitive.

It took many weeks of exploring, but eventually there was a breakthrough. Suspecting that Bernadette's strong feelings against penetration had some early cause, the counsellor encouraged her to explore her childhood. Bernadette had brought with her to the session some photos of herself as a young girl, on a camping holiday with her family. Suddenly, as she looked at the faces, she began to cry uncontrollably.

With the counsellor's support, she began to remember that one day, when the rest of the family had gone down to the beach, she had stayed behind. A teenage boy from a nearby caravan had started talking to her, and with no warning, had pushed her into the tent and abused her, thrusting his penis against her and finally into her mouth. He had then threatened that if she told anyone, he would burn the tent down at night, when she and her family were in it. He had stressed that 'I can see you from our caravan. I'll know if you tell anyone.' Terrified, Bernadette had kept quiet.

Over the years, she had successfully forgotten what had happened – but her body hadn't. She was happy with kissing and cuddling, but had held back from sexuality until she met Andrew. And then, on their wedding night, she was reminded of the childhood abuse by Andrew's erection. His passion, which seemed to her very close to the violent expression she had seen on the face of her abuser, had made her feel exactly the same emotions as she had felt when she had been attacked: terror and disgust.

Remembering this incident was only the start of the work Bernadette and Andrew needed to do, but it was the turning point. After they had understood what was happening, they knew that it was possible to heal Bernadette's wounds and for them to have a loving, passionate marriage.

If you know or suspect that you or your partner has been sexually abused – and such abuse is not something that only happens to little girls – then do get professional help. The horror of what happened is something that you as a couple shouldn't need to handle alone, because you are too close to each other to cope. Often, the person who has been abused feels so strongly about the abuse that he or she needs help just to be able to recognise and express those feelings. Often, the partner of an abused person feels strongly too – powerless, frustrated, guilty at not being able to help, angry at the accuser – so he or she can need professional help as well. Remember that a counsellor trained in helping people who have been abused will know how to take things slowly. You may not even need to explore the events themselves if they are too painful; what is important is to clear away the after effects.

SEPARATION

As a child, you depend completely on adults to be there to look after you. If they don't, when you are very young, you may actually die. So it's not surprising that if, as a child, you get separated from the important adults in your life, you will feel very strongly about it. If you have to spend time in hospital when you are four; if your father leaves home when you are five; if one of your parents becomes alcoholic when you are six, or if at seven you are sent away to school, you may panic, get angry, lose trust in everyone including yourself.

Debbie came to Relate because she no longer felt any desire for Paul, her partner of eighteen months. At first, they'd been passionately in love; now, the passion had died. The counsellor helped Debbie to explore her childhood by drawing a 'time line', a line representing her life on which she wrote important things that had happened to her. She pinpointed a time when, at three years old, she had been in hospital for several weeks because she had whooping cough. Her parents said that when she came back home, she was a changed child, anxious and silent: she'd reacted to being separated from her parents by cutting off from them emotionally and refusing to trust them any more. Even now, the more Debbie cared for someone, the more anxious she was about feeling dependent on them, or even good about them. As her relationship with Paul grew deeper, and they grew more committed to each other, Debbie protected herself simply by cutting off from her feelings, including her sexual feelings.

There is another way that being separated from an important adult can affect you. If you are left at home during the time that adult is away, you may end up acting the part of that missing parent yourself. You may have to grow up very quickly, look after yourself emotionally and physically, to perhaps support another adult who isn't quite coping with life because a beloved partner isn't there.

All this can result in a child who grows up to be an adult too old for their years. Then, when you are old enough to choose your own life, you drop the burden for ever, and become someone who never takes any responsibility whatever, expecting your partner always to take the strain. Or alternatively, you can't let your guard down because you were never able to as a child. You take everything very seriously and responsibly, and are never able to have fun.

GROWING UP

Puberty, when your body begins to change in preparation for starting a family, often affects you not only physically but also mentally and emotionally. If you're prepared for it when it happens, you will take it in your stride; if not, then you may actually get very frightened. A first period may convince you that you're bleeding to death; a wet dream can make you think you've got a fatal disease. And if the timing of when you begin puberty is unusual – you start your period a year before every other girl, or are still waiting for your beard to grow a year after every other boy – you may feel you are different, abnormal and strange.

Added to all this, the symptoms of maturity may be embarrassing. Your voice may break when you're saying something very serious in class; your period may start when you haven't got a sanitary towel with you. If so, you may feel that, when it comes to developing into an adult, you've got things wrong. You may start to lack confidence in yourself as a person.

You'll also be affected by how other people react to your physical changes. Fathers can be threatened by their sons suddenly gaining height and looking strong and masculine. Mothers, who may be going through the menopause and so feeling vulnerable anyway, may feel threatened by their beautiful, sensuous daughters.

Or, it may be the fathers who find their daughters hard to handle. One Relate client, Kim, reported that 'The day I had my first period, my father stopped kissing me good night. The message was that he'd stopped loving me.' Already a tomboy, she became very unhappy with her new 'woman's body', started to play truant, and suffered from eating disorders for years. She came to counselling when, having matured and found a partner with whom she was very happy, she was then faced with the challenge of his wanting them to start a family. Kim realised that she thought deep-down that being a woman meant that men stopped loving her. The idea of proving that she was a woman by having a baby was so threatening that she thought of ending her relationship rather than face the possibility of being abandoned again.

The fewer difficulties you hit during puberty, the more comfortable you will be being an adult, particularly a sexual one. The more difficulties you have, the more you may want to deny being an adult. You may play down your attractiveness, hide any signs of your growing up, become shy and introverted. This can last all the way through your teenage years, up to and including the time you take a partner. You may be timid and unsure, refuse to commit yourself, or seek a partner who because he or she is so mature and responsible, can allow you to stop having to be an adult and let you behave like a child again.

BOY MEETS GIRL

The first experiences you have of trying to form a partnership – let alone the first experience you have of sex – will create many of your expectations, hopes and fears for every other partnership you have. The problem is that these first experiences are often based on shyness, insecurity, lack of knowledge and lack of skill. With the right partner, the lessons you learn can be wildly exciting, a source of great confidence and an opportunity to mature. With the wrong experiences, the lessons you learn may be upsetting and unhelpful.

As a girl, you may learn from your friends that having a boyfriend is something of a status symbol. If so, you may feel reject-ed if you don't seem to appeal to the opposite sex, or if all your class-mates have boyfriends before you have. In fact, most girls feel like this, but you may still end up thinking that you're the only inade-quate one in your class. You may doubt whether you are attractive, or try to 'be nice' to boys by giving them attention (or more) in order to tempt one to go out with you. Then, as an adult woman, you may carry on believing that you have to be nice to your partner in order to keep your relationship together.

As a boy, your main problem may be feeling that you have to take the lead, even though, when it comes to dating, you don't really know what to do.

James and Marie entered counselling after being together for two years. James's possessiveness – which Marie had found flatter-ing in the beginning – had now begun to make her feel trapped and restless. Through counselling, James tracked back his insecurity to experiences when he was a teenage boy attempting to meet girls. Already very shy, he had interpreted the girls' nervous giggles as mockery, and convinced that he was unattractive to the opposite sex, had been very lonely until he met Marie. She was extroverted and confident, had taken James under her wing, and to begin with they fitted very well. But the more in love James fell, the more he believed that Marie couldn't possibly want him. The only way he felt he could be safe was to keep her away from other men, whom he was sure she would prefer to him if given half a chance. Through counselling, James worked through his early experiences and gained more confidence; Marie learned just how much she meant to him, and was able to reassure him that she really loved him and was not about to leave.

Above and beyond these emotional traps in early partnerships, there is the whole area of sexuality. The fact that young people often learn what to do from their same-sex friends rather than from opposite-sex ones means that they may not know anything about the reality of heterosexual love-making (or that they are pressured to ignore their own realisation that heterosexual love-making is not for them). So if, as a boy, you listen to all your friends bragging about how they 'did it' seventeen times last night, you may believe them. Then you may feel that you have to push ahead in getting a girl to have sex with you, whether she wants to or whether you do. If, as a girl, you want to keep up with the crowd by having sex, you may say 'yes' without learning how to make sure that your pleasure is taken into account as well as your partner's. Then you may be horrified at what an awful experience it all is. Both boys and girls can end up feeling guilty, uncertain, worried about how to give and receive pleasure.

GHOSTS FROM THE PAST

If you have had committed or long-term relationships before your present one, there may well be a concealed bomb just waiting to explode in your relationship. First, previous partnerships mean that you have a more complicated history. You already have clear ideas on how to run a committed relationship: on love; responsibility; how to live together; sex; perhaps even child-rearing and what it means to be a family. So when it comes to the nitty-gritty of how to celebrate anniversaries, who digs the garden, or how to cope if the children misbehave at school, you not only have deep-rooted memories of 'how things should be done' because your parents did them that way many decades ago, you also have a very recent set of memories of how things should be done because you did them like that a year or two ago. And, of course, these examples are ready and waiting to conflict with your partner's similar set of examples.

You may also bring with you, from a previous relationship, a feeling of failure. Even if your last partnership ended many years ago, and even if you weren't in any way the 'guilty party', you may still in your heart of hearts feel that you got it wrong. You may be wary of trying again. You may want desperately to get it right this time. This will put added strain on your current partnership.

Even though when you end an important relationship, you may say that you will never make the same mistake again, that may be exactly what you try to do. You may have chosen your present partner because he or she reminds you of your previous partner or allows you to replay parts of your previous committed relationship – in the unconscious hope of making it 'all right this time'.

! ─────────────── *Task* ───────────────

Life before your partnership

You'll need a large piece of paper (two, if you are both doing this task) and several coloured pencils.

You are going to draw on this paper a line that represents your life. Draw this 'time line' from one side of the paper to the other or from bottom to top, whichever feels right to you.

Begin by marking in the year of your birth at one end of the line. Write today's date at the other end of the line. Mark in one colour the following key events, and the age you were when they happened:

- The year you first went to school
- The year you left school
- The year you first took a job
- The year you met your partner.

Now mark, in another colour, three significant emotional events that you remember, up to the year you met your partner. If you can, write down the date of each event.

Now think about each of these many events. If you are with your partner, discuss them. What happened? Who else was involved? Why was each event important to you? How do you think it's affected the way you think and feel about things? How do you think it's influenced your relationship? How do you think it's influenced how you relate to your partner?

!

You may also bring with you parts of that relationship to 'haunt' this one. Such ghosts could be objects. One Relate client had unconsciously re-created the layout and style of his bedroom from a former relationship within the flat he had bought and furnished with his current partner. These ghosts could be secrets: perhaps you're hiding from your current partner how good a lover your past one was. These ghosts could be memories: are you unable to listen to a particular piece of music now because of the way it reminds you of your ex-wife? Or the ghosts can be real people. What about the former spouse whose brief visit to pick up the children always creates a Sunday morning row between you and your current partner? What about the children themselves, who because they are still attached to their 'real' mum or dad, try to undermine the 'false' one? One couple at Relate admitted that the wife's four year old from her previous relationship had driven such a wedge between her and her new husband that the child now slept in the bed, while the husband slept on the floor!

7

THE RELATIONSHIP PATH – FIRST ATTRACTION

In order to understand your relationship better, it's vital to explore the part of your life that led up to your meeting your partner. This provides you with your 'emotional dowry': the thoughts, ideas and feelings that you brought with you to your relationship, and which may now be causing problems between you. This part of the book, however, looks at what happens after you meet your partner and how that has affected things. Why were you both first attracted to each other, and how is that now creating problems? What were the original agreements you thought you made about running your relationship, and how are those now causing you conflict? And what has happened to you both since you met that has undermined your original attraction, and led you towards your current difficulty?

At the very start of your relationship, you both chose each other. Your first reason may have been physical attraction: quite simply, you fancied one another. Your second reason may have been common interests or background: you both like playing tennis, you both go to the same church. These reasons justified going out together for several weeks, months or even years. Then you made a commitment. How did you judge that your partner was the right person to commit to? The bottom line is that, in some way, you each felt that the other was meeting your needs, giving you what you wanted.

You might, for example, have chosen a partner who complements you. If you are nervous and full of energy and your partner is calm and reassuring, that can be an incredibly effective combination, making both of you much better able to cope with life. Your partner relaxes you; you energise your partner. You balance each other's weaknesses, fulfil each other's needs and are happy.

As mentioned earlier, hard though it is to believe, you may also choose your partner because he or she reminds you of someone important to you. You'll often, quite unconsciously, pick someone who seems as warm as your mother, as dependable as your father, as interesting to be with as your sister – because that's what you need. You may expect that with this person, you'll be able to replay the relationships you were most used to as a child. So you'll choose someone who allows you to be cared for, to feel wanted, or to have your own way, because that's what you did when you were a child or because that's what you witnessed your parents doing.

Or, you may choose someone precisely because he or she is not like someone important, because your relationship allows you to experience the direct opposite of what you went through as a child. The last thing you want is someone as scatterbrained as your mum, as unemotional as your dad, or as competitive as your sister. Or, the last thing you want is to be out of control, to have to be good, to feel bad all the time, so you choose someone who fulfils your need to take control, who allows you to be a rebel, or to act the angel.

Sometimes, as mentioned before, you may choose a partner with whom you have to 'replay' some of the more painful things in your childhood. It may hurt to be with someone who constantly fights you, just like your big brother did; but fights are somehow familiar; you need them more than you do long silences or gentle affection. And of course, there is always the hope that, as an adult, you may be able to get it right where, as a child, you got it wrong. You may hope to win with your partner where you always lost to your big brother; and so in some way, you even get to enjoy the rows because now, as an equal, you can fight much dirtier and hurt much more.

Whoever you choose, the ideal is that in some way, the two of you should fit together, like pieces of a jigsaw puzzle. In other words, in order to be attracted to each other in the first place, you both need to meet each other's needs.

_____FIRST ATTRACTIONS_____

Here are some examples of the kind of 'first attractions' that people can have for each other. It isn't a complete list, and these aren't separate categories. They overlap in many ways, and partners often mix and match their reasons for being together. Also, these attractions are all natural and understandable ways of meeting each other's needs within a partnership; many perfectly happy and successful relationships contain these elements. It is only when each person in the couple starts to fulfil the others' needs just a little too well – so that they never behave in any other way, or so that their interactions become painful – that things start going badly wrong.

See if you recognise some aspects of your own relationship and some of the reasons why you were first attracted to each other.

Mummy and Baby

In this relationship, one partner is dependent and the other does the looking after; or one partner tends to be slightly 'dizzy', and the other provides guidance and stability.

In fact, every relationship has a little of 'Mummy and Baby' in it. Everyone wants a partner in order to have someone to love and be loved by. Many of us like to be babied, because at some point in our childhood most of us felt a little neglected and want to make up for that. Most of us like to be Mummy because at some point in our childhood we were praised for taking responsibility and looking after the younger ones, or we felt powerful by caring for others.

The first attraction for both Mummy and Baby may well be immediate and dramatic. One of them feels truly supported for the first time in his or her life; the other feels strong and secure because of having the chance to really care for a partner.

A couple who had a Mummy and Baby relationship were Cathy and Alan. Alan had met Cathy when he had been a lab technician at her school and she had been in the sixth form. Because he was nearly ten years older than she was, Alan seemed to Cathy very mature and dependable; she compared boys of her own age to him and found them boring and rather silly. For his part, Alan's caring nature made him want to look after Cathy, who unlike many of her school friends, was in fact very inexperienced and not at all worldly wise.

Fire and Granite

Here, one partner feels all the emotions and provides excitement and exuberance. The other often seems to have no feelings at all, providing a solid, rock-like foundation for the other to lean on.

Perhaps the emotional one got lots of attention as a child for feeling strongly; or perhaps his or her parents were unemotional and the child rebelled by being the sensitive one in the family. Perhaps the unemotional one has been told that a particular feeling, such as anger or love, is unacceptably dangerous, then has cut off so as not to feel guilty or get punished.

The unemotional partner needs the emotional partner because he or she seems so alive. The emotional partner is attracted by the security of the other's less emotional outlook.With each other, maybe for the first time ever, they feel fulfilled.

This was the case for Rob and Ben. Rob, an attractive extrovert, lived his life on a roller-coaster of emotion. Ben was an academic from a top university, whose popular science book was published with the London-based company where Rob worked. Ben's calmness and certainty gave Rob a real sense of purpose. He began to pay more attention to his work and was soon in line for promotion. For his part, Ben loved the excitement that Rob's emotional outlook gave him. He would travel to London each weekend, and they would visit Rob's friends, talk far into the night, and make love. Ben felt that Rob had given him a new lease of life, after he had been feeling fossilised in his job.

Clinger and Puller

There are some relationships in which one partner always seems to be pulling away while the other constantly clings on. The Clinger is the one who makes the running – buying romantic cards, issuing invitations, slowly reeling in the Puller – who, even though he or she acts warily, is also strongly attracted in return.

The Clinger is often someone who, because of childhood experiences, feels strangely comfortable with rejection. But also, every time a partner doesn't reject, the Clinger feels that a victory has been won. The Puller may need constant reassurance that he or she is wanted; so how better to get that reassurance than by pulling away and so having to be chased? Often, the Puller has learned this behaviour from parents who withdrew love when the child was naughty. Or perhaps the Puller, like the Clinger, is scared of being abandoned – but has found a way of coping that involves trying to leave first.

Both of them find their clinging and pulling game familiar and therefore secure, even though it is painful to them.

Eve had suffered a stormy childhood. Her mother had left her father when Eve was five, and had then had a number of partners. Some of these men had had good relationships with Eve, but some of them had not been able to cope with the insecure little girl. Neil too came from an unhappy family: his mother had alcohol problems, and he too occasionally drank too much, but still had a good job as a television lighting cameraman. Both Eve and Neil had been divorced, and their relationship followed a clear pattern: when Neil returned from work abroad, they would fall back into each other's arms and plan to marry or start a family. Then, within days, Neil would get restless. Eve would panic, they would row, and he would move out and sleep on a friend's floor . . .

Devil and Angel

Here, one partner is 'bad' while the other is beyond reproach. For example, one has an alcohol problem, the other offers endless support. One has affairs; the other always forgives.

Either or both of them has, at some time, been given the message that they are wicked, wrong or unlovable. Perhaps Mum or Dad didn't make them feel cared for; perhaps an event such as a parent's being ill or depressed convinced them that they were to blame. Each partner has reacted to this differently, either by being particularly bad, or by trying to be particularly good.

They need each other because, as a couple, they can act out their roles. The Devil is drawn to the Angel because of his or her goodness. The Angel chooses the Devil because in comparison, he or she can feel perfect.

Charlie came from a very close-knit family. His mother was very strong and capable; everyone, including his father, worshipped her, and Charlie grew up believing that he would never be good enough to attract a girl and marry. He hesitated until well into his thirties, when he chose Judy, a young and lively extrovert whose sense of humour and naughty fun attracted him immediately. Her social confidence reminded him of his mother, and his calm good nature made her feel safe and accepted. Without their realising it, however, they were each looking for a way of feeling better about themselves.

Boss and Servant

In this couple, one gives the orders and the other obeys. This relationship is often seen in a traditional family where the man is the head of the house and the woman follows his lead. Of course, sometimes, things are actually the other way round: the woman makes the decisions and the man goes along with that.

Here, one needs to control, the other to feel controlled. The Boss probably had a childhood where he or she felt powerless, and wants to be in control in a relationship. Often, he or she has learned how to do this because of growing up in a family that was run in exactly the same way, with one parent giving all the orders. The Servant has learned that in order to be loved, he or she has to be obedient; that in order to be lovable, he or she has to be kept under control.

Both parties feel comfortable with their roles. And unfortunately this can even be true when 'control' means not only that one person makes the decisions, but that those decisions are hammered home by insulting words or even violence.

An example of a very traditional Boss and Servant relationship was that of Ken and Paula. They were in their late thirties, but behaved like a couple from a much earlier generation. Ken took complete charge of everything: deciding how the money would be spent, where their two children would go to school, and what sort of car they would have. Nothing was ever discussed. Yet Paula felt relaxed with this. She spoke gratefully of how her husband took all the responsibility from her, and how happy she was that he left her free to concentrate on the easy things in life.

ASSESSING YOUR RELATIONSHIP

By this time, you may be becoming clear about which of these various needs and wants first attracted you to your partner. The problem, however, is that there are built-in minefields in these initial attractions.

First, if you are attracted to someone because he or she seems to be able to meet your needs, what do you do when that doesn't happen? What happens when you finally realise that the partner you chose can't give you what you want, and has a separate and different set of needs and wishes? What happens when you have confused your partner with someone in the past and then you realise the bad news: your partner isn't your mum so won't look after you every minute of every day, or isn't your little sister so won't necessarily let you win all the fights?

If you choose someone complementary, then by definition, your partner is not the same as you are. Sooner or later, this will hurt because in time, your needs will start to clash. You'll want opposing things, and be unable to understand why. You'll put the bad feeling down to 'fault' rather than 'difference'. You'll blame your partner for being awkward or not loving you – when in fact they are just being themselves.

If you choose someone who allows you to re-create previous problems that you suffered or witnessed, you may also end up in a double bind. In this situation, what you really want is to resolve the old suffering: to feel good when last time you felt bad, or to win when last time you lost. But whatever your hopes are, you are probably not going to be able to solve the problem any more now than you were able to when it first happened. If you got hurt in the past, it's more than likely that you'll get hurt once again in the present. You choose your partner because he or she feels familiar and therefore comfortable, but you end up with exactly the same difficulties that you did last time round.

Or, strangely, in the end, you find that having your needs met is a two-edged sword. You spent your childhood taking responsibility, so you choose a partner who does that for you. You may begin by loving the fact that your partner takes all the weight off your shoulders, but after a while, it starts to feel as if you're never allowed to do anything by yourself. You loved being emotional as a child, so need to carry on being the only emotional one in your relationship, but over time, you just get tired of being with someone who never gets excited or enthusiastic. In a strange sort of way, you change the meaning of what's happening, so that 'supportive' at the start can become 'trapping' three years later; 'self-sufficient' in the beginning somehow becomes 'never lets me in' by the end.

RELATIONSHIP CRISES

For all these reasons, the relationship possibilities mentioned above can often, quite quickly, turn into relationship crises.

Mummy and Baby: one cares, the other is cared for

It is very wearying for one partner constantly to be looking after the other. You may find that while it felt lovely in the first years of your relationship, given time, it becomes a burden. If you are Mummy, you may find that you don't want to meet Baby's needs all the time. If you are Baby, you may start to feel trapped by being so dependent.

Cathy and Alan kept their relationship a secret until Cathy transferred to the local technical college. Then they announced their engagement and were married the summer after she got her A Levels. For a while they were very happy. They decided to wait several years to have a family because Cathy was so young, and so there was nothing to take their attention away from each other.

However, as Alan grew older and moved into a more responsible job, Cathy didn't seem to mature. The dependent schoolgirl of seventeen whom he had first met grew into a dependent woman of twenty-three. Alan was now in his mid-thirties. The clash in their outlook jarred; the fact that he had to constantly look after Cathy became tiring. He felt he now wanted an equal partner, to share the problems of life with. Cathy, though, increasingly complained that Alan wasn't looking after her; she felt that he didn't really love her.

Alan and Cathy realised through counselling that though their relationship had been based on a shaky foundation, they still loved each other. Cathy in particular saw that she had to take a more equal role in the partnership. She needed to support Alan in his job rather than expecting him to care for her the whole time, and they negotiated various practical ways that she could do this. The counsellor with whom they worked was optimistic that they would stay together.

Fire and Granite:
one feels strongly, the other is more emotionally stable

Here, complementary personalities may eventually conflict. The unemotional one may feel overwhelmed by the other's strong feelings and may shut down on his or her own emotions even more, to escape the threat. The emotional partner may begin to feel unappreciated because there is no one to really share feelings with – and is likely to get even more emotional, hitting out with words and actions to make the point.

Rob and Ben finally moved in together when Rob got a job with a publishing company in the university town where Ben worked. But the day-to-day reality of living with each other was very different from the excitement of weekend romance. Rob soon got bored and responded to the stress in his usual way, by being very emotional. Previously, Ben had been very supportive, comforting Rob over job disappointments, and talking things through when he got angry about something. Eventually, Ben got tired of the constant intensity; he wanted to live a life that was calm at least some of the time. Rob felt unsupported, and accused him of being a 'cold fish'.

In counselling, Rob and Ben looked at how their different ways of approaching life conflicted. Drawing out their family situations, they tried to understand how the past had added to their problems. Rob explored how similar Ben was to his father, who had also rarely shown his emotions. Ben had had a traumatic upbringing and had survived only by becoming very unemotional. They both worked hard at regularly communicating what they felt, and Rob in particular tried to learn to handle his emotions in a more useful way. In the end, however, they both decided that the gap between them was too wide to bridge. Rob started making contacts in his new job, and as he felt more confident of himself, he and Ben parted as friends.

Clinger and Puller:
one holds on, the other pulls away

This relationship often replays old problems, but rarely makes things better. The Clinger will probably get tired of always being rejected, the Puller may start being more outrageous in order to keep the Clinger interested. Or, the Clinger may find someone else more rewarding to cling to.

Neil and Eve's relationship was very unhappy, but for a while it was stable; every time they rowed, they went back to each other. But the rows got more bitter and the happy reunions shorter. Neil stayed away for longer and in the end one time when he was away, Eve met someone else. When Neil returned, they decided to come to Relate, but attended for one session only; Eve was clear that she had had enough. Her mind was made up and she chose her new relationship. But the counsellor was left with a sense of worry: Eve's new partner was married, and was still making up his mind which woman he wanted – Eve or his wife. The counsellor guessed that Eve was still clinging to someone who was pulling away. She had just got tired of clinging to Neil, and had found somebody else to fight for.

Devil and Angel:
one has a problem, the other is beyond reproach

It may seem that the problems here happen because the Devil will set out to be as 'naughty' as as possible. In fact, the Angel is unconsciously encouraging this because it helps him or her to feel 'good'. But the Angel then gets more and more annoyed, while at the same time trying to support his or her partner until the room is filled with what one Relate counsellor called the 'smell of burning martyr'.

Very soon after Charlie and Judy moved in together, they hit trouble. Judy seemed to spend most of her time out with friends, and Charlie started to resent her easy-going attitude to life. He panicked and nagged; she rebelled and started to spend even more time away from home. Charlie felt Judy was just being irresponsible, 'playing him up' almost as a teenager would. When he challenged her, she'd just stay out later and more often.

Charlie eventually came to counselling because he was frightened of the rage he felt that Judy was starting to stir up in him. He soon understood that because he had always felt inferior, he had chosen Judy so that this time, he could feel superior. It was almost as though the worse she got, the better he felt. In counselling, he worked hard to be more confident about his own life, and to fully realise how well he had done in his career. At the same time, the counsellor encouraged him not to nag Judy, but to give her more attention and love so that she felt better about herself too. Charlie returned three months later to report that Judy had responded to the change in his behaviour, that they were getting on well, and spending much more time together.

Boss and Servant:
one takes charge, the other obeys orders

This relationship may work at first, but if it all goes too far, it will become harder and harder for the Servant to accept his or her place.

For Ken and Paula, the problems started when Ken got a new job and started to spend more time away from home. Paula, left to herself, began to have to make more decisions about the house and the family, and began to gain more confidence. When Ken did come back for weekends, they began to argue over things, and in the end, he insisted that they go to Relate.

The counsellor was very pessimistic about how well Ken and Paula would do in counselling. It seemed as if both of them would be unwilling or unable to do things differently. If Ken changed, he would have less control in the relationship; if Paula changed, she would have to take more responsibility. In fact, the couple surprised themselves and their counsellor. Faced with the very real possibility of splitting up, they worked hard at learning how to communicate on an equal level, to negotiate so that both their needs were met, and to break free of the fears they both had of taking equal control. They felt much happier, and Paula looked years younger. 'It was as if they had gained a new lease of life,' said the counsellor.

! ================== *Task* ==================

What's the good side?

This exercise is best done only if you have begun to make improvements in your relationship and now usually feel good about your partner.

Think back to the very start of your relationship. What was it that attracted you to each other? Take a piece of paper and on the far left of it, make a list of six things that you really admired about your partner when you first met. Looks? Kindness? Generosity?

Now in a central column, write alongside the six things you admire, the problems which each has led to during your relationship. Perhaps your partner's being sensible has meant that you never feel you have any fun; perhaps your partner's liking for practical jokes has caused you embarrassment.

In a column on the far right of the paper, now write down opposite each of the six qualities you originally admired, the ways in which that aspect of your partner has, in spite of the problems, made your relationship better. Perhaps the fact that your partner is sensible means that, in fact, you have never been short of money. Perhaps the fact that he or she has a good sense of humour has meant that life has been full of laughter.

There are good and bad sides to everyone's strengths and weaknesses.

!

8

THE RELATIONSHIP PATH – THE FOUNDATIONS OF YOUR RELATIONSHIP

When you both first meet, and are attracted to each other, everything may seem totally natural and spontaneous. In fact, below the surface you are, even at your first meeting, laying down the foundations for how your relationship will be run. You are developing conscious and unconscious expectations about what you will or won't do on a practical, day-to-day level.

These aren't just short-term, 'courting arrangements', such as whether you split the bill or how far to go on the first night. They aren't just the more obvious agreements that you probably talked through when you made a long-term commitment, such as how to handle the finances and whether to have children.

Hidden deep at the bottom of your relationship are expectations about everyday living that are dangerous because you not only never talk about them, but often never realise that they are even there. How much time should you spend with each other? Should you keep up with your in-laws or not? What actually happens if one of you has an affair? The answers to these questions are usually based not only on the life rules you have learned, but specifically on the practical ways you have seen other people live out their relationships, or have yourself run partnerships in the past.

In many cases, your expectations are the same. You have a working arrangement, even if you have never talked about it. You make sure you spend time together every day; you do visit your in-laws regularly; you don't sleep around – just as you think you've agreed to do.

Often, however, as with all life rules, expectations differ. With a lot of these life-rule differences, although you may be frustrated by the problems they cause, you may recognise that there is little reason to expect similarity from someone who is a different person. But with these practical arrangements, the problems go one stage further. Here, because you have talked through and agreed many of the practicalities of life together, you may actually think that you have agreement on them all. You can believe that you've made arrangements about how *everything* should be done, simply because you've made arrangements on how *some* things should be done.

If you have the opportunity to check out your expectations – that is, if you know that your expectations need checking out – then you will realise that in fact many of the agreements you think you've made are just figments of your imagination. Well yes, you didn't actually ever agree that if your partner's mother became ill, she would come and live with you; and you never have actually discussed what will happen if one of you wants to take a year off work. But if you don't talk these expectations through – because neither of you had any idea that they existed – then when they clash, either or both of you can feel that a crucial agreement has been broken, and that the foundations of your relationship have been rocked.

An example of this happening is the story of Julia and William. They came to counselling shortly after they got married because things seemed to be going wrong. They had known each other for four years and had a little girl, Libby, of two years old. Up to this point, they had been happy, but now, Julia complained that William had completely changed.

Bill had spent the first few years of his life in a stable but unhappy family; his parents did not get on well, and he was always uneasy and insecure. When he was eight he had been away to school, where he had felt much happier with a more regular lifestyle. It could almost be said that he was glad to get away from home. But while he was at school, his parents split up, and his father moved out of the house. He came home to find his father gone, and after that lost touch with him.

Meeting Julia at first made him very happy. She was much younger than he was, and her obvious affection made him really enjoy life, and allow himself to feel secure. They moved in together and fairly soon Julia was pregnant; they were both overjoyed.

Then, having been together for nearly three years, Bill suddenly proposed. Julia, who hadn't really thought much about marriage, accepted happily. From that point on, things were different. Bill started to work harder and later, to put money aside and get very irritated if Julia dipped into it. He wanted to buy a house, he had to do it up, and everything had to be just so. He began to be much sterner towards Libby, getting more frustrated when she misbehaved. Although he was still loving towards Julia, he was also more critical of her and what he called her 'slapdash' ways.

Because the problems had begun at about the time that Julia and Bill married, one of the things that the counsellor encouraged them to do was to look at their expectations and agreements about what marriage meant. What they discovered was that where Julia really saw no difference between living together and being married, Bill did. He realised that he had been deeply upset about his parents' marriage breaking up, in a way that was out of his control and had even happened out of his sight.

Now, he wanted to be sure that he was in control of what happened in his own marriage. He said that he had waited to ask Julia to marry him until he was absolutely sure of her: they had slept together, they had lived together, he had even been able to 'check out' that Julia was a good mother when they had Libby. Once he was certain of Julia and had proposed, he then felt he needed to control everything else, just to be sure: the money, the house, their lifestyle, even Libby.

Bill had really understood what had happened, and why he had acted as he did. He began to see that his ideas were very different from Julia's. Julia, however, was very shocked. She said that she had had no idea that this was how Bill saw marriage, first of all as something that she needed to be 'tested for', and secondly as a relationship that was run along strict guidelines. Would she always be on trial? Was he always going to try to control everything in that way? While Bill was now feeling much more certain that he could take a more balanced view of things, Julia was much less sure of the relationship. She and Bill are currently struggling to match their ideas of what a marriage should be.

?_____*Quiz*_____

What are your agreements?

If you feel that your relationship difficulties stem from misunderstandings in your relationship agreements, then the first step is to become aware of what these are. Often, this is enough to allow you both to decide how you really want to arrange things.

This quiz allows you to do this, by asking questions to focus your attention on what these misunderstandings might be. Separately, using the questions as a guide, make notes on what you believe are the agreements in your relationship.

Now swap notes with your partner. Where are you amazed by his or her replies? Where are you startled? Shocked? Upset? Frightened? Angry? Delighted? Relieved?

Where do you disagree? Which of these disagreements do you now realise has caused friction or problems? You may want to read the chapters of this book on communication (pages 136–53) and negotiation (pages 165–9) and use the skills there to negotiate new agreements for your relationship.

Also, remember that agreements shift. It is a good idea to repeat this exercise at yearly intervals, to make sure that you and your partner are completely up to date with what you think you've agreed.

Money

- Who contributes how much?
- How is money divided?
- Are you both responsible if there isn't enough money to go round?
- How much can each of you spend without checking with the other first? (It may differ for each of you!)
- What is it acceptable to spend money on: yourselves, the children, essentials only, luxuries, donations to charity?

Housework

- Who does the housework: cleaning, cooking, washing, ironing, washing up, external maintenance, the car?
- What happens if the main houseworker gets ill?
- Are you allowed to get outside help for the housework?

Children

- If you haven't got children, will you start a family? If so, how old will you both be? What happens if you can't start a family (for example, no action, medical investigation, artificial insemination, divorce?)
- Who will do/does the child-rearing?
- How have your roles changed/will they change when the children arrive?
- Who will keep/keeps the discipline?
- What standards of behaviour do you expect from your children?
- Which children are the most important (for example, the girl or the boy, the older one or the younger one)?

Fidelity

- Is it infidelity to talk to another man/woman at work? At a party? In a disco?
- Is it infidelity if you kiss another man/woman?
- Is it infidelity if you have penetration? Have an orgasm but without penetration? Don't have an orgasm but give your partner one?
- Are your agreements on fidelity different according to which one of you is breaking them?
- Do the agreements change: if one of you is drunk, away from home, feeling very lonely, if you have had a row, if she is pregnant, if he is spending too much time with friends?
- What actually happens if the agreements are broken: tears, recriminations, separation, divorce, silent treatment, no sex for a month, attempted suicide?

Family

- How far away from your family is it acceptable to live?
- How often should you visit? When?
- How openly affectionate should you be to your family?
- What happens at celebrations such as Christmas and birthdays?
- Which family gets priority?
- What relationship secrets can be told to which family member?
- What happens if a family member needs money, gets ill, gets old, dies?

Your relationship

- How do you both show each other your love? Words, gestures, touch, sex, gifts? And how often? Daily, monthly, yearly?
- How much time should you spend together, apart, in the house but not interacting?
- How often should you talk, on your own, each week? How often do you need to do this to still feel close to your partner?
- How often should you make love? Who should start it? Is it OK to ask for sex? Who can do what to whom? Do both of you need to have an orgasm? Do both of you have a right to ask for an orgasm? What's not acceptable in bed? Is it OK to say no?
- What's an acceptable way to show that you are unhappy or angry with your partner? What ways are 'out of order' and unacceptable? Is there any difference between what a man is allowed to do, and what a woman is allowed to do? Is it OK to walk out during a 'row' or not?
- What is acceptable behaviour after a row: silence, steering clear, making up at once?
- What, if anything, could you never forgive your partner for?
- What, if anything, would make you leave?

?

9

THE RELATIONSHIP PATH – WHEN PROBLEMS START

As you and your partner begin your relationship, everything can seem wonderful. You make love a good deal and you cuddle a lot. When you talk, a lot of what you say is simply repeating how good life feels: each of you tells the other how wonderful they are; both of you talk about the exciting future you will have together. You rarely disagree because there is really nothing to disagree about; you feel and act the same, meeting each other's need for attention and affection, and maximising the feelgood factor. You are 'in love'.

Being in love is a wonderful stage in a relationship, and for many people it is a necessary part of becoming a couple. This is because through this stage, they form a close bond with their new partner.

In some cultures, of course, this bonding process isn't seen as necessary to forming a long-term partnership. The partnership is formed first, through an arranged marriage, and the bonding happens over a longer period of time, as the couple work to tackle the challenges of life together.

The problem is that although being in love is a natural part of the first stages of a relationship, it just isn't enough when it comes to forming a long-term partnership. Once you commit yourselves to each other, begin to build a home and perhaps start a family, you have to have extra skills: the more practical skills of meeting each other's needs on a day-to-day basis; getting things done in a way that you agree on; solving conflicts and difficulties between you. You need to know how to give support when one of you has failed at work; how to negotiate on whether to buy a new sofa; how to handle it if one of your children turns out to be uncontrollable. The ability to cope with these things, in a way that suits you both, lies at the heart of what we call 'love'.

FALLING OUT OF 'IN LOVE'

This sounds a very unromantic idea of how a love relationship should be. And here lies the first trap. You may not want to run your relationship in this down-to-earth way. You may be wary of the day-to-day routine of sympathising, supporting, and negotiating, even when it hurts. Instead, you may buy into the media myths that talk about 'lurv' as being an emotion, so you may be unwilling to believe that good relationships involve active doing not simple feeling.

This unwillingness is a particular problem because the 'in love' part of any relationship will fade away automatically as time passes. It is there to bond partners together, and although it may reappear at particularly happy times in a relationship, like a bonfire in the garden it isn't much good for keeping you warm long-term.

When this 'in love' feeling does fade, you may panic because you think it's the important part of your relationship. If you start to sleep together a little less, or disagree a little more, you pull out all the stops. You push down your bad feeling, try to be nice to each other, ignore your worries and panics, do anything to try to get the good feeling back.

If you can't get it back, then you may think that your relationship has died. You may feel you are facing a life without love. So you may up and move, to try to find the feelgood factor again and, because novelty does often go hand-in-hand with falling in love, you may well succeed. But sooner or later, however many relationships you try, the 'in love' will fade and you will be back to square one.

Interestingly, clients who begin counselling sometimes go through the same experience in relationship to their counsellor, beginning the counselling relationship feeling extremely positive about him or her, and then going through doubts before regaining trust and continuing with the work. Counsellors will often use their working relationship with clients as a practical 'lesson' for the couple in what is happening between them; this is one example of where what is happening in counselling can be an excellent parallel of what is happening between two partners, and can offer some very valuable lessons in how to relate.

This type of relationship difficulty is likely to happen early on in your relationship. So if you are in a fairly new partnership that is

! ——————————— *Task* ———————————

Improved with age

This exercise is best done only if you have begun to make improvements in your relationship and now usually feel good about your partner.

You may well think that when you first met was the best time of your relationship, because it was new and exciting, but take a moment to think of three ways in which your relationship has grown deeper over the time you've been together, possibly without your even being aware of it. Perhaps you have relaxed into each other, grown to know each other, developed mutual ways of pleasing each other. (Even though it may be tempting to remember how things have got worse, put those thoughts aside and concentrate on the improvements.)

If you can talk things through with your partner, spend some time sharing ways in which your relationship has deepened. Despite all the problems, remind yourselves of how your relationship is better than it was – and has improved with age.

!

hitting problems, you may want to explore whether you are doing so just because you are expecting the 'in love' feelings to last. If you are, then by moving on to the more practical ways of loving each other described in this book, you will give yourselves a better chance of winning through.

———WHEN NEEDS ARE A BURDEN———

Perhaps, though, you are able to accept that the strong 'in love' feeling will fade. Perhaps you are able to start really loving. You both honestly try to make your opinions coincide and your needs match as you live your life together. You learn to put aside your tiredness and listen to your partner's work worries. You manage to rise above your irritation and listen to your partner's jokes for the umpteenth time. You negotiate the house move, the job change, the overdraft crisis. If everything fits, you may indeed become a stable, happy couple.

Often, though, it all becomes a burden. Perhaps you each expect the other to meet your needs perfectly; perhaps your basic needs just don't fit; perhaps each set of needs has a reverse and painful side. You've chosen a partner who reminded you of someone important in your past – and only later discover that your partner just isn't that person, and just doesn't fulfil your needs in the same way. Or, in time, you discover that you didn't really understand what these needs were; your relationship agreements simply weren't stated clearly enough. Or, your original needs fitted, but a change in your circumstances has created a change in those needs. All of a sudden, you no longer blend with each other quite so well. You become irritated that she won't stay in and keep you company, yet again; you become frustrated that he won't come out and celebrate with you, yet again. Slowly, these things start to jar.

For unless your needs and those of your partner fit together very closely indeed, you will both naturally be in the double bind of every human being who has to live with any other human being. When needs don't fit, are you to meet your own or those of other people? Someone who only ever meets his or her own needs we call antisocial; someone who only ever meets the needs of other people we call a saint. Most ordinary people constantly have to make choices that balance out the two sets of needs. If they are living with someone day after day, as one is with a partner, then in the end, if these needs clash, they can get very tired. We may get tired of having to take someone else into account, tired of never really getting our own needs met. And because we only have basic skills in loving, we have no real ability to make the job easy and take the tiredness away.

Resenting your partner

If you get to this point, you can start to actively resent your partner's not fulfilling your needs. You start to resent your partner's having needs that you must fulfil; needs which, over time, you may start to see as pointless, then as misguided, wrong and finally bad.

You may then take a mental leap that completes your disappointment. You move from having a basic trust in your partner to having a basic distrust of him or her (often because, as a child, your basic trust in the world was in some way damaged). You start to believe not just that your partner's way of doing things is bad because it clashes with your way, but that your partner chooses that way deliberately, in order to hurt you. When he or she first fails to cut the lawn, because lawn-cutting isn't that important in life, you sympathise. After a while, you can start to criticise your partner as 'laid back . . . happy go lucky'. Your thoughts (and maybe words) become more bitter until your partner is seen as 'a slob . . . lazy'. You can finally end up believing that your partner 'just doesn't care what I want', 'does it to wind me up', 'obviously doesn't love me.'

Criticising yourself

Along with this you may well start to criticise yourself in exactly the same way. You see all the things you are doing wrong and feel bad about them. You catch yourself snapping at your partner and feel guilty. You may, or may not, feel as bitter about yourself as you do about your partner; you may, or may not, think as critically about yourself as you do about your partner. But you know deep down that things are going badly, and you feel deep down that it is your fault.

This is as natural a development in a relationship as passing from 'in love' to 'love', but it is far more upsetting. And, of course, it is a two-way process. Your partner is travelling down a similar mental road, until eventually they become disappointed with your behaviour and guilty about their own.

This relationship development is based on the thoughts you both have about each other. First, you are both upset because each of you doesn't always meet the other's needs; then, you think the worst of each other for that; finally, you feel bad about yourselves. If you can understand that this is what you are both doing, then you may have made the most important leap so far in improving your relationship. If you can understand that when your needs don't fit together, this is not a deliberate attempt to hurt, then slowly, you will be able to re-interpret much of what is happening between you in a completely new way – a way that may open the door to feeling good about each other.

!————————————— *Task* —————————————

The fear behind the anger

Next time your partner seems to be attacking or hurting you, ask yourself this question. Why is he or she on the defensive? What is the fear? That you will stop loving your partner? That you will take over your partner's life? You may know that you still care, that you don't want to control, and that you want to do your best – but your partner may still be afraid. Can you offer him or her genuine reassurance that these fears are groundless? If you can, you may find that mysteriously, the attacks stop.

!

————— RUSHING TO THE DEFENCE —————

If you are at the point where you begin to believe that the clash in needs between you and your partner is a sign of lack of love, then you will probably move to a new stage of relationship breakdown. Faced with what you honestly believe is attack, you will attack in return. You don't just think critical thoughts; you hit back.

You may do this in a number of ways. Which ways you choose will be personal to you, because you will have learned them from your personal past. As babies, human beings may learn to react to a problem by staying very still; by crying for help; by ignoring the danger; by yelling in fury. As adults, when we're threatened, we tend to do some of the same things, particularly if it is our love relationship that is being threatened. So when our partnership hits trouble, we do the adult versions of our baby reactions, such as keeping our heads down and pretending nothing's wrong; getting tearful; dismissing the problem as irrelevant; starting a row. She feels threatened by his attitude to her job, so gets angry whenever it's mentioned. He feels threatened by her attitude to the children, so stops even cuddling her any more.

This kind of reaction feels familiar, so you rely on it whether it actually works or not. It feels good to bite back, to play the martyr, to refuse to talk. But it only makes your partner even more certain that you are being cruel – as indeed, by this point, in many ways you are. Now your partner not only suspects that you are out to hurt, but has proof in your sharp words or 'brick wall' silent treatment. He or she will then begin to attack in return and soon you are at war.

Such in-fighting happens in every relationship that is breaking down. In the end, it spreads to every single interaction you have. She comes in from work and opens the fridge, takes out the ice-cream tub, finds it empty, tosses it in the bin. He thinks 'She's getting at me for eating the ice-cream. It's my house too; she never gives me anything.' He says, 'Don't you start. I can't do anything right.' She thinks 'We can't even be in the room together without being at each other's throats,' and responds 'What are you talking about? I didn't say a word.' 'You didn't need to say a word.. I could tell by the look on your face.' And on and on.

WHEN THERE'S A CRUNCH POINT

By the time you get to this stage in a relationship, both of you will be aware that there is a problem. But you probably don't know how to solve it. As day follows day of unhappiness, open warfare or simple silence, you may typically react in a number of ways, none of which are helpful.

You may ignore the problems and hope they will go away. Of course they won't, but in the meantime, you live in an atmosphere of rigid politeness because talking about what is happening is too scary.

Or you panic. Every time you conflict, you try to push the bad feeling down and kiss and make up. You both vow never to be defensive with each other again. Of course, when you feel bad about each other next time, exactly the same thing happens again.

Both of these reactions has a built-in snag. They don't address the root of the problem, that essential puzzle of how to meet each other's needs despite the fact that you are different people. These reactions don't allow you both to acknowledge those differences, understand each other, develop ways of meeting both your needs equally. To do this, you have to learn new skills, ones explained in more detail in the next chapter of this book.

If you don't, then sooner or later, you will hit a crunch point in your relationship. The fact that you don't quite fit together will become just too upsetting, the clashes between you will become just too threatening; the day-to-day irritations of living together will come to a head. Then one or both of you will, slowly or suddenly, decide that you can't take it any more. And then, as you know only too well, your relationship will be in trouble.

10
THE RELATIONSHIP PATH – TRIGGER POINTS

How does a relationship tip into real difficulty? Perhaps you have fought for years, over all the issues mentioned earlier. Or perhaps you have avoided clashes, naturally met each other's needs, and have lived together quite contentedly for years or even decades before it begins to go wrong.

Realising that you doubt your relationship can simply be a question of the straw that breaks the camel's back: one word, one action, one emotion too much, and you realise that this is the end. Relate counsellors also find that often, something actually triggers the problems, something that has come from outside the relationship. So what happens? What suddenly makes you disillusioned?

Change happens. It happens to every human being. Our age changes, our approach changes, our situation changes: because we move from adolescence to adulthood; because we commit ourselves to marriage, because we are suddenly made redundant.

It would be boring and sad if life always remained the same, and many life changes are exciting and full of new possibilities. But change also creates problems. Short term, it sets off a whole series of physical, mental and emotional reactions that can rock a relationship. You get stressed by the alterations that a new job brings. You don't know what to do when your father develops Alzheimer's disease. You get scared by the future when your children leave home. In this kind of situation, you both need things from each other far more than you normally do, simply because you are suffering from life's natural knocks. So suddenly, what you need is just too much for the relationship to sustain.

Long term, life change also alters your approach to life itself. You shift in your goals: what you want out of work, out of play, out of other people. You shift in what things mean to you: whether you are impressed by status, disappointed by job failure, delighted when you make a new friend. The bottom line is that you both shift in your needs. Suddenly you are completely concentrated on the new baby; so where before you relied on your partner for a good social life, now your need is for help with the nappy-changing. Suddenly, your partner's job is under threat; where before, she relied on you to persuade her to overspend on clothes, now she needs you to help her to economise.

If you are both aware that you are changing, and are able to see that change as opening new doors and making new things possible, then you can adapt. In fact, you may welcome the new approaches and attitudes that you are both taking on. If you aren't aware of the change, or if you don't realise it can create clashing differences, or if you start to resent the differences it does cause, then you can both feel very betrayed. All the things that originally attracted you, all the needs you originally had, and all the things you originally agreed, can seem to become irrelevant overnight. Where before you were meeting each other's needs happily, now they start to grate and jar. They become a burden, where they weren't before. The phrase that Relate counsellors hear again and again is 'My partner has changed the rules on me'.

As with so many relationship difficulties, the main weapon you have in coping with life changes is communication. If you can talk about what is happening, how you are feeling, and in particular how you are altering, then you have a much better chance of weathering the storm. As well as supporting each other by talking through the problems, you can update yourselves on how things are altering, and so be aware of each other's changing needs and how to meet them. You can also start to concentrate on the positive aspect of things; for almost all these life changes can, with the right approach, be challenging, interesting and great fun.

LIFE STAGES

The simple fact that you get older can shift your outlook on things. Counsellors speak of 'stages', through which people pass as they move through life. If you're happily settled, both enjoying the responsibilities of what you are doing, then the life stage you are in probably isn't adding stress to your partnership. But if one of you hates where you are in life, it might well be triggering conflict. And if you have just left a life stage, or are just approaching one, then either or both of you may be suffering from regret, anxiety, or shifting viewpoints that need exploring and resolving.

The life stage of reaching independence

This life stage is about breaking free of the influence of parents and family. This may happen quite informally, when you start going out late, choosing your own clothes, forming your own friendships. Or it may happen formally, as you go to college or get married. This stage is about being able to make your own decisions in your own life; it's an essential and fulfilling stage on the way to becoming a mature adult who can happily form a partnership with another mature adult.

If you don't ever reach this life stage – as many people don't – then you may be unable to really feel yourself part of a couple; your loyalty will always be back home. If you reach it well after you are actually living with or married to your partner, maybe because your parents die or re-marry, then this can be very upsetting. You may feel insecure as you face up to being your own person for the first time; you may need lots of reassurance. Or you may feel you need to have a period of complete independence, living your own life completely, and this may conflict with your commitment to your partner. Many a forty-year-old man, on his parents' death, suddenly makes a bid for freedom, to the total horror of his partner and children.

The life stage of reaching commitment

This life stage is about feeling able to commit yourself to another person in a one-to-one relationship: through engagement, marriage, living together; or simply through a personal but meaningful promise to each other. Though it's a wonderful thing to do, this step isn't easy. To move into this life stage, you have to accept that in future, you will have to compromise on what you yourself want; you will often have to put your own ideas aside in order to meet your partner's. In fact many couples who live together or marry find that, having formally committed themselves, they are not ready to make an emotional commitment. They need to reassure themselves that they are still their own people; so they may have affairs, spend more time with friends than with their partner, or overspend on themselves. Many couples say that, in fact, they are several years into their marriage before they realise that they have really entered this stage of commitment.

The life stage of having a family

One of the key stages in life is the one in which you face up to having children. This is a life stage, whether or not you actually do start a family. If you decide not to, then taking that decision may well involve you in just as dramatic a shift in your idea of yourself and your life as if you did have children. This shift in outlook – perhaps on to career or achievement – may not cause conflict if you both agree on it. But if one of you does want a family and the other doesn't, this may cause a gulf between you that you can't actually bridge. Faced with the choice between children and relationship, some partners choose the former and let the latter go.

This issue can be particularly heart-breaking when you conceive mistakenly and have to decide whether to have a termination or a child. Here, whatever you decide can affect you even many years later, as one of you regrets the decision or feels that he or she wasn't really consulted.

If, on the other hand, you both desperately want to start a family and find that difficult, this will also cause you a great deal of strain. You may spend a great deal of time, money and nervous energy trying to conceive. Either or both of you may feel as if you've failed, and blame each other as well as yourselves for that. You may feel that, without children, your partnership is pointless, and if so, there may well be hurt and bitterness between you.

If you do have children, then this can be a marvellous life stage, with all the joy of seeing your family grow and develop; but it is also a very challenging stage. You have to take responsibility, possibly for the first time in your life, for a small person who is so dependent on you that if you aren't there, they will die. This can be a huge burden, and faced with it, you may well feel afraid that you will fail, sad that your old happy-go-lucky existence has gone for ever, angry that this new arrival is now ruling your life.

For all these reasons, many couples find it very hard to adapt to having a baby, particularly the first one, which marks your entry into this life stage. One partner may try to pull back from the work and the responsibility involved, and the other one may then feel let down and abandoned. If the reverse happens, and one of the couple – usually the mother – finds herself compulsively drawn to looking after the baby, the father may then feel locked out and so become even more unhappy.

The rest of the family life stage also has an impact on your partnership. Faced with the reality of caring for your children, protecting them, and disciplining them, either of you may seem to undergo a total personality alteration. An easy-going, calm wife who needs very little support can turn into a frenzied and disciplinarian mother-of-twins who has a temper tantrum every evening! You can find yourselves arguing with each other, particularly if your life rules on child care differ, instead of presenting a united front. This is particularly true if some of the children you are caring for are not your own; then there is all the extra stress of being a step-parent and so possibly feeling unaccepted, untrusted or unloved.

As the children grow up, you may be threatened by their youth, their beauty, their seeming self-confidence. You feel inferior when compared to them, and take out your feelings of inferiority on your partner. You may actually get jealous of your children having the rest of their lives ahead of them, and want some of their independence and potential. Then the other partner may discover, as one Relate client put it 'a fourth teenage son in my house, on top of the three I conceived'.

The time when the children leave home marks the end of the family life stage. Despite the fact that you may both love having more time to yourselves, it may be very difficult for you to adapt to being a couple again. It was hard to adapt, twenty years ago, to the addition of a baby that meant you had no time for each other. Doing it in reverse, and having all the time in the world for each other, can be just as challenging. You both need to commit yourselves to each other as lovers again, rather than simply as Mum and Dad.

The life stage of reaching your plateau

At some point in everyone's life, usually in middle age, there comes a point when they realise this is as good as it is going to get. Perhaps you have recently been passed over for promotion, or begun your menopause. Perhaps you realise that you're never going to make the local football team, ever again. You have to come to terms with the fact that you have reached that plateau. You may be happier or more content as time passes because you are no longer striving and fighting, but you will never, now, achieve all the dreams you had.

If you can't face this fact, then you may get depressed at the thought of what will now never happen. You may rebel, going back to adolescence in an attempt to re-create your youth. You may try to make a new start, taking a different job, moving house or beginning a new relationship. You now need an injection of hope and excitement for the future, which your partner may either not realise or not be able to provide.

If you do the opposite – accept that you have peaked in your achievement, come to terms with your life, and start living for the present – then you may start to head for security and stability. This can mean you settle happily into this life stage and really enjoy it, although if your partner hasn't kept pace with you and still needs achievement and a sense of the future, he or she may start to feel trapped.

The life stage of reaching old age

Some birthdays are more upsetting than others. As they mount up, sooner or later you have to face facts. You may, as you did when you reached your plateau, try to avoid this life stage by starting new things. Or, as you reach retirement, suffer your first major illness, or hear of an old friend's death, you may also give up hope. You may panic that your life is nearly over, resenting the fact that you are old. What you need, actually, is immortality; when your partnership can't give you this, you may resent it deeply.

Such feelings can come to a head quite unexpectedly, as Henry and Norah discovered. Norah was just seventy, Henry a few years older; it was a second marriage for both of them, and had lasted happily for twenty years. Both had retired, the mortgage on their semi was paid off and they had no financial worries.

Henry had told Norah that he had something to say to her, and suggested they talk while they were driving across to see her son on his birthday. Norah agreed, imagining that Henry wanted to plan next year's holiday. Instead, he announced that he was leaving. He said he had been feeling trapped by their marriage for some years, but over the last few months, had realised that he really felt nothing for her. He had become convinced that he could have a better life outside the relationship.

Norah was shattered. Everything she had imagined for the future was now at risk. The couple arrived at her son's house drained of all emotion, and spent large parts of the birthday itself in their room, Henry quietly stating that he was leaving, Norah alternately pleading with him to stay and insisting that he pack his bags immediately.

Norah's son suggested they go to Relate, and when they were back home again, they decided to do so. Henry was clear that he was attending only for Norah's sake; he wanted the counsellor to explain to her that it was all over. Norah wanted the counsellor to tell Henry that he must stay. (Needless to say, the counsellor's role didn't allow him to do either.)

Instead, he encouraged Norah and Henry to look at what had triggered this sudden change of heart within a relationship that had up to that point seemed to be stable. What came to light were the differing expectations that each of them had of retirement and old age. While drawing out their family trees, it became apparent that each family had had a very different way of coping with old age. Norah's parents had enjoyed their later years; they had had a lively social life and her widowed mother had been active and healthy up to her death at eighty-five.

Henry's father, on the other hand, had died of cancer a short while after retiring; his wife had missed him dreadfully, and faded away three years later. To add to this awful message of what it would be like to be old, Henry also had a history of failure at key points in his life. His first marriage had collapsed within a few months of his realising that he would get no further in his job. Some part of him believed that he would always be deserted at the point where things started to go downhilll, and he had unconsciously decided that this time, he was going to be the one to cut off emotionally and leave.

By the time Henry and Norah had understood all this, they were feeling very much closer to each other. The counsellor had suggested that they take time each day to talk, and despite the fact that they had been living together for many years, they were amazed at how many new things they learned about each other. Henry admitted that he was rediscovering the pleasure in Norah's company that he thought had gone long ago.

Both of them also realised that they had been expecting their old age would be a time to narrow their horizons. They had planned to sell their car and to pave the garden so that it was easier to manage. They agreed that instead, they would plan ahead in a way to broaden their horizons. They would keep the car, which would give them more independence; leave the garden as it was for a few more years; use a small part of their savings to travel to America and see Henry's daughter. The couple spent a number of sessions on positive goal setting, and left counselling feeling good about their future together.

‘ ═══════════════ Talking Point ═══════════════

Where are you now?

It's worthwhile checking just which life stage you are in at present. Are you independent? Have you reached your plateau?

What stresses are being placed on your relationship by being in this particular life stage? If you are just coming up to a life stage or just leaving one, what difficulties do you think this may be creating for you?

Which life stage do you think your partner is in? It is more than likely that you will be in the same one, but if you are in different stages, this may be making it hard for you to understand each other.

If you can swap notes with your partner, talk through where each of you think you are now and how this is affecting your relationship. How can you improve things by being aware of what life stages you are both at?

’

LIFE EVENTS

Life events are ones which are not inevitable. They may happen to you, but just as often, you may avoid them. Because they are often unexpected, these events not only affect your relationship with all the long-term effects mentioned before. They may also create an instant shock wave that leaves you reeling. If you are currently hitting relationship problems because of a life event, make sure you are getting here-and-now practical support as well as exploring the emotional issues with your partner.

Love life events

Studies report that up to seventy per cent of men and sixty per cent of women have an affair outside their main relationship. You should be prepared for one or even both of you to be unfaithful during your partnership. In fact, an affair, unlike many other life events, always comes from what is happening between you as a couple. One of you has needs that can't be met within your relationship: to be comforted, to have sex, to seek novelty. You turn to a lover to meet these needs. Or one of you wants to communicate something to your partner: that you are unhappy, that you are jealous, that you want to leave. You use an affair to communicate these things.

The problem is that, whether or not an affair is out in the open, it will always change your relationship, and this will create strain and stress between you both. Your communication will get worse, your willingness to meet each other's needs will die away. You may actually have fewer rows because the person who is having the affair feels so guilty or so scared of discovery that he or she simply aims to please. But the quality of your partnership will fade because one of you isn't putting one hundred per cent into the relationship.

Once discovered, even if it then stops, the affair will change things further. Facing up to infidelity will create very strong emotion: a loss of trust, a drop in self-esteem, a flaring of possessiveness, a backlash of guilt. Sex between you may stop for a while; you may not feel good about each other for a long time. The one who has had the affair may feel ashamed or defiant; the one who hasn't may take a long time to forgive. At this point, you will both need all your resources, first to fight the temptation to punish each other, second to try to understand why the affair has happened. Third, you will need to change what is wrong with your relationship, so you don't need to have affairs again.

Career life events

If one of you takes a new job, or is promoted, all sorts of pressures can build up. There may be more money, and the partner with the new job may gain confidence, but may also be more under stress. The partner who hasn't got the new job can feel resentful, and try to undermine the more successful one. All this pressure will be increased in the special case of a 'returner', perhaps a wife who goes back to work after having had children, because everyone in the family will need to adjust to Mum's not being there so much of the time.

Of course, if one of you loses your job, perhaps because of redundancy or even retirement, similar things can happen in reverse. With redundancy, the one who has lost the job may need a great deal of support. If they don't get it, they may instead try to undermine the one who hasn't. Both of you may somehow feel that the job loser has failed in some way, and there may be a great deal of blame flying about. The longer the period without employment, the worse things can get, as the jobless partner feels more and more rejected. And if there has to be a role shift – so that the jobless or retired partner has to take on the housekeeping while the previous 'housekeeper' takes on a new job – the problems can double.

This is what happened for Pat and Derek. Pat was in her late forties, a small, energetic woman who was very house proud. She had always enjoyed working part time as a sales assistant. The couple had shared interests in travel and cooking; at weekends, for example, Derek would often make Sunday lunch, or in the summer, prepare a barbecue. He was a good cook, if anything better than Pat.

Then the electrical goods firm for which Derek worked got into difficulties, and he was made redundant. At first they coped well; their children had left home, so they only had themselves to support. Pat raised the hours she worked at the department store, and they cut back on spending. Derek was happy to help around the house, particularly with the cooking. All in all, they thought they would manage.

Within two months of Derek leaving work, they were sleeping in separate rooms. They were both short tempered with each other, both felt irritated when the other was around. They explained to the counsellor that they had believed they had a very happy marriage, but now were not sure. Perhaps the fact that they were spending more time together was only just bringing to light the difficulties between them.

The counsellor said afterwards that looking back into the past gave Pat and Derek very little help. They had been together for so long that they had probably worked round many of the vulnerabilities that had come from their past, and ironed out many of the main conflicts between them. Up to Derek's redundancy, they had indeed had a good working relationship where their needs had complemented each other. So what had gone wrong?

The counsellor asked Pat and Derek each to write down what their 'jobs' in the family had been up to the time Derek stopped work, and then to write down a similar list of what each of them did now. There had been many changes. Previously, Pat had most of the responsibility for the house, including the cooking; Derek had helped out only occasionally; his role had been the traditional one of earner. That was an arrangement that they had negotiated over the years, and which had worked well for them both.

Now, while Pat was home less of the time, Derek had taken over. He was doing most of the cleaning, most of the cooking, and he was slowly going round the house redecorating and smartening things up. Pat felt totally shut out from 'her house'. While Derek was no doubt feeling low at having lost his job, he had in fact passed the problem on to Pat by taking over her role. She was the one who was actually redundant.

Both Pat and Derek recognised immediately that this was at the heart of their problem. They felt very relieved that in fact, there was nothing basically wrong with their relationship, other than that their situation had changed. What they had to do was to make sure that this change didn't affect either of them badly. They were well used to talking things through and to negotiating what met both their needs. Once the real problem had been pointed out to them, they were able quite quickly to arrange a way of organising their work-load, both in and out of the house, that made them both feel useful.

Not all career life events are as easily solved as Pat and Derek's. But if you have a solid relationship that has been affected by a career change, you can often, by common-sense planning, remove most of the friction very quickly. Talk carefully about what each of you really needs, how the career event has altered how those needs are being met, and how you can both reorganise your lives to keep meeting those needs. To underpin all this, offer reassurance all round that the career change doesn't mean that either of you has failed.

Physical life events

Physical life events that may affect your partnership include illness, mental illness, being the victim of a crime or having a serious accident; all of which are deeply upsetting and stressful. Serious accident or illness of anyone in the family can make you both very scared of the possible future ahead, and needy for reassurance. And if the person who is ill is the one who has been strong in the relationship so far, then they may suddenly need support – which the other partner, who may have leaned up to now, just can't give.

Mental illness can create even more insecurity. If one partner is depressed or has a nervous breakdown, he or she may feel incredibly guilty and full of self-blame; meanwhile, a partner may feel let down, may worry that the relationship is no longer secure or stable. In all these situations, wherever possible, lift the strain with outside help, nursing care or crisis support, leaving you free to deal with the underlying emotions.

If one of you is the victim of a crime, it may create in both of you all kinds of feelings of fear and vulnerability. Also, you may be tempted to blame yourself or your partner for what the criminal or attacker did. In particular, when one partner is raped or abused, then he or she will often feel guilty. While the vicitim's partner will often be very supportive, there have unfortunately been many cases where doubt has crept in as to whether the raped partner 'asked for it'. If this kind of doubt starts to come between you, get professional counselling as soon as you can to deal with the immense hurt that both of you will be feeling.

Parenting life events

Once you have formed your partnership, perhaps the most important life event that will happen to you is child-bearing. Of course, starting a family is also a life stage of up to twenty or more years, and throughout the whole of this time, you will have to take on new and challenging responsibilities. But having a baby, particularly your first, is also a life event, which at the time it happens can rock you physically and financially as well as emotionally.

A case in point was Rochelle and Winston, who came to counselling a year after their first baby was born because they had stopped sleeping together. They were both in their early twenties and had moved to a new town about a month after the baby arrived, so that they could have a house with a garden. Rochelle had had a bad pregnancy. After that she hadn't wanted to have sex for a while and Winston had been very understanding.

Since then, though, they had never really felt like having sex. Both of them had been shocked at how their lives had changed. 'It's much more rewarding than I thought it would be,' said Winston, 'because Nathan is so wonderful; but it's also much more demanding.' They said that, not surprisingly, they were both tired most of the time, and Rochelle felt that even when she and Winston were just cuddling together, she had to keep one ear open in case Nathan cried.

As mentioned on pages 116–17, in many cases where couples come to Relate with problems just after the birth of a baby, the problems are to do with adjusting to having a new person in the family. The counsellor sensed, though, that this wasn't true for Winston and Rochelle. Both of them seemed delighted at Nathan's existence, and both seemed equally involved in caring for him. Instead, the counsellor felt strongly that the problems were practical ones. Rochelle and Winston had moved to a town they didn't know, away from their families, and away from friends. They were trying to cope almost entirely alone with a lively one year old, and Rochelle in particular, at home all day, was exhausted and had no friends. The counsellor helped them to organise practical resources, putting them in touch with local parent support groups, for example.

Rochelle and Winston also worked out a way to take time together as a couple, something they had never really done since Nathan was born. They arranged to spend just one hour a week together, added on to the hour of baby-sitting they had had to arrange in order to attend the Relate session. One week they would go out for a quick meal, the next week go home and snuggle up on the sofa. By the time they were due to collect Nathan, they felt a lot more relaxed.

It also helped for Rochelle and Winston to understand that what they were going through was very typical. Rochelle cried when the counsellor pointed out how much they were coping with. 'I thought I was doing so badly, and now you're telling me that it's OK.' Both of them had felt failures for not being able to cope; when they realised that they weren't expected to be perfect, they felt a lot better.

Several weeks into the counselling, Winston and Rochelle came into the session looking smug. During their 'free hour' following the previous session, they had ended up in bed, made love, and thoroughly enjoyed it. Both felt very relieved that their desire for each other hadn't died and that they were still able to enjoy themselves as much as they used to, even though 'we felt we needed a bit more practice'. They had arranged to visit Winston's mother the following weekend, leave Nathan with her and have the day to themselves. They and the counsellor both felt that given only a little more time and practical support, they would be back on track again.

After childbirth itself, other parenting life events usually centre round childhood emergencies. A child's illness or death is very often a trigger for relationship problems because of the different ways that each person may handle the worry and the grief. Often Mum gets all the professional support and attention and Dad feels left out. Or, in his attempt to be strong, Dad fails to show his real feelings and Mum feels unsupported. Relate counsellors report many cases of couples whose problems come almost completely from one partner's feeling that the other 'didn't care', when in fact the 'uncaring' partner says that he or she didn't dare to show any feelings because those feelings were just too painful. An example of this is the story of Yasmin and Deepak, told later in this book on page 185.

Life events concerning your parents

What happens to your parents can be a life event for you. More and more old people are living longer; they may be ill and need caring for, or be left alone through divorce or death and need your support. The practical aspects of this can be a strain, particularly if one of you resents caring for the other's parents. The emotional impact of seeing people you love slowly fading is also likely to create stress; you have to re-think your own relationship to them; start seeing them

!——————————————— *Task* ———————————————

Life since your partnership

Go back to the time line you drew in the task on page 85. You will already have marked on it the important events in your life that happened before you met your partner.

Now mark in another colour any of the following key events that have happened to you, and the ages each of you were when they happened.

- The year you became engaged
- The year you started living together
- The year you were married
- The year your first child was born
- The year your children left home
- The year you each retired
- Also mark in three other significant events you remember which happened since you met your partner. If you can, write down the date of each event.

Now think about each of these many events. If you are with your partner, discuss them. What happened? Who else was involved? Was each event important to you? How stressful was it? How do you think it's affected the way you think and feel about things? How do you think it's affected the way you relate to other people? How do you think it's affected the way you relate to your partner?

If an event seems to mark the beginning of difficulties you have had in the relationship, look at it particularly carefully. What shifts in your attitudes might have happened because of that event? How might these have caused you problems?

!

as fallible; realise that you are now responsible for looking after them.

When your parents die, even if you haven't been close to them or seen them for years, it can affect your relationship. You will need to pass through various stages of mourning – of not quite believing that they are gone; of being angry with them for all the things you think they did badly; of being sad that now you will never get to say the things that you wanted to. You may simply miss your parents, or you may panic that you are wasting your life as you think they did.

As well, you will almost certainly change your attitude to life now that your parents are not there. As mentioned before, your parents' death will push you into the life stage of independence. As you adapt to this, you can find yourself needing to take things more seriously, to give your own children more time and attention, to put more energy into fulfilling your ambitions. Your partner may find that he or she has a whole new person to deal with once your parents have withdrawn from the scene. And this can create a whole new relationship between you.

PART 3
CHANGE

11

FACING UP TO CHANGE

In order to move to deeper commitment in your partnership, you have to change things. The way you both relate to each other can't remain the same if you want to avoid further doubt or future crisis.

Once you begin to understand the reasons behind the problems in your relationship, you will almost certainly find that the problems themselves are starting to shift. Understanding itself creates change, because it alters the way you see things and so alters the way you feel about them and what you do about them, and because it brings you closer together in the way you think and feel. So if you have both begun to understand yourselves and your partnership, then you will already have begun to ease the problems.

Almost certainly, not everything in your relationship will need to change. You probably have whole areas of your partnership where you are doing well, even though you may have lost sight of them underneath all the conflict; but these are the areas you may have to look at closely.

Possible changes

● You may have to change the way you both communicate: listening, talking, sharing. Once you do this, you will be able to explain to each other just what you really think and feel. You will be able to swap notes on what you have begun to understand about yourselves and the relationship, so slowly start to appreciate each other's differences and not feel threatened by them.

● You may have to change the way you are both acting, particularly the ways in which you are meeting each other's needs and your own. If you can both begin to improve your skill in meeting needs, then you will start to feel more motivated to do things for each other, and will gradually build up trust that you can get what you want from the relationship.

● You may have to change the way you both cope with emotion. If you can feel better, and so be less tempted to defend and attack, every aspect of your relationship will improve. Resolving any painful emotion that you still feel about past events may well remove much of the bad feeling between you in the present.

● You may have to change your love-making if, for any one of a number of reasons, you are finding it unsatisfying. For while a poor relationship can all too easily lead to a poor sex life, the reverse is also true. If each of you can't give the other pleasure, or can't gain pleasure yourself, then your partnership is quite simply not fulfilling its potential.

● You may have to change the amount of energy you put in to making your relationship enjoyable, and to creating good times within your partnership. Spending time together, celebrating each other and planning for the future are all essential elements of a good partnership. You may have to learn, all over again, how to do these things with each other.

CAN YOU CHANGE?

You may feel that you don't need to change. You may think that if you change, you may seem to be admitting you are in the wrong in this relationship, and that your partner is in the right, when you are sure that it's completely the other way round. In fact, if you really want your relationship to come through this bad patch, you need to let go of this kind of blame. Neither one of you is really in the wrong; your relationship has simply developed in a hurtful direction because of your conflicting needs.

You may believe that you can never change. Perhaps you think that the way you have grown up has made your 'personality' unshiftable. Or you may believe the same of your partner, that he or she is never going to change, is in fact going to be the same for ever – and you may resent that. In fact, neither of these beliefs is correct.

It is possible to shift opinions; it is possible to behave differently. Once you have experienced that and know it's true, change becomes easier just because you know it can happen. Relate counsellors say that once a couple starts to believe things can alter, the battle to rebuild their relationship is almost over. Once 'he never has and he never will' turns into 'he can and he does' one counsellor commented, 'then I know that the couple will make it.'

What if you are scared of changing? The previous part of this book, on Understanding, explored how very stressful change in human life can be, because it is unknown. If we change, we never know what might happen. If in your past, a change has left you feeling hurt, you can be wary. Maybe you moved house and never made new friends; your mother re-married and you never did get on with your stepfather; you lived through a war or a recession and everything was swept away. If these things happened to you, change may be the last thing you want.

You may have reason to be anxious. Changing the way you handle your relationship can cause problems because, once changed, you realise you are still dissatisfied with your partnership, or are even more dissatisfied than you were. This is what happened for Jacky and Trevor, who came to counselling when their youngest boy went to secondary school. Jacky felt trapped by their relationship and thought she needed more freedom 'so I don't feel like a little housewife'. But in what seemed to be a very easy few sessions, the couple agreed that Jacky should go back to her work in tele-sales; they knew that this would alter the way they organised things, but they were prepared for that. They seemed to have negotiated the change well, with Trevor supporting Jacky not only emotionally, but also by picking the children up from school and helping around the house. They were confident that Jacky's job would help her not to feel so imprisoned in the relationship, and would, long term, improve their marriage.

A year later, though, they were back in counselling. Jacky's supervisor had offered her training in preparation for a better post; Jacky realised that she did want to do the training and that starting work had made her more dissatisfied than ever with her marriage. She was now even considering leaving. Trevor was very bitter: 'I thought supporting you to go to work would help, and you would be happier ... If only I'd said no, we might never have been in this situation.' In fact, the relationship had deteriorated not just because of

Jacky's job. There had been many other reasons why it was going wrong. The changes they had made to their partnership had highlighted their problems, because by seeing more of the outside world, Jacky had not felt less, but more trapped. Both of them had to look much more deeply at what was going wrong in order to begin to solve their difficulties.

HOW CAN YOU CHANGE?

Trevor and Jacky's story is unusual. In most cases, changing means you will be able to rebuild your relationship to be more, not less, stable than it was before. But there are guidelines to making that change work for you in the best way.

Taking responsibility
The bottom line is that you have to change if the relationship is going to. Even if you feel that it is your partner who is causing all the problems (or that it is your family who is creating all the difficulties) you won't be able to *make* anyone else change. Other people may be willing to change for you, but on the other hand, they may not be willing. Or, they may seem to change, but then, once you take the pressure off, mysteriously flip back to their original way of behaving. However, if you yourself genuinely shift what you are doing, then your relationship will shift. If you find out what you are doing that is adding to the problem and alter that, then automatically, things will improve.

Being realistic about your goals
Remember that this is relationship Mark 2 rather than Mark 1. There won't be any point in aiming for the incredible romance and the emotion you felt when you were first 'in love'. You can't ever have in reality what one Relate counsellor called the 'rosy cheeked babies and pine furniture' fantasy of partnership. Instead, focus your 'wish list' for the relationship on one particular thing that you want to achieve, such as getting your sex life back or dividing the housework more equally. Relate counsellors report that for most couples, one main relationship problem sticks out like a sore thumb, so find your

equivalent and do your best to concentrate on that. You can concentrate later on your other problems; they won't be forgotten and may even disappear on their own if you work on the main difficulty.

Going back to basics

You may feel that the simple suggestions included in this book won't solve your tricky problem. Counsellors say that some clients resent being asked to 'sit down for five minutes and talk'; it can seem, after having run a relationship for fifteen years, that going back to basics will do no good at all. But what you are both trying to achieve is exactly that: to go back to the basics of running a relationship, such as communicating, meeting each other's needs, handling your emotion, in order to make sure you are providing a solid foundation in your partnership. What Relate has done is to identify the basics, and to provide tried-and-tested ways of using them.

Not expecting to do it all at once

If you hope change will happen immediately, you may be lucky. One or two counsellors spoke of couples who identified their problem and their solution within a few sessions and then walked off hand in hand into the sunset; but this is unusual. It is more likely that you will improve one bit of your relationship at a time until eventually everything feels good, in the same way as when you learn to drive, you need to learn about the brakes, then the gears, then the indicators. You experiment with changing different parts of the way you relate, seeing what works, exploring what doesn't work, keeping going until you meet success.

Sticking with it

You may hit setbacks when you try to change your relationship. It is worthwhile remembering that everything you do is a rehearsal until your new skills become second nature. As with any rehearsal, things will go wrong; the rehearsal itself is the way you get to put them right.

Even when things change for the best, you may be unsure; you may panic, want to turn the clock back, not know what to do with this new and unfamiliar situation. This is exactly what happened to Salma and Phil. They came to counselling because she was tired of his working long hours and never spending any time with her. She wanted a fulfilled relationship; one where they were a couple again.

Phil seemed to completely understand Salma's unhappiness and want to meet her needs. He worked in a high-powered repping job and really saw himself as someone who was happy with change, and could be different if people needed him to be. He was proud of how he and Salma had adapted when their first baby was born, how he had supported her in those early years, and how flexible he had been as the children grew. Salma and Phil liked the idea of the communication exercises that the counsellor suggested; they talked daily for a while, and then began, with the counsellor's help, to negotiate exactly how their life would be different. Phil began coming home earlier, rearranged his job so he travelled less, began to take Salma out. He enjoyed the new depth that he saw was possible in their relationship.

Then Salma began coming to the sessions very angry with Phil. She would complain that he was always under her feet. She kept finding other things to do at times when they had negotiated to be together. He had changed his whole life in order to live with her, and she was frantically getting him to change back again.

At first, when the counsellor pointed this out to her, Salma was furious. Then she realised that what the counsellor was saying was true. Salma had what she'd asked for, but was now having to live with the results. She, as well as Phil, had to change. Up to now, through all her twenty years of child-rearing, she'd had very little opportunity to be close to Phil. She'd wanted that opportunity, but now she'd been given it, she had to respond to it: talking to him, sharing with him, opening up to him. Scared of having to do that, she was pushing Phil away in order to protect herself. Once Salma had realised that this was what was happening, she was able to begin to explore and resolve her fears about being close to her husband.

This part of the book is about how to change various aspects of your relationship in order to change the whole way you relate. Each of the chapters deals with a different aspect, and each is as vital to rebuilding your relationship as the rest; they often overlap. Relate counsellors work with their clients to decide where the vulnerabilities are and which area of the relationship needs the most work first; but in general, all the areas mentioned here need to be strong for a partnership to begin to improve.

! ————————— *Task* —————————

Abracadabra

You've probably noticed that it may literally take just a fraction of a second to change your mind about something. It can take only that much time to decide that you are going to behave differently in some way in the future.

Choose a very small part of your behaviour that you know your partner wants you to change. Don't choose something that causes much bad feeling between you. Rather, choose something small, such as remembering to shut the fridge door when you open it, or tidying your work-top every day. Change your behaviour now, and keep it up for exactly a week, no more and no less. Don't get upset if your partner doesn't even notice; you are making this change for you, to prove you can do it.

At the end of the week, make your own decision about whether you are going to continue with the change or not.

!

12

GOOD COMMUNICATION

Communication is the basis for any relationship improvement. You need good communication between you to swap thoughts, goals, ideas and feelings; to tell each other what you need and want; to negotiate shifts in your relationship; to check that those shifts have happened as you wanted them to.

You also particularly need to communicate about the past. You have probably realised by now that in order to fully understand what is going on, you have to explore your past, particularly your very early life or any important life changes that you've experienced. To move towards deeper commitment, at some point you will both almost certainly have to share what you've explored with each other, so that each of you appreciates what the other has gone through. If you don't communicate the tension you had in your relationship with your mother, the fear you always felt of not passing your college course, or the horror you experienced during the miscarriage three years ago – or whatever else has been important for each of you – then you will never begin to contact the real tenderness for each other that underpins every truly loving relationship.

And, once you've resolved the past, and even once you feel confident that your relationship is completely solid, you will need to keep on communicating. You both have to continue updating each other on your different and changing thoughts and feelings, often on a day-to-day basis, otherwise problems will build up again.

WHAT BLOCKS COMMUNICATION?

Real communication is a skill, and often, we never learn it. Our early experiences – things we do ourselves or see other people doing – teach us a lot about communication, but what we learn may not always be helpful. As a child, your parents may have shouted at you or at each other. You may have learned to block off these frightening words by simply not listening to them; now, when your relationship gets tough and your partner screams at you, you cut off and don't pay attention. As a child, you may have learned to keep quiet because you got bullied if you said something stupid. Now, in crisis, when you think about confiding in your partner, you feel scared, and don't talk; you pull back from being honest, and never really tell your partner everything. As a child, you may have been able to squirm out of trouble simply by what you said; now, when you are in conflict, you use your words to create a smokescreen until your partner just gives in and gives up.

The way communication can actually lie at the centre of the problems in a relationship is shown clearly by the story of Jamie and Janice. They sat in the counselling room as if they were strangers, tight-lipped, turned away from each other, not even able to look each other in the eye. The counsellor learned that they had been married for twelve years, and had tried to have children for six. For a while, they had remained optimistic, through medical examinations, fertility treatment, more examinations until eventually they had said 'enough is enough' and decided to stop 'trying' and relax. Since that time, two years ago, their relationship had gone downhill. They had each withdrawn into themselves, lived their lives as best they could and tried to carry on. Both worked long hours, and when they were at home at the same time, they reported that they had very little to say to each other. Things had got worse over the last few months, since Jamie's sister had had a baby, which had made them remember their problems all over again.

As part of counselling, Janice and Jamie were asked to try the communication exercises that underpin most Relate work. Regularly, for just a few minutes, they each took turns in talking about something that was important to them. The counsellor explained that only by beginning to really communicate with each other could they begin to rebuild a relationship that seemed on the rocks. They were pessimistic. 'I'm not sure what we would talk about,' said Jamie, but they agreed to try.

It was hard for Jamie and Janice. They found it difficult both to concentrate on what the other was saying, and to talk when it was their turn. They reported long silences, embarrassment and feelings of resentment. After the third week, they both came back to the session saying that they weren't prepared to try any more.

The counsellor explored with Janice and Jamie individually just what was stopping them communicating, and found that it was almost the same thing for both of them. Both, in their own ways, were frightened to speak or to listen; they were frightened of what they would say if they did open up, frightened of what they would hear if their partner opened up. The whole issue of not having a baby had built up so much guilt and resentment between them that it was like an unexploded bomb.

With the counsellor's encouragement, Janice and Jamie began to try to explain their feelings to each other in the session. The results were remarkable. Their emotions were incredibly similar: a mixture of fear, guilt and anger. It turned out that, because the results of the fertility tests had been inconclusive, each had imagined that the other was blaming them for not being able to start a family. At the same time, each of them did feel angry in case it was the other's 'fault'. Over time, they were able to see that 'fault' wasn't a relevant word to use, and that had they been able to talk through their feelings at the start, they would have been able to face the problems as a couple. Instead, they had simply stopped communicating altogether.

Janice and Jamie had a great deal more work to do in counselling. They needed to explore what having a family meant to them, their own past family life and how that had affected them, and what they wanted to do in the future. But now, they had the tool of communication to help them through. Also, having realised what lay behind their lack of communication, they were actually getting on very well as a couple. In the end, they left counselling with exactly the same decision they had previously made: not to go for fertility treatment, but to keep on trying to have a baby. The difference was that they both knew that whatever happened, they would stay together.

! ——————————— *Task* ———————————

Hand over your mouth

Whenever we have a bad experience of communicating, this makes it less likely that we will be able to communicate well in future. Of course, whenever we communicate effectively in a way that helps, we learn to do better next time.

Complete each of these sentences with as many words as you like. Then think through what you've written. What lessons have you learned in life about listening and talking? Have these lessons helped you communicate well or badly?

- I remember a time I was afraid to talk because . . .
- I remember saying something I regretted when . . .
- A time I said something that really made a difference was when . . .
- I remember a time I misheard something and it caused trouble because . . .
- A time I listened to someone and really helped was when . . .

If you can swap notes with your partner, say more about the sentences you've written. Do you think any of the events you've remembered may have influenced the way you listen and talk to your partner now?

!

LEARNING TO LISTEN

The most basic communication skill is listening, and yet it is often the most difficult. First and foremost, you have to let your partner reach you. It is very easy to be physically present when someone talks but, somehow, not quite mentally present.

You may find yourself blanking out, switching off as if turning down the volume, particularly if your partner is explaining something that means a lot to him or her but which cuts across your ideas. Or you may listen outwardly but talk inwardly, holding your own little conversation about what you are hearing, or rehearsing what you are going to say next. Your own 'inner voice' totally drowns out that of your partner.

Then, you may be tempted to let your 'inner voice' find its way into your mouth. So when your partner stops to take breath, you make a 'rubbishing' comment that shows clearly that he or she hasn't reached you at all. Perhaps you cut across your partner's words, so making your point seem more important. Perhaps your response, instead of showing respect, contradicts your partner's feelings or suggests that they are misplaced.

All these things – blanking out, talking inwardly, 'rubbishing' your partner's comments – have one very simple cause. At the bottom of them all is actually a single emotion: fear. You may feel irritated, frustrated or defensive; but underneath that, what is really going on is fear. Perhaps you are frightened that your partner is somehow proving that you are wrong. Perhaps you're frightened that if you let your partner go on speaking, he or she will eventually overpower you, take you over with words. Perhaps you're frightened that your partner's anger will harm you or that criticism of the relationship will mean that in the end, he or she will leave.

It's difficult to put the fear to one side, particularly if your relationship has been going through problems and much of your recent communication has been angry and hurtful. Relate counsellors find that the key is to practise listening to each other regularly, taking turn and turn about. Clients often learn their first lessons about this from the fact that the counsellor is willing to listen to them; he or she models out what would be helpful in a loving partnership by including it as an integral part of the counsellor–client relationship. Then, clients are encouraged to listen attentively and respectfully to each other during their session, followed by 'homework' of spending just a few minutes of listening while the other talks, then building up to half an hour each, or more. It can begin by feeling quite uncomfortable, but soon you will start to feel more at ease with concentrating on the other person, and really taking in what he or she is saying.

The experience of Relate counsellors is that when you begin to listen openly, something shifts. The person who is listened to starts to put aside the defensiveness and the need to attack which underlies so much of the pain. By listening, you don't actually give the other person power over you. Rather, you offer a chance for self-expression which, in the end, will take away bad feeling and make your partner much easier to be with.

To help you listen more openly, even at the start when you are unused to it, try doing some of the following things.

● Do your best to give your full attention to your partner. Concentrate on what he or she looks like and sounds like, focus your attention on face and voice; try not to notice anything else.

● If your own thoughts start to intrude, don't fight them. Intruding thoughts are like children: the harder you try to get them to be quiet, the harder they winge. Instead, try turning your attention gently back again to what your partner is saying and letting the intrusive thoughts fade away.

● Once your partner stops speaking, try not to jump in immediately. Try counting to at least three before you open your mouth; this will give you time to think about what he or she has been saying and will give the message that you have really been listening.

● If what your partner is saying is full of emotion that is painful to you, the guidelines on pages 183–4 offer suggestions to help you cope.

Encouraging your partner to communicate

Good listening is active; you don't just sit there and take it all in. When you listen well, you actively help your partner to speak. While he or she is actually talking, you are giving positive signals by your body language; when he or she pauses, your comments are encouraging more words.

Unfortunately, all too often people don't do this. As we listen, we can turn away slightly, lose eye contact, let our expression show boredom or disagreement. When we speak, we can say something that leads the conversation off in another direction.

Once again, it may be fear that drives us. We don't want our partner to talk, simply because we are afraid of what he or she may say. Something in the words is frustrating us and we just don't want to even think about it. Interestingly, boredom with a partner's conversation, though it may seem to be the result of too many years spent together, can also be one way of feeling irritated or anxious. We really want our partner to talk about something other than what he or she is talking about – perhaps about us. Rather than admit that, even to ourselves, we push down the anger and feel bored and restless instead.

It is actually very simple to encourage a partner to talk, and doing so can make a huge difference. This is because long-term partners are unused to being positively encouraged to speak; over the years you may both have lost the knack. So if you do offer encouragement, and show that you are really interested in what your partner has to offer, then you may both very quickly start to feel better about each other and be more willing to trust and share.

Try making body language positive. This means turning towards your partner; trying not to block with your gestures, but leaving your arms open; keeping your face turned towards him or her; looking interested. To begin with, using these body-language signals of interest may seem false, so use them carefully. In a very short while, they won't be false, because surprising as it may seem, if you take on the body language of interest, very soon you will become more interested. Your mind will reflect what your body is doing.

You can also use some 'acknowledgement signals', such as a slight 'mm' sound, a nod, a 'yes' or an 'OK'. These are ways of telling your partner not that you necessarily agree, but that you have heard the words and accepted them. If you already use some of these signals when you talk to each other, then use them more; if not, then develop some between you. (Try not to use signals that have developed between you to mean the very opposite of acknowledgement, signals that say, 'I want you to think that I'm listening, but in fact I'm not', such as the classic 'Yes dear'.)

Finally, use your words to encourage. When a partner pauses, you can ask a short question which will lead him or her to say more. Or, you can say something that comments on what has just been said: 'You must have felt very sad when that happened.' Then pause, allowing your partner to take up on that, and say more about exactly what those feelings were.

Hearing what is really said

Very often, you think you know what your partner means when actually, you don't. You may hear what you want to hear. You may 'mind read', thinking you know what is meant, but actually not interpreting your partner's words correctly at all.

And of course, especially if your relationship is under strain, you may assume the worst in your partner's words. So when your partner says 'I love you' what you hear is 'I want something', and when he or she says 'I'm tired', what you you hear is 'I don't fancy you any more'. You put the unhappiest interpretation on what your partner is saying and believe it to be true: because you ignore other, more positive evidence; because you generalise and think that one negative comment means that everything is completely negative; because you magnify your partner's comment out of all proportion.

An example of this taken to its extreme was the case of Marian and George. He had suggested they come to counselling because she had had an affair. A gentle couple in their late fifties, they had moved towards early retirement as they had planned, living in an old house in a leafy suburb. A few months previously, the last of their children had left home and it was after this that Marian had begun to go out with, and then to sleep with, a fellow student in the French class that she attended every week. She had not told George about this openly, but she hadn't hidden it either, and when he challenged her, she had admitted what was happening. George had been very shocked, and had immediately suggested that they seek outside help.

George was distraught. A small, rounded man who loved walking – he worked as a postman – he sat in the counselling room crying, rocking backwards and forwards like a small child. Marian cuddled him. She seemed to be keeping all her emotions tightly under control, though she said that she did 'sometimes panic if I feel things slipping away'.

To the counsellor, there seemed to be something that wasn't clear. It was almost as if each of them had their own idea of what had happened, which didn't quite match. It very soon became obvious what it was. They began to explore what had happened to trigger the affair. George said he suspected that it might have had something to do with their children leaving home, or could it have been that they were hesitating over their round-the-world trip, which because of lack of money, they had talked about postponing? Marian looked at George, amazed and angry. 'Don't twist things,' she said. 'The travel was off. Everything was off. You said so.' George looked completely confused.

Slowly the story emerged. When their youngest child had left, and before they were going to travel, George had really wanted to 'enjoy the house'. Also, he was feeling a little anxious about being alone in the house with Marian after twenty-three years of the children being around. They had never been a couple to talk in depth, and they had completely lost the knack over the time it had taken them to rear their family. So George had said that he wanted more space, and moved upstairs, setting up his own room with his own special things around him. Sometimes he even slept up there. He was aware of tension between them, but had not seen it as anything particularly threatening. They would work it through; they had the time.

To Marian, however, George's 'wanting space' and taking a separate room was quite simply a code for 'the relationship is over.' She had imagined that George didn't want to spend the final decades of his life with her, travelling and working abroad. She had slowly withdrawn from him, quietly and unnoticeably panicking as she saw everything 'slipping away'. Very soon, meeting a kind, considerate man who seemed to like her, she started what she thought was a brief affair, which she would use to recover from her failed marriage and give her the courage to move out.

George was horrified. He couldn't understand why Marian had believed he was going to leave or, if she did, why she had just accepted it. The answer seemed to be down to her panic, which made her always fear the worst, and then not have the courage to challenge it. Once Marian had heard the truth, it was as if she had a new lease of life. The two of them began to work on improving their communication, and slowly built up more trust; both of them seemed fully committed to making the relationship work.

Then, another crisis occurred, and this time the counsellor saw the problem being acted out in front of her. George arrived at counselling very happy, saying that it was working well for him, but that he'd like a month's break, to think things through. As she listened to him, Marian became very still, smiled, and patted his hand gently, but the counsellor sensed that underneath, something much stronger was going on. 'Marian, what have you just heard George say, and what did you think that meant?' Once again, Marian had interpreted George's words as meaning the worst; that he wanted to stop counselling and that everything was over.

The counsellor helped Marian to hear the real message of George's words, and they negotiated that he would take four weeks' break from sessions. During this time, Marian worked on her own, tracking back to her childhood her fear of being left, and also her inability to challenge what people were doing. By the time George returned to counselling, Marian was far more able to hear what he was really saying rather than the things her fear made her hallucinate that he meant. George, on the other hand, had learned from the way the counsellor had questioned Marian that he could do the same if he felt that he was being misinterpreted. Both of them had realised, from their interactions with the counsellor, that deep miscommunication could happen in their relationship, and that the way forward was to realise that and to challenge it – another example of how the actual counsellor–client relationship can be a vital way of changing things for a couple. .

What George and Marian failed to do was what in fact you have to do every time you listen to your partner: check out if you're unsure. What does your partner really mean when he or she speaks? Read the signs.

This will mean listening carefully. Some of the words that your partner says may sound more 'weighty' than the others; which are they? If your partner comments lightly that he is 'a little tense' at work, and the word he stresses is 'tense', then he may not actually mean 'a little'; hear the signal that he needs help and respond to it. If your partner says that she isn't irritated by the fact that your mother is coming to stay, does she actually want you to hear the word 'irritated' and ignore the word 'isn't'? If so, maybe this is something that needs talking about.

You can also often see or hear the emotions in your partner's body language. Look particularly for signs that your partner is saying what he or she thinks you want to hear, but really thinks something else. If her words say that 'she's fine', but her voice sounds as if she's tired and anxious, she probably isn't fine; ask about the anxiety. If his words say 'it doesn't matter', but his face looks tight and tense, then it probably does matter; ask what you can do about it.

Also, of course, when listening to your partner, be prepared to explore further, even when under attack. If he or she says something hurtful, then ask, without a sense of challenge, what the real emotion is. You may then get to see the fear behind the anger, and once you've understood that, then the hurtful comment can lose its sting. Chapter 14 of this book, on emotions, gives further guidelines for communicating with partners who feel strongly.

! ———————— *Task* ————————

Your turn

One of the key exercises that Relate offers is regularly listening to each other for just a few minutes. If your relationship is starting to improve, and you feel that both of you would be willing to listen to each other, then try this exercise. Set aside at least a quarter of an hour of uninterrupted time.

The talker

One of you talks for five minutes; the other should do nothing but listen. (If you keep forgetting who's supposed to be talking, let the talker hold something – an ornament or a stuffed toy. If you are not holding that thing, you must just listen.)

To begin with, try to avoid talking about your partner or about the relationship. The one who is talking should stick to 'safe' subjects, perhaps telling your partner about something neutral that you did recently, what you liked and disliked about it, what was interesting, what was boring. Try to avoid talking about your partner at all to begin with.

The listener

The listener has most of the work to do! You should sit silently and concentrate on listening as carefully as you can; allow yourself to be interested in what your partner is telling you. You can make an enormous difference by listening well.

When one person has finished talking, the other can take a turn. When you swap over, don't comment or react directly to what the other has said.

Try to do this exercise at least twice a week. You'll find that it gives you the opportunity to practise your skills so that you become a much better listener.

In counselling, once you have developed basic listening skills through doing these exercises, you progress to harder tasks. You may be asked to spend a longer time listening; to repeat back what you have heard; to allow the talker to speak about things that he or she feels strongly about.

!

'————————— Talking Point —————————

Retreat

The ideal relationship gives you the opportunity to communicate, occasions without interruption where you can listen and talk about how you think and feel. Often, though, it just doesn't happen like this. When you try to talk, the family interrupts, or the phone rings.

Do a communication survival plan. Together, decide the following things to make it easier for you to spend at least fifteen minutes a day communicating with each other.

- When exactly can you take fifteen minutes on your own?
- Where will you go that will be private: into your bedroom, out in the garden, away from the house?
- How will you make sure that there are no distractions: take the phone off the hook, pin a note on the door?
- How are you going to tell the people who need to know – children, family, neighbours – that this is your private time and nothing is going to disturb it?

What exactly will you do if someone tries to interrupt? It's good to have a form of words ready in advance to say to anyone who interrupts you, such as 'I hear that you . . . (need the video switching on). Mummy and I are talking, and want to carry on talking until four o'clock. You can wait until then. Go downstairs and we'll be with you in about six minutes, at four o'clock.'

'

LEARNING TO SHARE

The other side of listening is talking; in order to communicate with your partner, you need to say things and be willing to share yourself freely. Perhaps the first thing to look at is just what you are saying to each other, and particularly whether you are really interacting.

For example, when you first met your partner, you probably both talked a great deal in order to learn all about each other. To start with, this may have been well balanced, with both of you asking questions, giving answers to questions, and making points that weren't in response to any question but seemed relevant. This balance probably made you both feel good; you liked talking about things, you liked being asked about things, you liked asking, you liked answering .

As a relationship develops, people tend to ask questions and to answer them less and less. This is a natural development; we do know many things about each other now, and so do need to ask less. But we may reach a point where we feel we know all about each other. So we only ask questions such as 'What time will you be home tonight?'; forget to ask questions such as 'How are you feeling?'; give answers of one word or even just a grunt. Eventually, we only ever speak in unrelated statements, giving each other information but not expecting or inviting intimacy. One way to improve a relationship very quickly is to start asking more questions and giving fuller answers when you speak.

Another problem that can happen in a relationship is an imbalance in who does the talking. You are afraid of hurting your partner, or of a negative reaction if you say something he or she doesn't like. So one of you may stop talking almost completely. You change the subject if the conversation starts to reach an important point, one that means a lot to you or that may force you to face painful issues. You answer questions such as 'How are you doing?' 'Had a good day?' on the most superficial level possible, so that you won't break down and reveal just how bad you are feeling. If you have a lot to hide, you may actually shift your body language and voice so that your real thoughts and feelings don't show, blanking out your expression and your voice tone so that you are not really communicating at all.

An instance of a couple whose balance in communication caused immense strain is that of Fiona and Stuart. Fiona was very unhappy, because, as she put it, 'he never talks to me . . . He will never ever tell me what he feels'. She was angry and frustrated, felt locked out from Stuart's thoughts and was beginning to think that he didn't love her or trust her.

When the counsellor turned to Stuart, it seemed clear that this wasn't so. He was very much in love with Fiona, and kept repeating that he would do anything not to hurt her; he had great difficulty in understanding why she was so upset, and why she had thought it necessary for them to come to counselling.

The counsellor encouraged each of them to talk about how communication had been handled when they were young. What came out was that Stuart's father, who had died when he was sixteen, had been a psychiatric nurse, working with very difficult patients at a high-security prison in the West Country. Every day, when he came home off shift, he was tired and tense. All he really wanted was peace, and if he didn't get it, then his wife and children had to pay. As Stuart spoke about this, his voice became quieter and quieter, and it was obvious that the memories upset him a great deal.

Fiona was riveted by what Stuart was saying. Never having met his father, she had had no idea what had happened. She was astonished, and very eager for him to tell her more, to let her into his memories as well as his feelings about them. This itself came as a big surprise to Stuart. He had learned to keep his feelings in so as not to be beaten by his father; now he was still keeping them in because he thought that was the way to best love his wife. And here she was telling him to do the exact opposite. When the session finished, they went home and talked all night, catching up on Stuart's history, and all the upsetting things he had never dared tell Fiona. Suddenly everything fell back into place for them, and they were able to begin to rebuild their relationship.

Fiona and Stuart were able to confide in each other more or less right away once the reasons behind their problem were clear, but regaining trust in your relationship can take a while. Relate clients often take months before they can truly open up to their partners and reveal their innermost feelings. Don't expect to drop your guard immediately; it will feel unsafe talking about things that you are not sure your partner will accept. But at some point, you do have to make a leap of faith, and confide: perhaps about how sad you felt when your brother stopped speaking to you, perhaps about how angry you felt when you lost your job. If you do confide, you may be amazed at how easily your partner also begins to share things with you; if you trust him or her with your feelings, it makes it much easier for mutual trust to develop.

What if you are actively keeping a secret from your partner? The ideal is that, as you feel more committed, then you can both tell each other everything. But this is very hard if you have a secret that you fear will make your partner hate or withdraw from you: such as the fact that you had an affair, a termination, or a spell in jail. If you know that your secret will hurt your partner deeply, you do have to stop and think. Are you opting for total honesty in order to improve the relationship, or just in order to make yourself feel better? If it's the latter, and speaking the truth will only hurt your partner and harm your relationship, think carefully before breaking your silence.

KEEPING THE PEACE

The most unhelpful thing you and your partner can do when you talk to each other is to attack. If you do, then very soon you won't want to listen to each other. Eventually, you may well stop talking altogether. Here are some typical 'battle responses':

● Blame: telling your partner that something is his or her fault. 'You spoiled the evening by telling that joke.'

● Accuse: saying that your partner 'made' you feel something. 'You made me feel so angry when you overspent on our joint account.'

● Tit-for-tat: taking each statement your partner makes about how bad he or she feels and claiming that you feel worse. 'I know the children played you up; they play me up every day.'

● Nag: telling your partner, again and again, what you think ought to be done. 'I've told you a hundred times to clean the car.'

● Dump: telling your partner every single bad thing you think her or she has ever done. 'Everything you do is awful.'

● Cringe: using a scared voice tone, or body language, to give the message that you're frightened of your partner.

● Shout: raising your voice in order to try to get your message across, often with a pointed finger or aggressive body language.

● Give commands: telling your partner that he or she 'should' help you unpack or 'ought to' ring the office, when in fact, it is just your life rules telling you that these would be good things to do. Remember that your partner's life rules are not the same; he or she probably has no deep inner belief that these things 'should' be done.

● Make excuses: saying that you can't do something because you haven't the time or the energy when the truth is that you don't want to or choose not to.

As mentioned before, many of these responses link back to ways of coping that, when you were a child, made you feel better. The problem is that while these ways of communicating may help each of you to feel better, they do nothing to help the relationship. If you blame, nag or shout, your partner will feel bad. Even the less obviously threatening reactions, such as cringing, are a form of attack; if you cringe, you give your partner the message that he or she is a bad person who actually frightens you.

In fact, you may deliberately, though unawares, be choosing the way of communicating with your partner that is most threatening. You do this because over the years, you've learned that this will make him or her back off. So each partner in a couple will, when rowing, often behave in the way that most winds the other up.

This is illustrated by Sarah and Maggie, a lesbian couple who came to Relate. They were slowly making progress, and on one particular occasion, Maggie started to speak about how well things had gone. Sarah was delighted at this, and for about half the session, they talked around the issues, with the counsellor's help, in a very positive way. Then, Sarah began to talk quite angrily about something that had happened at work. Immediately, and in front of the counsellor's eyes, Maggie's behaviour changed. She turned away, answered in single syllables, used a flat, expressionless voice. Within minutes, Sarah was in tears. Maggie responded by turning away even more. Both of them, by this time, were feeling terrible.

The counsellor, struck by the dramatic change, asked them both if they would try an experiment. They agreed, and under the counsellor's direction, Maggie turned towards Sarah, looked at her, answered her questions, and tried to respond in a more animated way, as she had done before. Sarah immediately brightened up and stopped crying, whereupon Maggie, feeling less threatened, visibly relaxed and opened up. The counsellor pointed out that both of them were actually making things worse by their reaction, and they realised that they had choices in the way they behaved.

Sarah and Maggie remained in counselling for a long time. They tracked down the past reasons for Maggie's reacting to anger by shutting off and the reasons why Sarah got so upset when she did that. Maggie, who had been fiercely bullied when a child, had learned to 'put on a hard face' and ignore anyone who got angry with her – an effective way of making the bullies lose interest fairly quickly.

Sarah's mother, on the other hand, would usually follow up any childhood punishment by 'cold shoulder' treatment for days at a time. Sarah's angry tone had reminded Maggie of previous bullying – even though Sarah hadn't actually been angry at Maggie – and she had shut off. Maggie's shutting off had reminded Sarah of her mother's rejection. When the relationship had entered its crisis, they had both, completely without meaning to hurt, learned which behaviour would most push each other's buttons. Then they had used that behaviour more and more.

As counselling progressed, both Sarah and Maggie tried to relearn ways of behaving that got positive rather than negative reactions. Maggie learned to keep in contact with Sarah, to keep talking, to keep looking. Sarah learned that a particular angry tone of voice would always make Maggie feel bad, and consciously avoided using this, expressing any frustration she felt out of earshot, or by using an expression and voice tone that didn't upset Maggie so much.

The lessons that Maggie and Sarah learned is true for all the 'battle responses' listed on page 150. If you can hold back from nagging, blaming, or using a particular tone of voice, then your communication with your partner has a much better chance of working. Instead, try using clear, non-threatening ways of communicating with your partner. Here are some you can use.

● Instead of blaming, take responsibility: rather than 'You spoiled the evening' try saying 'I didn't enjoy the evening, but that's my problem'.
● Instead of accusing, admit to your feelings: rather than 'You made me feel . . .' try saying 'I feel . . .'.
● Instead of 'tit-for-tatting', acknowledge your partner's feelings: rather than 'Well, so what; they play me up every day' try saying 'I'm sorry the children played you up'.
● Instead of nagging, make constructive suggestions: rather than 'I've told you a hundred times to clean the car' try saying 'Why don't we clean the car together?'
● Instead of dumping, stick to the matter in hand: rather than 'Everything you do is awful' try saying 'One thing I'd like to change is . . .'
● Instead of cringing, use a clear voice and steady eye contact.
● Instead of shouting, use a calm voice and gentle movements.
● Instead of giving commands, make requests: rather than 'You really should help me' try saying 'I'd love it if you'd help me unpack.'

- Instead of making excuses, use a clear 'no', or open a discussion of how to achieve what your partner wants.

! ——————— *Task* ———————

Dear . . .

Not all forms of communication involve talking. If you enjoy writing, try scribbling a short letter to your partner. A good subject would be how you spent your day: couples often misunderstand this, each partner thinking that the other has had a much more interesting day than they've had!

Write your letter, including what you did, who you met, what you thought and particularly how you felt. Try to avoid negative comments about your partner; on the other hand, if you thought about him or her lovingly during the day, be sure to put that in.

!

! ——————— *Task* ———————

I really heard what you said

If you have already tried the short exercise on page 146, and have completed it successfully for several days, then you can add an extra piece to it.

Take five minutes each to talk, just as in the previous exercise. Follow all the guidelines, as outlined on page 146.

At the end of the five minutes, when each person has finished talking, the listener should briefly repeat back the basics of what he or she has heard. Don't try to do this word for word, but do give back an accurate account of the main points. The person who did the talking can correct you if he or she thinks that you have misunderstood.

Don't discuss this, but move on immediately to the other person's turn to talk.

In time, you will both become much more accurate in hearing each other. And as you each begin to feel that your partner is listening to you more closely, you will find that your trust in each other will improve.

!

13

MEETING NEEDS

Every human being has needs that must be met. These may be physical needs such as food, drink or warmth. They may be emotional needs, such as love, warmth, affection, support. Most of us have the same sort of physical needs, but our emotional needs will vary according to who we are and what our past has been like. We may need to be cuddled when we get upset, or simply to be allowed to cry. We may need to rush out and celebrate when we hear good news, or just like to curl up quietly and enjoy the moment.

However self-sufficient anyone is, it's impossible to meet all our needs ourselves. Human beings are social creatures, and we want to talk, to laugh, to make love. So when we form a partnership, it's usually because we feel that the other person is going to meet our needs well, and that we will be able to give in return. Falling in love is such a wonderful experience because there is such a huge sense of possible fulfilment as never before, and we hope that our needs for attention, support and company are going to be satisfied for ever.

Unfortunately, for many reasons, this just doesn't happen. We may not know what our own needs are; or they may contradict each other; or they may be just too huge ever to be met. We may not even be able to tell our partner what it is we want – and if we do, he or she may not understand. Or our partner simply can't meet our needs, because of who they are or because their needs don't fit with ours. And, of course, all this also happens in reverse; our partner may be just as disappointed as we are, because just as few of their needs are being met.

When we first meet, to some extent, we can ignore these difficulties. But eventually, as explained more fully in Chapter 9, they can become a burden. Either immediately, because our needs don't fit from the start, or eventually, when a change in one or both of us makes needs suddenly start to clash, we can find it all too much. We get tired. Bad feeling builds. We start to assume the worst. In a few months or a few years, we can reach a situation where we can feel that our partner is doing nothing for us, and we have no wish to do anything in return.

In order to have a working partnership, you have to get to the point where, in general, you are both fulfilling and being fulfilled. This doesn't mean that one of you gets all the goodies or the other doesn't; it doesn't mean that one of you does all the taking and the other all the giving. It does mean that you have to change your relationship so that both of you feel that your needs are being met, most of the time.

BEING AWARE OF YOUR OWN NEEDS

It may seem strange to begin by talking about your own needs, because love is often said to be about forgetting yourself and thinking of your partner. However, if you don't know what you want, it can be bad news for you and for the relationship. People who aren't aware of their own needs tend to be cut off from their own ability to be happy or to really enjoy life. They can be martyrs, making it really uncomfortable for their partner because they will never accept anything as a gift of love. Such people will probably, in the end, resent the fact that none of their needs are being met. So if you don't keep track of your own needs – even though on occasion you choose to set them aside in order to avoid conflict – then in the end, you will feel disappointed with your partnership and bitter towards your partner.

Very often, you don't know what your needs are because you are afraid to find out. All of us feel can like this, because all human beings are encouraged, as children, to put ourselves second and others first. How many times have you heard parents say (or caught yourself saying) 'I don't care what you want; we're doing it this way', or 'Don't be so selfish; give some to your sister.' Of course, we have to be taught these lessons, because otherwise the world would be full of people who just grabbed what they wanted and never thought of anyone else. But we often end up thinking that what we need doesn't matter.

There is also a temptation, particularly if you have been together for a long time, to forget your own needs completely and concentrate only on your partner's. You can 'blur the boundaries', think that what your partner wants is what you want, and then feel unhappy when yet again you go to your in-law's family rather than yours for Christmas.

Finally, you can think you know what your needs are, but in fact have only identified the surface demand. There may be other, deeper needs underneath, and you will be more likely to get what you want if you are aware of that. If you want your partner to help with the dishes, it may only be that you want the task finished more quickly. However, it could be that you would feel more supported if your partner helped; that you like the feeling of working togther; that your partner's helping you with the dishes would be a sign of love for you.

If these are your hidden needs, then if your partner refuses, you may well be far more upset than if your agenda is simply to finish the dishes in time to watch your favourite television programme. Being aware of these 'hidden agendas' will help you to explain to your partner more fully and more convincingly what you really want. It will also, very often, help your partner to understand just why you are asking for some particular thing. And if a partner really understands your deepest needs, he or she will almost always be more prepared to say yes to you.

! ——————————————— *Task* ———————————————

Giving yourself a gift

Decide on one thing that you really want and that you can give yourself. It might not be anything expensive; it could be an evening alone with delicious food and drink, a walk in the country, or a day spent sunbathing and reading a book.

Give yourself this gift. Take responsibility for arranging it and making it happen. Don't expect other people to do it for you; do it all for yourself. Enjoy it even more because you now know that you are able to give yourself a present.

!

TAKING RESPONSIBILITY FOR MEETING
YOUR OWN NEEDS

We often think that as a couple we have to be everything to each other. If we are not, then we think there's something wrong. So we blame our partners if they don't make us happy, accuse them of disloyalty if they aren't there for us all the time, think that they don't love us if they don't meet our every need.

One of the most important steps in rebuilding your relationship is realising exactly what your partner can and can't do for you. There will be some things, of course, that you will rightly expect of your partnership: probably love-making, certainly companionship, possibly financial support. But there are many other, day-to-day things, that a partner may not be able to do for you, simply because they are only one person. The fact is that your partner can't do everything. It isn't that he or she doesn't want to; it is that, having a certain personality and upbringing, a certain outlook on life, and certain strengths and weaknesses, your partner just cannot provide all you need.

There are also some things that are simply outside a partner's control, and in the end, however much it hurts, there may be nothing that either of you can do about that; the alternatives are to spend the rest of your life bitter and resentful, or to accept what is happening and work with it.

This is what happened for Jean and Bernie. They came to counselling at the point where they were about to split up. Both in their late fifties, they had just celebrated their silver wedding anniversary, and seemed to have done well in life. Bernie was a manager in a large corporation, with a salary big enough for Jean not to have to work. She had brought up their two children, and for the past five years had done voluntary work and entertained Bernie's business contacts.

Bernie came into the counselling room ready to leave his relationship there and then. He was tired of Jean's nagging and blaming, which over the past few years had reached crisis point. He said that he couldn't walk into the house without her criticising him for something. He had been very much in love with her, had enjoyed family life; now, he would rather be alone for the rest of his days than put up with her nagging.

The counsellor suggested that the couple use a time-line exercise to explore their history. When they reached their mid-twenties, and the point at which they met, Jean spoke enthusiastically about how impressed she had been by Bernie – his intelligence, his sense of achievement, his air of 'going places' – but slowly, as she talked her way along the time line to the present day, she grew less and less enthusiastic. Her tone became very bitter as she spoke of how Bernie had been passed over for promotion, and had not been able to rise as high in his profession as she had expected.

Bernie admitted that he too had been upset that his career hadn't risen to the heights, but he had come to terms with it. He had, over the past few years, started to turn his attention to enjoying life here and now, spending more time with his family, developing his interest in sport, doing his job as well as he could despite the fact that he hadn't done as well as he thought.

Jean was still disappointed. In her eyes, Bernie had let her down. She saw her disappointment as something Bernie had caused; if he had really loved her, he would have done better, worked harder, risen higher. Bernie assured her that he had done his best. In any case, there was nothing they could do about things now.

The counsellor felt that they were stuck. Jean was blaming Bernie for not achieving something that meant a lot to her; if she continued to blame him, their relationship did indeed seem to be at an end, because she was destroying it with every word she said.

The counsellor gently asked Jean to consider what her options were. There seemed to be three of them. First, she could decide that Bernie wasn't what she wanted, and leave. Second, she could carry on as she was doing, nagging and blaming. Then, if Bernie didn't leave her, in ten years' time she would be exactly where she was now, disappointed and stuck, and ten years nearer the end of her life. Or, she could let go of the past, accept what was actually happening and work to improve it.

These options shocked Jean. She sat in the counselling room, thinking deeply for a long while, then said that she needed time to decide. When she returned to counselling the following week, she had made her decision: to stay and make the most of what she had.

Once Jean made her mind up, she did change her approach; she realised that rather than undermining Bernie for what she wished he could be doing, she had to learn to support him in what he was actually doing. Having taken that step, she and Bernie were able to re-contact the trust they had lost and work towards rebuilding their relationship.

If you are aware that your partner isn't meeting some of your needs, there's no point in trying to pressurise; this will just make him or her less likely to want to change. Once you are sure that your partner has understood what it is you want and your reasons for wanting it, then accept a 'No' when you hear it. To go further means that you are demanding, not asking.

Instead, with day-to-day issues, why not take responsibility for meeting your own needs, or supplying your own needs from other sources? As long as you aren't meeting needs outside your relationship that you have agreed to meet inside it (such as love-making, for example), there is nothing wrong with this. Perhaps you can go to an evening class with a friend instead of expecting your partner to go with you; perhaps you can make your own meal instead of relying on your partner to be there to do it for you. If you do, that doesn't mean there is anything wrong with your partnership. It just means that you are realistic in what you expect from your partner.

! ═══════════════ *Task* ═══════════════

Letting go

Make a list of ten things you think you need in your relationship.

Then divide the ten into three lists: ones you absolutely have to have for the relationship to continue, ones that you would like but could settle for an alternative, ones that in fact, you could let go of.

What does this tell you about the things in your relationship that, actually, you could do without? Which things could you compromise over, if wanting them threatened to create a conflict with your partner?

If you can talk things through with your partner, do. Which of your partner's needs are a surprise? Which ones didn't you know about? Which of your partner's 'didn't know' needs can you, actually, start meeting immediately now that you know they exist?

!

COMMUNICATING YOUR NEEDS
TO EACH OTHER

There is a myth that partners should each know what the other needs without being told. This myth comes from our childhood; because our parents were often good at guessing what we wanted, particularly before we could talk. As a result we get the impression that people who love us should instinctively know what we need.

In fact, we can't mind read for each other. Even if we could, often our needs are so different from our partner's that we would mind read inaccurately. We actually don't know, fully, what each other is thinking, feeling or wanting. So one of you may love to sit in the dark with the light off, but the other may not understand why; to him or her, it's important to see things clearly, to turn the lights full up. What happens then is a startled and impatient yell, but not an explanation of just why you occasionally like to sit in the warm, intimate, comforting dark.

You may both be wary of admitting your needs to each other. As mentioned earlier, because of childhood experiences, you may feel guilty about having needs in the first place, and even more guilty about discussing them. But if you can do so, then you may be surprised.

Craig and Maureen had started to live together two years before, shortly after their baby, Lindsay, was conceived. They had both wanted a place of their own but with a new baby due, money was short. So Maureen had suggested that they move in with her father, who was retired and was more than happy to let them have the spare bedroom.

From the start, things weren't right. Maureen had been very worried about Lindsay because she was quite ill in the first few months of her life. Craig, an easy-going man who had been brought up to handle matters lightly and not take things to heart, tried to support Maureen by his calm and slightly jokey approach. Maureen, though, interpreted this as meaning that he didn't care; she felt he was immature and irresponsible. Slowly but surely, she turned back to her father for support. Her father, there all the time whereas Craig was at work, was delighted to help look after his grand-daughter.

As Maureen and Craig saw it, there was never any one time when things went wrong, but the more Maureen saw Craig as irresponsible, the more she shut him out. The more she shut him out, the more he laughed and shrugged it off. The more he did this, the more she turned to her father for support. Eventually, as Craig put it, 'I did what I was expected to do: move out and leave them to it. Now I'm just the guy who calls round from time to time.'

The counsellor suggested that Maureen and Craig look at what they both wanted in the situation. How could they re-work their relationship so that both of them were getting their needs met?

The key issue for Maureen seemed to be Craig taking responsibility. She was convinced that this was the last thing he wanted to do, because he seemed so unconcerned about things. But when it came to Craig's turn, he said that his main need was to be 'included, trusted, allowed to help'. The counsellor then asked him to be specific; what did 'included' actually mean in terms of practical action? Craig wanted to spend more time with Maureen, to be given jobs, to help far more with caring for Lindsay, to go out more as a family.

In many exercises that Relate clients do to work out just what partners want, the needs of each partner may only overlap very slightly. One person may want to live one kind of life, the other person may want a completely different kind of life; it may seem as if there is no meeting of minds at all. Then, the challenge is to find ways of meeting both sets of needs by negotiating.

To the counsellor, the surprising thing about Maureen and Craig's lists was that their needs were actually very similar. Both of them wanted Craig to take more responsibility. Their problems had arisen firstly because Craig's way of approaching matters had convinced Maureen that this was the last thing he wanted. Second, she had made him feel excluded. In fact, Craig's jokey approach to life had in the past made many other people assume that he wasn't to be trusted; he remembered many times feeling shut out. As a result, taking responsibility was the one thing that he deeply wanted to do.

Maureen and Craig were able to work towards a solution that suited them both. Maureen needed to allow Craig his place in the household, and get her father to pull back. She needed to trust Craig more and let him into her life. Craig needed to realise that his way of behaving convinced people that he couldn't handle responsibility, and that if he wanted to be trusted, he had to prove himself. As a first step, he immediately moved back in with Maureen and Lindsay; they planned to get a place of their own as soon as possible. When the counsellor last spoke to them, things were going well.

Communication strategies

Most of us don't misunderstand each other's needs as much as Maureen and Craig did. However, you may well have misinterpreted what your partner wants, particularly if your relationship difficulties mean that you are not talking easily day to day. The way to be sure, the way to find out your partner's needs, is quite simply to ask.

When you first met, you probably checked out what your partner thought and felt because you wanted to build a good relationship; it's a good idea, when rebuilding your relationship, to start 'checking out' again. Use 'I heard you say . . .', 'I think you mean . . .', 'I think what you want is . . . am I right?' Then, really listen. Take a careful mental note of what is said, querying anything you're not sure of, checking out as you go whether you've understood correctly. As your relationship begins to gather strength again, you probably won't have to check out nearly as much – although if you want to maintain your progress, it's a good idea never to take anything for granted.

In just the same way, when you have a need that you want your partner to hear, you will always get the best results by communicating that clearly and cleanly. Choose a good time, when he or she isn't trying to do something else, isn't talking to someone else. Avoid all the 'battle responses', such as nagging or sulking, that were mentioned on page 150. Instead, simply ask for what you want, briefly explaining why you want it.

It's very tempting, particularly if your relationship is in crisis, to start with what you don't like. 'I need you not to be so irritable . . .', 'I need you to spend less money . . .' Your partner feels criticised and, not surprisingly, doesn't want to meet your needs. Instead, try to be positive. Talk about what you actually want; that will motivate your partner far more. There are very few people who can refuse a request that they really feel will make their partner happy.

As well, be specific. It's difficult to get needs met if either of you are unsure what they are. So try not to talk in terms of huge concepts, such as 'love', 'respect', 'loyalty'; these words mean so many different things to so many different people that they can be worse than useless. If one of you asks for more respect, the other may start opening doors more or walking on the outside of the pavement, when what is actually needed is to listen more carefully or to criticise less.

Finally, remember that when you are negotiating about needs, you are not telling your partner to do something, but asking your partner to do something. So request, don't demand. This means replacing words like 'you must', 'you should', 'you ought to' with ones such as 'I wonder would you . . . ?' 'Can I ask you to . . . ?' 'Would you like to . . . ?' It also means saying please and thank you.

COMMITTING YOURSELF TO ___ MEETING YOUR PARTNER'S NEEDS___

In order to improve your relationship, you have to commit yourself to meeting your partner's needs. If you want to take, you have to be prepared to give. But actually, you may not always feel able to do that. Particularly if you haven't been getting on too well, you may have a number of reasons why you feel you can't give your partner what he or she wants. It's worthwhile looking closely at these reasons, because if you undermine your trust in each other by failing to meet needs, in the end, it will build up resentment between you.

You may feel that there are simple practical reasons why you can't give your partner what he or she wants. Your partner suggests going out together on one evening a week; your immediate response is that you couldn't possibly spare the time. Your partner really enjoys playing squash and suggests that you learn so that you can play together; you are certain you haven't got the energy. Or your partner suggests you go out on Valentine's Day, but you know for a fact that you can't get a baby-sitter, so you are sure it's a doomed plan.

If there are practical blocks to doing what your partner wants, but otherwise you are really keen to meet his or her needs, then you may not be thinking flexibly enough. So often, we think that everything depends on money, time, energy, when in fact given some creative thinking, we can get the result we want with less resources than we thought. If you think you haven't got the energy for squash in the evening, could you play at the weekend? If you can't get a babysitter for a romantic Valentine's dinner, could you stay in and have salmon and bubbly instead?

The other possibility, however, is that you are using practicalities as an excuse for not meeting your partner's needs. Often, we do this because of hidden resentment. We tell our partner that we have no time, when in fact, if we really tried, we could make the time. We plead tiredness but in fact we have plenty of energy for other things in our lives. The fact that we don't want to agree to what our partner wants is because we are afraid or angry; we are defending ourselves or attacking our partner. We may fear that if we agree to one request, our partner will simply keep on asking more and more, or that if we say 'yes' now, our partner will expect us to say 'yes' for ever and ever. Particularly if we don't feel good about each other, we may already feel that we have given too much, and that to give more would be pointless. Often, we feel that our partner has lost respect for us, or thinks we are stupid for agreeing to requests so often.

If these thoughts are blocking you, then you need to dissolve the painful feeling. This may well be down to understanding. As always, if you talk through your fears and worries, it can be that you can reassure yourselves and regain the trust you have lost. Or you may need to resolve some past resentment that has built up between you, healing your grudge, again by talking things through.

Yet Relate counsellors find that in many ways, the speediest route to being able to meet each other's needs is simply to start doing so. For miraculously, if you both begin to try to fulfil each other's wishes and do that with energy, then all of a sudden, you start to regain energy for the relationship. When you know that your needs are being met in a positive 'tit for tat', you start to feel that it is all worthwhile, and to look forward to the future. In a very real sense, the more you meet your partner's needs, the more you will want to do so. Bad feeling has a strange habit of just fading away if you do good for each other.

NEGOTIATING YOUR NEEDS

You've communicated your needs, and committed yourselves to meeting them. What next? What happens if there are clashes? What happens if you disagree? What happens if you get stuck? Clients at Relate are often actually taught, step by step, how best to negotiate their needs. These lessons will often start when a couple have to negotiate the actual nitty-gritty of the practicalities of counselling: between themselves, or even with the counsellor, they learn valuable things about just how they operate as a couple. Next, they may move on to negotiating what they want within their relationship. This often involves sitting down together, listing out what each person needs in a 'wish list', and then talking through just how possible each 'wish' is. This is useful not only for ordinary disagreements, when you argue simply because one of you wants one thing and the other wants another; it can also be vital when you make major decisions and realise that your needs may not fit at a very deep level.

The way this can work is illustrated by the story of Kitty and Adam. Adam was a car restorer, Kitty worked from home as a skilled seamstress; they had lived together for several years, and now had two children. When they came to counselling, they seemed locked in a battle of wills. Adam complained violently that Kitty didn't love him, was always trying to avoid him, never really wanted to be with him. She felt that he never left her alone. 'He works in the house all day; at night he expects me to talk to him all the time. I just need some space.'

Coming to counselling seemed to allow them to express their feelings in a way that reassured them, and within a week or two, the counsellor was able to suggest that they begin to negotiate a solution that worked for them both. He asked them each to write down what they really wanted of each other. Adam's list was long, and went into detail about all the ways he wanted Kitty to be with him; to talk to him; to share her thoughts and feelings with him. Kitty's list contained more of this kind of thing than Adam had expected, but top of the list was her need for space, time on her own and privacy.

The single issue that seemed to be typical of what they were talking about was the issue of sharing a bed. Adam wanted them always to sleep together, in a big double bed that he had designed and which a carpenter friend of theirs had made. Kitty wanted, just sometimes, to sleep alone, downstairs. Adam saw this as a complete rejection, a symbol of the fact that their marriage was breaking down, while Kitty reassured him that she simply wanted her own space. They were able to negotiate that on two nights a week, Kitty would sleep downstairs, and on that the other nights she would sleep with Adam.

The following week, the couple reported that on the first night Kitty slept downstairs, Adam had become violent when left alone, and had thrown a vase against the wall, though he had made no attempt to stop Kitty. On the following day, when Kitty returned to their bed, Adam said that he had felt very relieved, 'I thought that she wouldn't keep her side of the bargain, but she did.'

Adam had learned the lesson that many of the Relate exercises set out to teach. When it comes to meeting needs, we have to know that we can trust our partners to do what they say they are going to do. Once we know that they will, it is a lot easier to meet their needs in return.

Adam and Kitty continued to work down their list of needs, negotiating each week to meet more of them. Kitty agreed, for example, that they would eat lunch together each day and have a chance to talk, but in return, Adam would stop 'popping out' from his work every few minutes to interrupt her and demand that she pay him attention. They also agreed that one day a fortnight, Kitty would visit friends while Adam looked after the children; the next week, they would leave the children with friends and go out for the day together.

While they were practising negotiation, Kitty and Adam were exploring why they had such very different needs. Kitty was the second youngest of a large family; she had never had her own room, never really had privacy. She had enjoyed the first years of their married life, when Adam was working in a garage and she was at home, first just working alone and then also bringing up the children. She loved the feeling of freedom, of having her own place where she could wander round all day, though she would welcome Adam home each evening very happily. But when Adam had decided to go freelance and set up his business at home to save money, she had felt very intruded on. It was at this point that her wish for 'space' had started.

Adam, on the other hand, had some very particular childhood memories that he realised explained a lot of his unhappiness. His father had been away from home constantly when he was young, and his mother, desperately lonely, had never really let the little boy out of her sight. She insisted he come home from school to spend time with her, and often even slept with him in the same bed. No abuse had taken place, but Adam had felt trapped and stifled. In a sad but very typical 'passing on' of the problem, Adam was now demanding of Kitty what his mother had demanded of him when he was young.

Adam and Kitty's negotiation of needs made a start. Then, their exploration of the past made them able to stick to their negotiation in the long term. They were able to understand their own and each other's feelings and so start to come to terms with them. Slowly, Adam began to trust that Kitty's needing time alone wasn't just a sign that she was losing interest in him; he grew to value the much higher quality time they spent together when they both wanted it. Kitty, free of the constant pressure of Adam's requests, began to enjoy being with him again; she started to believe that her need for space and time would be met in the future. So by the time they finished counselling, she was happy to sleep with Adam every night, knowing that if she needed time out again, he would be happy to agree to that.

Building up negotiating skills

If you want to practise negotiating your needs with each other, don't begin by trying to resolve the issue of the overdraft, or whether her mother will come to live with you. You have to build up trust and skill in negotiation by working on small things before big ones. So try first deciding which television programme to watch tonight, or which of you will go to the supermarket on Saturday. The following guidelines may also help.

Being clear about what you will and won't do

You may not be able to give some things that your partner wants, because you feel they are too risky, immoral or illegal. If a partner asks you to fly to the moon, or take part in a bank raid, you may simply have to say no. Be prepared though, before refusing, to discuss the issue in depth so that you really understand your partner's needs. You may find that what you think is needed is not what is really needed at all.

Being prepared to accept no
Equally, if your partner says no, particularly once you have fully understood each other, then accept that if you can. Remember that your partner's needs are simply different to yours. If you genuinely feel that your partner's 'no' is a sign that he or she doesn't respect you, care for and love you, then you need to check that out. But you also need to ask yourself whether you are expecting your partner to give up his or her principles in order to make you happy.

Being prepared to give
Keeping a relationship together is often about doing things you don't want, or giving up things you do want. Making a cup of cocoa for you both even though you feel tired is a deposit in your relationship bank balance; on another day, your partner will do something loving for you. You may need to offer something in order to set the scene for receiving something in return.

Being flexible
Be prepared to negotiate and compromise to get your needs met. Accept alternatives, perhaps as to the time something will happen, the date or the situation. If there isn't the money to take a week's holiday, offer a weekend instead. Also, help your partner think of other ways to meet his or her needs, of other people who could help. If you can't do ballroom dancing, encourage your spouse to find a dancing partner that he or she can go with.

Being prepared to ask for help
When negotiating big decisions, such as whether to marry or have a child, you can benefit from discussion with the help of a Relate counsellor even if you are not otherwise in counselling. Counsellors will not take sides, but will support both of you to explore what your needs are until you reach a deep understanding of each other and are sure you are both making the right decision.

One of the most welcome things that Relate clients realise as they learn to meet each other's needs, is that they will not only have to give, but can also take. If one of them meets the other's needs, then if the relationship is working as it should, they will have their needs met in return. Often, neither partner's needs are met completely; there is usually some element of compromise; but there will be equality, and once a couple has started to believe that need-meeting, in a mutual way, is a real possibility, then everything else falls into place.

! ================ *Task* ================

Meeting the need

This exercise is best done only if you have begun to make improvements in your relationship and feel good about each other most of the time.

Each of you should think of one thing you would really like your partner to do for you. It should be something that you know your partner wouldn't find unpleasant; that he or she could do without worrying about money or time; that you have never disagreed over; that is simple and straightforward. Write your requests down and give them to each other.

When you receive your partner's request, fulfil it. Take a leap of faith and do it even if you don't know why your partner is asking, and even if it is not something that you think is important. Trust your partner to ask for whatever he or she needs, even if you don't understand why!

When your partner has done what you asked, show and tell him or her how pleased you are and how much it meant to you.

!

14

COPING WITH EMOTIONS

We all feel emotions, every day. In a partnership, because everything is so important, we are likely to feel a variety of emotions very strongly indeed. When you first meet your partner, you may feel excited when you are with him or her, lonely when you are separated. As you make a commitment, you may feel hopeful that things will work out, yet anxious that they won't. And when a relationship hits problems, you can get overwhelmed by the panic, anger and grief that you feel as one disappointment follows another. It is how you cope with these emotions – particularly the ones that are painful for you or your partner – that makes your relationship a success or a failure. So if you are not coping with painful emotions, or if the ways you are coping are hurting your partner or yourself, then you need to change.

__WHEN EMOTIONS CREATE PROBLEMS__

Emotions are just one way that our body draws our attention to things. If we see a good friend coming towards us on the street then we may feel pleased. That tells us how good we feel about our friend. We get a smile on our face and an extra bounce in our step, and we say hello to our friend in a positive way, which will make both of us feel good.

Alternatively, let's take another example. We hear our partner coming home. We know that this morning we left on bad terms. We feel anxious because we wonder whether we are again going to row. We feel irritated as we remember what the early morning argument was about. We feel sad as we compare how bad things are with how good they used to be. All these feelings draw our attention to the arrival of our partner, and prepare us for when we say hello.

These emotions themselves are not a problem, even though they may be painful. In fact, they are useful because they draw our attention to things. It's important to be aware that our relationship could be better, and being anxious, angry or sad increases that awareness. But what happens next, the response that our emotions lead to, may well be a problem.

Our response could be based on the lessons we learned when we were children about how to handle emotion. Perhaps our early experiences have never taught us how to cope with painful feelings such as grief, fear or anger. The end result is that we are frightened of these emotions and we simply can't handle them. We try to control them but they overcome us and just burst out; or we succeed in controlling them, and completely push them down.

So, we may let our painful emotion explode. As our partner walks in the door, we look up angrily. Our partner, having completely forgotten what happened this morning, is taken aback, and asks in a confused voice what the matter is. We slam down a coffee cup. They walk into the living room and turn the television on. We snap. They shout. War is declared.

Or, when our partner comes in, we may simply push down the emotions, often so quickly that we ourselves aren't even aware of them. We'll block out any feelings of anxiety, irritation and sadness, either because we don't want to hurt our partner, or because we don't want to show our vulnerability. But in doing that, we may also have to push down any positive feelings of remorse or sympathy, so what our partner gets is a blanked-off face and a toneless voice.

Letting our emotion burst out may make us feel better in the short term, but in the long term, letting emotions rule how we behave puts other people on the defensive. They will feel bad, let their own emotions out – and end up on a merry-go-round of bad feeling. In the long term, this can escalate into strong language, throwing things, or even violence.

Interestingly, while dumping emotion on our partner leads to disaster, keeping our feelings completely to ourselves isn't helpful either. We may do it because we feel that it's going to cause more trouble, but it stops us really exploring what is happening and sorting it out, and it prevents us being truly honest with each other. In the long term, simply pushing down our emotions may lead to other problems that can affect our whole life, such as lack of concentration, illness, feelings of sadness, and deep depression.

Alternatively, and almost unbelievably, we may find that rather than pushing down our emotion or letting it out, we are – as a couple – dividing these options between us. This can be both painful and confusing.

Christine and Michael came to counselling worried about the fact that she seemed to be always angry with him. Christine had been married before, and that partnership had broken up four years ago because, as Christine put it 'my husband just couldn't put up with my rages'. Now Michael had asked her to marry him, and she felt she loved him, but was she right to marry when she spent so much of her time being angry? Michael seemed very calm and cheerful, and said that he didn't like being blamed and shouted at, but that personally, he didn't have any doubts about the wedding. 'Coming to counselling is for her, to help her sort herself out,' was the way he expressed it.

The counsellor got Christine and Michael to track back their past history, drawing out their family situations with a series of circles in much the same way as Stephanie and Barry did on pages 47–9. In this case, the counsellor encouraged Christine and Michael to indicate on the drawings what kind of emotions had been part of their early childhood. It soon became clear that for both, anger had been a key thing in family life. Christine's father had been a very angry man, sociable outside the house, but at home full of rage against the world and his family. Though he was also very loving, he would shout at the slightest thing, and Christine had grown up with memories of her father's angry voice echoing through the house. Michael, on the other hand, had lived in a family which denied that there was any such thing as anger. Although his mother and father, now divorced, admitted that their marriage was unhappy from the start, they had lived in a very 'civilised' fashion, never raising their voices. However, even as a child he had been aware of an undercurrent of bad feeling in the family that was never talked about.

Both Michael and Christine gained a great deal from beginning to understand their family backgrounds. As they did this, Christine was also trying to handle her anger in a better way. The counsellor offered both of them helpful guidelines, and at first these began to work; but after a week of peace, they turned up to the next session very upset. They had started rowing again. Christine was confused: 'I try to hold my tongue,' she said, 'but it's almost as if Michael knows what to say to wind me up. I just find myself getting angrier and angrier.'

The counsellor, knowing that both of them wanted to understand what was happening, asked them to explore the following possibility. Perhaps both of them were angry underneath, but it was Christine who was expressing the anger for both of them. Why might this be happening? Michael's family had never really given him any models for being angry; in fact, he had learned that it was dangerous to express critical feeling. But in all relationships, some irritation and anger does exist, and has to be resolved. Maybe Michael's way of resolving it was to encourage Christine – who had learned from her father how to be furious – to get angry for him.

This idea did make sense to Christine, who also linked it back to experiences in her former marriage. 'I'm not sure whether I'm just trying to shift responsibility, but I do feel it is like that. Michael is so loving, so calm, so peaceful all the time that I sometimes think it's not real. It was like that too with Rob, my former partner. Perhaps it isn't real. Perhaps he's being calm and I'm being angry for both of us.'

Michael found much more difficulty in accepting the possibility that he was adding to the situation, but he agreed that over the next few sessions, he would look at what he might be angry about. He worked with the counsellor individually, and as he began to feel safer, found an amazing amount of resentment. He felt bitter about his mother, who he always felt had never loved him; he felt angry with an older sister who had bullied him. He also realised that he felt angry towards Christine, who had for a long time refused to come and live with him; when she had, he began to feel safe enough to allow anger into their relationship, but not safe enough to express it himself.

As Michael began to express his anger more openly in the counselling sessions, things eased remarkably at home. When the two of them began seeing the counsellor together again, they were much more content with each other, and reported that Michael was now able to say clearly when he was irritated, and that Christine was feeling less angry a great deal of the time. They both felt that although there was work to be done, they had begun to be able to take equal responsibility for the emotions in their relationship.

! ================= *Task* ================

Emotional lessons

It's our family who teaches us most of the lessons we learn about how to handle painful emotion.

Choose one painful emotion. It could be fear, sadness, anger, jealousy, resentment, or any other. You may want to choose an emotion that now, as an adult, you are wary of: maybe you pull back from feeling that emotion yourself, and get uncomfortable when other people feel it. Now fill in these sentences about the emotion you chose.

- In my family, we handled our own (painful emotion) by . . .
- The girls/women handled this emotion by . . . ; the boys/men by . . .
- In my family, we handled someone else's (painful emotion) by . . .
- The girls/women handled this emotion by . . .; the boys/men by . . .

So how did the members of your family handle this emotion: feeling it themselves, being with other people when they felt it? Notice how males and females handled different emotions in different ways: for example, often it's fine for boys to show anger, and girls to show grief, but not vice versa. How do you think the lessons you've learned from your family help you in coping with emotions in yourself and in your partner? How do you think what you've learned may be causing problems in your relationship?

If you can talk to your partner, swap notes about these things. How do you each cope with the same emotion in different ways?   **!**

! ═══════════════════ *Task* ═══════════════════

Button push

What's one thing you do when you're with your partner that makes him or her upset or angry? It will probably be a small thing, a word, phrase, sound or expression.

Try, one day at a time, simply not doing this thing. Instead, genuinely try to do something that shows your love for your partner. Does this make any difference to the way he or she behaves?

!

EMOTIONAL MANAGEMENT

Coping with your own emotions

So how should you cope best with emotions? The first step is to become aware when you are experiencing painful emotions, to recognise what you are feeling and accept what is actually going on for you. Second, you need to investigate your emotions, to interpret what is happening. Then, if it's appropriate, you need to find a good way of expressing your emotion; a way of handling it that is not going to bounce back on you, your partner or your relationship. Finally, you may need to take action, to do what needs to be done to resolve the issue.

Recognition and Acceptance
We all know what strong painful emotion feels like and looks like. If you or your partner get furiously angry, or deeply tearful, then that is obvious; but you also need to recognise emotion before it becomes strong, when it first starts to bite. That way, you can act immediately to reduce the problems almost before they start.

Try to become aware of the first thing you notice when you are feeling a painful emotion. Some people find that they feel a strong sensation in their stomach, or tension in their back or jaw. Often you will start to feel shaky or cold, have a faster heartbeat or a dry mouth. These are all signs that your body is rushing into action, and that the next step along the way is probably going to be to say or do something that expresses your emotion.

Once you've recognised an emotion, do your best to accept it. This may be hard. As mentioned before, we are often brought up to feel bad about our unhappy emotions. This is particularly a problem for men, who may believe that in order to be manly, they have to think, not feel. They may never lose their temper, never cry, never feel anxious. But the end result of this blocking process is that some men can also find it very difficult to feel sympathy, excitement, joy, hope or happiness.

In fact, feeling is a totally natural human response; it's good to celebrate the fact that, as human beings, we can experience a wide and full range of emotions. While the expression of some feelings isn't always helpful, it's always helpful to accept the feelings themselves: to pause for a moment, the minute you are aware of them, and think 'Yes . . . OK, I'm feeling resentful/anxious/frustrated'. If you do this, then strangely enough, painful emotions themselves are often easier to handle; they tend to come and go much more quickly; they aren't felt as strongly; they are, in the end, much more easily managed.

Investigation and Interpretation

After acceptance, comes investigation. In order to really deal with what you are feeling, you have to understand what has led to it. So let's say that, one sunny Saturday morning, your partner simply sighs heavily when you pass a comment at the kitchen table. You immediately feel angry and a little anxious. Now it may seem as if it is the sigh that is directly responsible for your feelings, but that's not so. In fact, in between your partner's action and your painful emotion lies something you have been thinking. It's a kind of 'negative-thought sandwich', with the thought in the middle. Something happens, you think the thought, you feel the emotions.

For example, the thoughts rushing through your head could be any or all of the following: 'S/he's irritated with me.' 'What have I done wrong?' 'This is unfair.' 'S/he doesn't love me.' 'There's nothing I can do about that.' And these thoughts will seem real and true; they won't, at the time, seem in the least misguided or inaccurate. It's no wonder, having besieged your brain with these negative thoughts, that you feel angry and anxious. You can plummet into such a negative spiral that the next moment you are snapping at your partner, and ten minutes later you are in the middle of a blazing row.

You probably weren't aware of your negative thoughts as you were thinking them but, in fact, a vital part of managing your emotions is to become aware. For if you can start to be conscious of such thoughts, you will be more in control of them. You can start to find out what is really going on, to investigate whether what you thought was actually true.

Because often, we feel painful emotions inappropriately. We feel irritated when in fact there is nothing to be irritated about, we feel panicked when in fact we don't need to be afraid. We simply don't appreciate what is going on for our partner, or we simply underestimate our own power to deal with that. All too often, as explained earlier in Chapter 9, we think the worst.

Begin by looking for evidence. What evidence do you have that your partner is irritated? What evidence is there against that? Can you check, can you ask? If he or she isn't irritated, what evidence do you have of what might be happening instead? And if your partner is irritated, do you have evidence that you have done something wrong, or that you can't do anything about that?

By looking, listening, and asking, you may, for example, realise that:

• there's no other evidence that your partner is irritated; up to a few minutes ago, everything was fine.

• your partner's not irritated. When asked, he or she claims to have been thinking happily about the holiday you've got planned and so simply didn't hear what you said.

• your partner is irritated, but about something completely outside your situation, something that happened at work that day.

• your partner is irritated, because he or she forgot to buy you a birthday card.

• your partner is irritated, but when you talk about it, you both realise that underneath the irritation is some much more acceptable emotion: anxiety about money, or sadness that your son has failed his exams.

• your partner is irritated with you, but when asked, genuinely says that he or she feels sorry for being irritated, and wants to make amends.

• your partner is irritated with you, but over something you didn't realise you'd done. Knowing about it, you can act and solve the problem.

• your partner is irritated with you, but that doesn't mean he or she doesn't love you; your partner is irritated over something trivial that doesn't affect love at all.

• your partner is irritated, and you can do something about it; offering a cuddle makes all the difference.

• your partner is feeling bad, but it's not irritation. It's regret that, because he or she got home late, you weren't able to make love last night.

Realising even one of these things may be enough to make you feel completely differently about the situation. You may now feel relieved, sympathetic, apologetic, loving or – if the answer your partner gives is the final one – you may now feel lustful! Having correctly interpreted the meaning of what is happening, you may well feel so much better that you can't even remember what it was you felt bad about. Instead of shutting down or snapping at your partner, you will be able to smile and reach out. You will move closer together rather than further apart.

It isn't easy to learn to reverse negative thoughts. If you and your partner have been in conflict for a while, expecting the worst of each other may have become so much part of your way of life that it's difficult to stop. You need to practise constantly every time you have a negative thought, checking it out mentally, checking with your partner, finding a correct interpretation for what is happening. Counsellors find that the overwhelming majority of painful emotion in relationships can be eased by simply investigating and truly understanding what is happening. Changing even just a few negative thoughts to positive ones can reverse the whole trend, because you are then reacting to your partner optimistically rather than assuming the worst.

What if, having investigated, you find that in fact, none of the above-listed explanations are true? Your original idea was correct. Your partner admits that yes, he or she is irritated and yes, it is with you.

In this case, you still need to investigate further. You need to support your partner and find out just what it is upsetting him or her. You need to bring all your skills of communication into action to try to understand your partner. You need to really try to appreciate what is going on in the present and perhaps even what went on in the past. Because, as explained earlier in this book, if you begin to understand, then your painful emotion often dies down. You are able to say 'Oh – that's why you didn't hear me,' and offer support and help. Coping with Your Partner's Emotions, on page 183, offers further guidelines for how to handle this situation.

Relevant expression

Of course, even if you learn to re-interpret negative thoughts and really appreciate what is going on for your partner, there may still be times when you feel emotional about what is happening. It may simply be impossible to 'investigate' without your partner getting even more upset, so you are left on hold, with your emotions unresolved. It may not be possible to check immediately with your partner what is happening – and until you do, you feel bad. Or, in the general chaos of a relationship in difficulty, there is so much going on that you are in a constant state of stress, and this makes you emotional. Sometimes, you simply have no choice but to feel.

You do have a choice about expressing those feelings, however. You may feel sad but not cry, feel disappointed but not say so.And while expressing many emotions – such as happiness, excitement, anticipation – is wonderful, expressing many others simply causes trouble. If you are frustrated, angry, disappointed or disgusted with your partner, then expressing these emotions may be a bad thing. Such expression stirs up just as painful emotions in your partner and then you will find it next to impossible to sort things out in a constructive way.

So how can you hold back? You can, if you choose, simply hold your tongue when you feel bad. Or you can wait just a few seconds to avoid saying or doing something you may regret. You can often, by taking a deep breath and letting it out again, begin to relax, release the tension, and so control any instant emotional reaction such as a snappy comment.

When you do speak, you can simply mention that you are feeling bad and that you don't want to interact right now; then do something else for a while until you are feeling slightly better. You can alert your partner to the fact that you are feeling bad, but hold back from dumping everything on him or her. You can find your own way of taking your mind off things, such as doing the washing up or walking round the block, until you are ready to talk things through.

Of course there are times when the emotion you feel is so strong that you just have to let it out. If so, unless your emotion is about something completely unlinked to your partner, aim it away from him or her. Relate counsellors have gathered a whole list of good ways of letting off steam that they suggest to their clients: play squash; yell into a pillow; hit a cushion; scream at an empty chair; go out in the car and turn the stereo up; write a furious letter (but don't post it).

On the other hand, don't underestimate the effect of the short, sharp scream. It can be a useful tool if you make it clear what you are doing and don't turn it into a blaming session. Denise was in counselling because she was feeling trapped in her marriage. She was in her mid-forties, just approaching her menopause and worried that this was the end of her life. In particular, she felt unable to express her needs; she felt her frustration building up at her husband, at her two teenage daughters, even at the dog. But she felt that if she expressed her rage, she would hurt someone. As a result, she never showed her feelings, and was often depressed.

While a lot of the work that Denise did in counselling was about tracking down the reasons for her frustration, she also learned ways of expressing it directly and without danger. She started to find ways of coping with strong emotion that didn't overcome her, by stating clearly what was bothering her and then negotiating for things to change. By doing this, she started to feel much more in control of her situation.

One breakthrough event for Denise happened during the school holidays when she had been out shopping, leaving the house spotless. She came back in, not expecting anyone to be at home, to find her two daughters and their friends spread out all over the kitchen. They had been snacking: breadcrumbs and jammy knives were on the table, the radio was on and the smell of burnt toast filled the air. Although she knew that her daughters would eventually clear up, Denise felt invaded, her sparkling kitchen destroyed.

Before going to counselling, Denise might have tiptoed past and then felt depressed for days because she had simply 'given in'. Or, she would have rushed about, nagging, tidying,and making the girls feel bad. She told the counsellor in her next session that what she actually thought was: 'Well, it's their house and they have every right to be here and to do this; and it's my house and I have every right to be irritated.' What she actually did was drop her shopping bags, let out a stress-releasing scream, and then turn to her daughters quite calmly and say; 'It's fine; I'm angry, but it's not your fault.' She had learned the difference between being frustrated, and dumping that frustration on to other people.

Sometimes, the right expression of emotion is not just to let out the tension, but to tell your partner exactly how you feel. This is usually true when you know that you have never really explained your real emotions to your partner, and because of that, he or she doesn't understand your feelings about a particular issue. We're not talking here about the situation where you have nagged for a month about the unplumbed-in dishwasher, and where you are simply adding more nagging to the pile. We are talking about really communicating how sad, angry, upset or afraid you are over an issue that is important to your relationship.

In this case, if you want your partner to really appreciate your point of view, you need to express your emotion in a way that he or she can hear. This may mean, at first, exploring the issues only within the safety net of a counselling session, or after you have built up considerable trust between you. Even then, you need to take care how you express yourself. Remember all the guidelines to good communication (pages 136–53). You can talk about you; what you feel, what you think, what your emotions are. You can talk about the actions or events that triggered your emotion.

Even so, don't attack your partner. Never blame him or her for making you feel an emotion, never say that your feelings are his or her fault; you choose what you feel. Don't winge, nag or accuse. Don't rake up the past. Simply say what you have experienced, and the emotions it created. Don't worry too much if your partner doesn't hear you first time; Relate counsellors often find that it takes several 'goes' at expressing emotions before one partner really understands what was happening for the other. Once they do, however, they really appreciate their partner's viewpoint and are able to sympathise.

Action

Denise was very clear that she didn't need to take any action about her daughters' behaviour. She was frustrated, and wanted her right to express that frustration, but she didn't need the young people to do things differently. She knew that they had every right to be in the kitchen, and that they would eventually clear up after themselves.

Often, however, your emotions get triggered because you want something to happen; you need something. You are anxious because of the lack of money; you want your partner to find a job. You are sad because your partner has stopped communicating with you; you want him to start. You are frustrated because your partner comes home late; you want her to come home earlier.

All these situations require action, from you or from someone else. You probably have to tell someone about what you want, ask someone to support you in doing it, or ask someone to do it themselves. Remember that this action is not the same as expressing your emotion; it is about meeting your needs. In fact, often, expressing the emotion without thought will stop you from getting your needs met because your partner will feel so threatened that he or she will be unable or unwilling to respond.

So step outside the raw emotion. This means not screaming, 'Why don't you come home early for once?' but instead saying 'I really would like it if you came home earlier from work just one night a week. I'd like to spend just one evening with you, talking and being happy together, maybe making love. Friday would be good, but if not, then Thursday. If it means you have to work late another night, that's fine.'

You can use all the guidelines offered in the chapter of this book on Meeting Needs to arrange with the other person exactly what can be done (page 154). When you have decided what you need, set your aim: make it positive and specific. Do your best to get your timing right. When you do communicate, ask for what you want and say why you want it. Be prepared to do your bit to get action; to be flexible, to offer something in return, or to suggest what else could be done if what you're asking for just isn't possible.

Coping with your partner's emotions

There will be times when your partner is feeling emotional and wants your support. Here, you may find it helpful to use a modified form of Acceptance, Investigation and Action.

Once you've spotted, through body language or words, that your partner is unhappy, then try checking out for yourself whether you are at ease with that. Can you comfortably accept it? If so, it's useful to tell your partner that you don't find that emotion a problem; so often, we feel bad about something, and then feel even worse because we think our partner can't handle it. So if a partner is anxious about work, for example, and you can easily understand that, why not say you sympathise and reassure that it is fine to be anxious? Add a hug if your partner wants that.

It's much more difficult if you aren't at ease with your partner's emotion. Perhaps your partner is anxious about work and so are you; your partner's anxiety is adding to yours, making you really wish that he or she would keep quiet and not panic. Or perhaps your partner is anxious about work and also angry because you've added to the problem. In both cases, you may not be able to accept your partner's feelings fully.

You can, though, do your best to accept those feelings partially. First, try not to argue with your partner or defend yourself; if you do, your partner will feel criticised rather than accepted, and will get defensive or attack. Second, try listening as your partner talks, giving signs of acknowledgement (see page 142). Whether or not you agree, if your partner feels listened to, he or she will start to relax, and you will both start to feel better.

Then, it is time to investigate. Asking what a partner really means can be helpful and reassuring for both of you. If your partner says 'I'm furious that you forgot to pick me up from the station,' you can help both of you to clarify what that statement really means. 'Were you angry because you got wet and ruined your new suit? Was it that you were scared that something had happened to me? Did you think it meant that I don't care for you?' It can be useful to summarise what you've heard, both to be clear in your own mind and to reassure your partner that you've really understood. 'So you got angry because you felt that other things were more important to me than you were. Yes, I've got that.'

If you can, offer some action that will help your partner. See it as an exercise in meeting needs. For example, your partner needs you to remember to pick him or her up from the station in future. Using the guidelines about meeting each other's needs, offered in Chapter 13, do what you can. Be clear about what you will or will not do; be prepared to give; be flexible. If you forgot to pick him or her up from the station because your watch stopped, get the watch mended. If you forgot because the friend you were visiting was in need of support, then see if you can agree that, if such an emergency happens again, you'll ring your partner and warn him or her that you'll be late.

If your partner feels that his or her emotion has been recognised and understood, and that in future, you will take action to change things, then he or she will feel much better. And if you both continue to respond to each other's anger by accepting, investigating and taking action, then you will start to trust that you don't need to get angry or upset with each other. All you need to do is ask.

' ===================Talking Point ===============

Time out

Violence is never a relevant expression of emotion, but a large number of otherwise positive relationships do contain a tiny element of violence: a thrown cup, a raised hand, a push, a pinch. A way of coping suggested by one counsellor is based on the principle of taking 'time out'.

If either of you feels likely to throw things or hit the other, or are scared that your partner will do so, you give a pre-arranged signal (a word, phrase or clear gesture) that you want to leave the room. Then you leave. You don't leave the building, so that your partner doesn't feel abandoned. Then you return after a pre-arranged time – say, half an hour. This means that neither of you is giving up on the situation; you are just taking time out for safety reasons. If when you return, violence threatens again, you leave again.

If you (or your partner) are tempted to violence, however irregularly, talk through this strategy; arrange your signal and your time limit. If this strategy doesn't work, or if the violence starts to get at all worse, go for professional help.

'

CLEARING THE EMOTIONAL BACKLOG

It may seem, in the middle of a painful interaction with your partner, that most of your emotion is being caused by what is happening now, in your relationship. In fact, this may not be so. Things that have happened in the past, either distant or recent, will have caused you to feel hurt; these emotions may well be affecting you now. A backlog of painful emotion will always add to the hurt you feel in the present. This will be particularly true if your bad feelings were constantly triggered over a long time, such as regularly feeling abandoned because your mum left you alone every day; or if what happened in the past was very upsetting, such as being abused, injured or bereaved.

Such events can actually cause a backlash in your relationship even many years later. Yasmin and Deepak married in their early twenties, and within a year had a baby daughter. They loved being parents, and thoroughly enjoyed caring for the little one as she grew up. Two years later, ready for another addition to their family, Yasmin became pregnant again. Seven months into her pregnancy, she tripped while doing the gardening. That evening, she felt labour pains start, and although Deepak rushed her to the hospital immediately, she lost the baby.

The first memory she had, recovering from the anaesthetic, was of Deepak leaning over her, kissing her, and saying 'Don't worry, love, we'll try again'. She felt terrible. She wanted to think about the baby she had lost, grieve for it, and spend some time recovering. Instead, Deepak seemed to have just pushed away the baby as if it had never existed. She fell asleep again feeling bitterly unhappy. Eighteen months later, they did have another child, this time a boy.

Twenty years later Yasmin and Deepak were a seemingly happy couple. Certainly not even Yasmin knew that she had never resolved her feelings over her dead baby. Then her mother developed cancer, and it seemed certain that she was going to die. Faced with a new bereavement, Yasmin started to feel all the emotions that she had so successfully buried for so long. She was tearful, anxious, and seemed to constantly criticise Deepak, who not surprisingly was confused and resentful.

When the couple came to counselling, they were both unsure what was happening. Tracing back with the counsellor the experiences in their lives, it soon became clear that the miscarriage was something they had never really talked about. The event itself was a desperately tragic one, but they had never even discussed it, certainly never expressed to each other what they were feeling. The counsellor encouraged them to try.

What came out, on Yasmin's part, was a huge amount of grief. In a very moving session, she cried for her baby, cried for the child that baby could have been – and cried too for the fact that, over that miscarriage, she had lost faith in Deepak. Previously, she had seen him as a kind and caring man; from that point on she had doubted him.

Deepak was appalled. His only concern had been to spare her pain, by encouraging her to put the loss behind her and look to the future. He had had no idea that she needed to grieve, no idea that she had needed something from him that he had not given her. They clung to each other in the counselling room, and wept for their baby together.

Later, with the counsellor's help, Deepak and Yasmin planned a way of mourning their baby. Yasmin wrote a letter to the child, expressing all her thoughts and feelings. Together, they bought a rose bush which they planted in their garden, as a tribute. And they both made time to tell their other two children that part of their family history that they had never known.

Handling the past

Yasmin and Deepak didn't realise until they reached counselling that the problems in their relationship were being triggered by something that had happened in their past. So how can you tell if you need to sort out past issues? There are guidelines, though ideally you need the specialist help of a counsellor to help you track down any emotional upheaval in your past.

● If you feel an emotion which seems out of all proportion to what's happening here and now: if for example, you regularly panic if your partner simply leaves the room.

● If the emotion you feel seems unlinked to what's happening here and now: if, for example, every time you think about cooking for your partner, you feel incredibly sad.

● If whenever you feel the emotion, you also remember a particular past memory: if, for example, whenever you make love, you feel bad because you recall an earlier unhappy sexual experience.

● If whenever you feel the emotion, you remember clearly someone who isn't present: if, for example, you think of your sister every time you feel irritable with your wife.

If you are aware that some or all of the above are true for you, you may want to explore your past to see if some key event is adding to your pain. The first step is to try to track down that event, recognise it and talk about it. Particularly, it will help to talk about the emotions. The wonderful thing about a past, painful event is that once you have recognised it and spoken about it, it loses its impact on you, just as in many fairy stories, the monster, once named, becomes powerless. You will still be able to remember what happened to you, but as you bring it into the open, perhaps sharing your memory with a counsellor, perhaps eventually talking to your partner about it, the emotions will fade away.

If the memory is deeply painful, maybe such a memory will never actually feel completely positive, although one Relate client, having spent many sessions describing fights he had with his first wife, suddenly burst into laughter because 'we must have looked so stupid chasing each other round the garden'. Your memories will slowly lose their effect on you here and now. You will eventually no longer feel so betrayed when you remember the affair, you will no longer feel so angry when you remember the violence.

If what happened in the past is something that involved your partner, then it will almost certainly help to share what you felt with him or her. Yasmin needed not only to remember her miscarriage and grieve for her baby, but also to tell Deepak her emotions about the way he acted. Such feedback can be difficult to give and to hear: you or your partner may get upset or angry with each other; you may learn things about each other that you never imagined were possible. (This is another reason why exploration into the past is often best done with a counsellor there to support you.) But often, just telling your partner how he or she hurt you can help you begin to get things into proportion.

Sharing with your partner feelings about the past may also help you to forgive. As one counsellor said 'If a client can make emotional sense of what's happened, it can often feel OK, even many years later.' Exploring the past helps you to make emotional sense of things by helping you to understand why they happened. If your partner can then explain to you what he or she was thinking and feeling when the hurtful incident happened, it can also help a great deal.

Forgiveness is also possible even if you don't understand, if only you know that your partner does love you. Often, looking back, a partner will realise that he or she regrets what happened and now loves you too much to repeat that mistake. If you can hear your partner express this regret, often your bitterness will fade away. You may look clearly at what happened and know that it was painful. But then, because you have now both re-contacted your love for each other, you may be able to put the pain firmly behind you and refuse to allow it to affect your relationship any more. This is what forgiveness is all about.

Working with a counsellor

If you work with a counsellor, he or she will provide a safety net, giving you ways of coping with strong emotion that will, as one counsellor put it, 'heal and not hurt'. A counsellor – unlike a friend or even a partner – can support you to talk through a painful memory again and again until it begins to feel better. You can express your emotion quietly and privately, or if you want to, you can shout and cry and scream time after time.

On the other hand, a counsellor will never push you to feel more emotion than you want to. Instead, he or she will support you to understand exactly what happened; why it is affecting you; and what problems it is causing. After this, you will be able to start to let go of the pain.

You may have worries about what happens in such a counselling session, concerns which it is worthwhile checking out. Here are a few of the most usual worries that people have about counselling.

● I will have to express my emotions in front of my partner. It often helps to express your feelings when both of you are in the counselling session, but no one will ever force you to. Often a counsellor will suggest that you explore a particular past incident privately with him or her; afterwards, if you want to, you can share with your partner what you discovered.

● The counsellor will tell my partner what I said. A Relate counsellor will never pass on to a partner emotions or information you have shared with the counsellor privately. On the other hand, if a counsellor feels that it would help your relationship to tell your partner what you feel, then he or she may suggest to you that you do that.

● I'll shock the counsellor. Counsellors have heard and seen most things. Also, and perhaps more importantly, all Relate counsellors have themselves felt strong emotion. They won't be shocked by what you tell them.

● I'll say something I don't mean to. Yes, of course you will. When you are exploring strong emotions, often the result is that you say things that, afterwards, seem stupid or misguided. But once you have expressed the emotion, you will realise that you didn't mean what you said, and will be able to see things more clearly. The counsellor realises this and will never use against you afterwards things that you say in a session.

● If I express all the emotion I feel, I'll explode – or never stop. If you have been bottling up your emotions for a long time, it can feel like this. But remember that if you are feeling happy, you don't worry that you'll never stop. Unresolved painful emotion is like an unburst boil: as soon as you begin to express your feelings to a counsellor, the chances of their being a problem are immediately reduced.

! ─────────────── *Task* ───────────────

Strong feelings

This exercise is best done only if you have begun to make improvements in your relationship and in general feel good about your partner.

As a couple, you have almost certainly been through many strongly emotional events together. Some of these will have been wonderfully positive, others will have been incredibly painful. This exercise can help you rebuild your emotional connection very quickly.

Each of you should choose four events in your life together that have been strongly emotional for you. Choose two emotionally positive ones and two emotionally painful ones. Try to avoid any events that involved clashes or conflicts between the two of you. You should each arrange the events in order, so that the happiest one is marked 1 and the most painful is marked 4.

Compare notes. Don't worry if you have listed different events or marked them differently. If you have listed the same event, perhaps as number 2 on one list and number 4 on the other, then cross out the first mention (number 2) and renumber the rest of that list.

Then begin with number 1 on one of your lists. Take it in turns to each describe what you remember about the event, and particularly how you felt.

Then move on to number 1 on the other list. Talk about that.

You will probably take several sessions to complete your lists. If you both start to get angry with each other, then stop, though you may find that other painful feelings, such as sadness or regret, give you an opportunity to comfort each other. If you can each really listen to how the other feels about each event, you will understand a great deal. In the end, you will feel much closer to each other than you did before.

!

EMOTIONAL MINEFIELDS

When a relationship is in difficulty, much of what you each feel will centre around the conflict between you. However, there are other emotions that can cause stress in a relationship. The final part of this chapter covers in more detail three of these difficult emotions.

Grief

Grief is usually triggered by the fact that you lose something. Most often, this is a person – a parent, a child, a close friend – but it may be the loss of a thing, such as a house that has been repossessed, or a promotion that's been missed. In today's world, we often expect to bounce back from such 'bereavement' in a very short time; but in fact grief, though a positive, natural healing process, can take many months , and in some cases years, to be fully complete.

If you are grieving, you go through a process that is clearly marked in stages, and will probably affect you very deeply. At first, there may be a sense of shock, which can make you forgetful or confused; you will need practical support through the first few days or weeks, and the opportunity to talk things through, often over and over. Next, you may start to fight your sense of loss; you may get angry with yourself, the world, or particular people, including sometimes a person who has died. You may become very sad and burst into tears at the least thing; you may have times when you refuse to believe what has happened. You may have a period of depression, as you start to accept that the loss has happened; you will have little energy, and may constantly think pessimistic thoughts. Some of these feelings, such as anger, can seem unacceptable, so you may need your partner to be particularly understanding and reassure you that what you are feeling is only natural. Eventually, when the natural process of grieving has run its course, you will start to recover, starting to put energy back into life again and looking forward to the future.

If you've both suffered a loss, both of you may go through these stages, sometimes together, sometimes at different rates. And there is a twist. If one of you is grieving a great deal, the other may feel that he or she has to be strong and unemotional and not grieve; as a result, that person may get stressed, irritable, depressed with life. Then often, the partner who has grieved sees the one who hasn't as being heartless, as in the story of Yasmin and Deepak mentioned earlier in this chapter.

If you do need to grieve, support each other as much as you can, with tears and talking. Get professional help if you feel you need it, because grief, though natural, can be something that affects the whole of your life. If you share what you are feeling together, then it can also bring you incredibly close, and once you are through the grief, your relationship will actually be stronger for the experience.

Jealousy

When you feel bad because you think that your partner is giving elsewhere something that you feel belongs to you, then you are jealous. Sometimes of course, you are right; if your partner is sleeping with a lover or spending more time with friends than with family, then your feelings are understandable. Yet often we are jealous not because of what is happening here and now, but because of our past experiences.

For almost all of us, at some time in our early lives, find ourselves part of a triangle, a relationship between three people. We usually form this triangle with our parents, but it can be with others, perhaps grandparents, brothers and sisters or friends.

Triangles have their problems. We can never be sure whether we're important or not, because the other two people may well shut us out: children often feel shut out anyway because their parents are older, taller, have control over them, and speak their own private 'adult language'. So we may feel jealous of Dad for taking Mum's attention away when he arrives home. We may feel that Grandma is monopolising us when we visit, and never letting us really get to know Grandpa. We may feel guilty, even though pleased, if we seem to be ganging up with our older brother against our younger brother. And whatever we experienced as a child, we'll re-create it in some way with our partner.

So you may find it hard to allow your partner to spend time with friends; you may try to prove that your partner has a greater commitment to you than to work or hobbies. One Relate client followed her husband to work every day for a year– a journey of many miles – convinced that he was having an affair. Another kept his wife locked in the house and monitored her phone calls to friends. Both believed that their partners couldn't possibly love them, and so had to protect their relationship by being constantly jealous. You may even, sadly, find it hard to adapt to having a baby, because the fact of having an extra person added to your partnership unconsciously reminds you of having to 'share' someone you loved when you were young.

If you or your partner are actually giving to another person the love or sex that really should only be given to each other, then it's only natural that you should feel strongly about that. You do need to choose: you either need to make each other the most important person in each other's lives, or you need to consider seriously whether you do want a relationship with each other.

However, if your feelings of jealousy or resentment are actually being triggered by a memory of what you experienced in triangular relationships in the past, then what you need to realise is that you are feeling past emotions rather than present emotions.

Then you need to change your feelings. It will help if you can build your self-confidence and independence. Start doing things on your own, things that show you that you are valuable and worth loving, to build your confidence that your partner does love you and will stay. Ask for reassurance from your partner, then believe it. Learn to trust your partner; he or she will respond to that.

If your partner is jealous of you, try to appreciate why. It may be nothing to do with you and everything to do with childhood experiences, or with the fact that he or she was betrayed in a previous relationship. Try to build your partner's confidence: this could mean showing when you feel particularly loving and affectionate; supporting your partner to do well in things that are important; celebrating when your partner has a success. If you are in a situation which might raise your partner's jealousy level, make sure you do nothing to actually increase his or her anxiety. It will help if, when you are out, you ring if you going to be late; if, when you are in company, you regularly glance across at your partner, chat to them or give them a quick hug. Always show that he or she comes first with you, and that there is no reason to doubt that.

Anxiety

It may seem as if there are very few things in life that we are truly frightened about. In fact, a low-grade version of fear – anxiety – probably runs throughout our whole lives. We can be anxious about losing our job, fearful for our children's safety, wary that our partner is losing interest in the relationship. When we feel this low-grade fear, it can make us edgy and uncomfortable, particularly if we have been brought up to believe that we shouldn't be frightened of anything (as many boys, in particular, are). And if real panic strikes – as it can when we are made redundant or we find out that a close friend is terminally ill – then we can feel paralysed.

If you yourself feel anxious, the best way to handle it is to be clear about what you feel. If your partner isn't willing or able to discuss your anxieties, then you could find a friend, or better still a counsellor who will help you to express your worries, to explore whether they are realistic, and then to take practical action to reduce them.

If it is your partner who is anxious, it can seem as if that emotion is bringing your whole relationship to a standstill; the anxiety stops him or her from taking action to improve things. This was what happened for partners Greg and Hugh. Hugh came alone to counselling because Greg had left him, and he needed support to come to terms with this. Hugh was a quiet man who, at the age of forty-five, had suddenly started to re-think his whole life, and find it a failure. He had worked hard to become a certified accountant, but had been a good solid workhorse rather than an inspired professional go-getter. Now, he began to see that life was catching up with him, and he was scared. He remembered his father, who had died of a heart-attack just before retiring, and he worried that he too would get ill. He looked around at all the other accountants in his firm, and wondered if the management would get rid of him during the next cost-cutting exercise. He began to be so nervous that it affected his whole life, and he got to the point where he was tense about leaving the house.

Hugh's partner Greg had become frustrated at his constant anxiety and had left, but when he heard that Hugh was in counselling, he agreed to come along too. He turned out to be a sensitive man, still committed to Hugh, but unable to understand what his lover was worried about. He often brushed away Hugh's concerns, literally with a wave of his hand. 'It'll never happen, and if it does, we can cope!' was his favourite phrase.

There was no dramatic breakthrough with Hugh and Greg, but there was steady progress. Greg had to learn to acknowledge Hugh's worries, and not just dismiss them; then Hugh was able to feel as if he was being heard and so begin to move on to take action. Greg also had to slowly begin to share his own fears about the future, which he had had to push down in order to reassure Hugh, and then Hugh had to learn to listen to those fears and realise that they were just as important as his own. Both of them had to see that the problems which might come in the future were probably never going to be as incapacitating for them as Hugh's anxiety was, and so it was vital that they work together to solve that problem.

In the end, Greg and Hugh were able to support each other much more fully. The last time the counsellor was in contact with them, they were living together again, and Hugh was beginning a night-school course to extend his qualifications and so make it less likely that the worst would happen.

15
SEXUAL SKILLS

Making love is such a vital part of your relationship that if you are suffering difficulties, very often your love-making is the first thing to show the strain.

If you and your partner don't understand each other, this will spill over into your love-making. If your partnership is triggering a memory in your past that isn't resolved, you may feel nervous about sex. If you aren't communicating with your partner by talking, often you won't feel like communicating by making love. If painful emotion has built up between you, you may find that you don't trust each other enough to let go in bed. And if your needs are not being met in your relationship, you may well feel so resentful that you will block off your desire and never get aroused at all.

Because there is such a direct link between how you get on outside the bedroom, and what happens in it, a Relate psychosexual therapist will usually ask clients who have sexual problems to look first at what's happening on the emotional side of their relationship. If you both improve your understanding, communication, emotional coping skills and your ability to meet each other's needs, it's very likely that without doing anything else at all, your sex life will improve.

Sometimes, however, this doesn't happen. You can rebuild your relationship to be even stronger than before, and still have sexual difficulties. Perhaps you look back and realise that you haven't made love for months. Perhaps you just don't want to make love any more; the spark isn't there. Perhaps you can't get an erection, can't have an orgasm, come too soon or are anxious about penetration. This part of the chapter offers some suggestions for how to trouble-shoot, to change things so that your love-making reflects the improvement that is happening in your partnership as a whole.

CHECKING PHYSICAL PROBLEMS

Your problem could be physical, particularly if your sex life used to be good, but has only now hit difficulties. Having said that, don't automatically jump to the conclusion that it is. Thinking that all your difficulties are down to your health can be an easy opt-out if you don't want to face up to a more in-depth relationship problem. However, any of the following things could be causing difficulties:

Stress, strain, overwork

If you are putting most of your energy into your family or your job, there may be none left over for your sex life. One Relate therapist, whose clients were mostly young, overworked commuters, called his town the 'Gone-off-it centre of the universe'! Worry and stress not only lower your need to have sex; they may make a man less able to get an erection or a woman less able to reach her orgasm. So build your health. This means taking more time off if you are overworking; getting enough sleep; eating healthy food; going on holiday; and taking regular exercise, particularly when you are very stressed.

Hormonal changes

Some women's desire for sex falls according to the time of the month; other women are affected by the contraceptive pill, pregnancy, hysterectomy, menopause, all of which can alter your hormone balance. Recent research also suggests that it is possible that men may also have a midlife 'menopause', when their ability to get an erection falters. Hormone supplements can help, but don't always do so; talking through the problem with your GP will allow you to decide whether hormonal problems are an issue, and if so, what to do about it.

Child-bearing

Childbirth is a key stress time for relationships; and not only because you both have to adapt to your new roles in life. The sheer physical strain of childbirth; the disturbed nights; the worry and responsibility of a new person to look after; the fact that you are constantly on call; all these may mean that sex is the last thing on your mind. Try to get as much support as you can from other people, and remember that children do grow up and eventually become less of a dampener on your sex life!

Alcohol

Drinking affects hormone levels in your body, so you are less likely to feel desire. It then makes the genitals less sensitive so that really sensuous sex is less possible. And alcohol creates difficulties in performance: for up to twelve hours after drinking six pints of average strength beer, for example, many men find it impossible to get and maintain an erection! Make sure that both of you are keeping well within the guidelines of 21 units a week for men, 14 units a week for women, and if you do drink regularly, have at least two or three days without alcohol every week.

Illness

Any kind of illness will make your body concentrate on getting better rather than feeling sexual. On top of this, surgery or a disability may make you embarrassed to take your clothes off, and anxious about the intimacy of making love. Watch out too for specific conditions that can affect you: diabetes can cause erectile difficulty; the onset of multiple sclerosis can mean that you feel fewer sexual sensations. Medication for a number of conditions such as epilepsy, glaucoma and hardening of the arteries can create problems in male sexual performance. So if you are receiving medical treatment, check specifically with your GP or consultant that there are no side-effects of the condition itself, or of the treatment or drugs you are receiving, that might be affecting you.

TAKING THE OPPORTUNITY

If you have both been together for a while, one of the main things that may be stopping you having good sex is the opportunity. This is particularly true if you are suffering from lack of desire or a feeling of dissatisfaction with your sex life rather than one of the more specific sexual problems; you may have stopped wanting sex because you know at the back of your mind that you won't actually have the chance all that often, and that when you do it will all be rushed and stressful. When you were first together you probably spent long evenings cuddling, touching, arousing each other; now, you may be very lucky if you get ten minutes together in bed on a Sunday morning before the children are awake. Your job, your home, your hobbies, your family: all these may make you feel as though you are never able to relax and become sexual people again.

If you suspect that your love-making has declined because of these factors, you have to change things. If you don't, quite simply,

---

! ━━━━━━━━━━━━━ *Task* ━━━━━━━━━━━━━

If I could choose anything

This is an exercise to do on your own, at least at first.

Choose a time when you are alone and not likely to be interrupted. Make sure that you can be alone for at least half an hour, and take the phone off the hook. Get yourself really comfortable, perhaps on the sofa or lying on the bed. If you want to, close your eyes.

Now imagine you are having the best sexual experience of your life.

What setting have you chosen? Indoors, outdoors, somewhere exotic? What are your surroundings like? Is there food and drink? Is there music or other sound? Are there soft rugs, leaves or sand to lie on?

Your experience might be with your partner, or it might not be; this is only a fantasy, remember. Your experience might include lots of other people or just you on your own. It might begin slowly, or it might be sudden and lustful.

Take your time to run your fantasy right the way through from the beginning to the end. Enjoy yourself.

Are there any parts of the fantasy that you want to bring into real life? If you can talk things through with your partner, are there any parts of your fantasy you want to share with him or her? (You don't have to.) Perhaps your partner could help you act out parts of your fantasy, if you want that.

!

you may never have a good sex life again until the children leave home or until you retire. Can you set aside just one occasion a month when your toddler can go to Grandma's? If you have older children, can you sneak off upstairs in the afternoon? One Relate couple, in their forties, regularly used to creep out and up to the woods at the back of the house for an hour in the evening while their teenage sons were doing their homework. 'They used to think we were simply going for a walk . . . it may have been cold, but it seemed ever so romantic and urgent!'

However little opportunity you have for full sex, always make sure you have some 'passion on the run'. Many couples don't get physical with each other unless they are making love, and because they then don't have the opportunity to make love, that actually means that they rarely touch. You can keep desire alive, and reassure each other that you still care, by seizing every opportunity. Have a cuddle on the stairs, a romantic kiss as you go to bed, a quick fondle over the washing up. Such things don't have to lead to sex, but they do act as a constant reminder that you still love and want each other.

YOUR SEXUAL HISTORY

As mentioned in Part 2 of this book on Understanding, your ability to be sexual is often formed in your past. In fact, all the lessons you learn, even those that don't seem to be directly about sex, add or take away from your ability to be intimate and confident in your love-making.

The extent to which you learn to trust yourself and other people at a very early age lays the foundation for whether you are able to be intimate with your partner. The extent to which you feel that you are 'good enough' and deserve love affects just how much you can let go sexually, confide your desires to your partner, feel that it's OK to have your sexual needs met. All the direct messages you received about sexuality from the physical affection you got as a child will leave you feeling more or less relaxed about your body and being touched. And all the more indirect messages you were given about sex by your parents, your teachers and your friends also combine to leave you happy or unhappy, anxious or secure, at ease or disgusted. Finally, any specific sexual experiences you may have had before you met your partner will also help you think of yourself as a skilled and successful lover, or as one who doesn't really get it right.

This was certainly what happened for Tina and Chris. They came for sex therapy because he was having difficulty in getting an erection. Chris was a man whose good looks hid a shy personality; Tina was five years younger, tiny, dark, with a boyish figure that made her look almost like a little girl. She kept glancing across at her partner, reaching over to touch him, leaning towards him, but also tended to take what he said about his problem as a joke, and often laughed about it. Chris seemed hurt by this, and on one or two occasions when she touched him, moved away.

They had been together for just a year, and the erection problems had started about six months ago. At first, they had enjoyed making love a great deal, but slowly, Chris had lost confidence. He said that he felt threatened by what he called Tina's 'teasing'. Tina was worried by Chris's lack of erection, but also angry about it. She said she only joked, 'because otherwise, to be honest, I might hit him! He really winds me up.'

A number of things linked together meant that Tina and Chris were making each other unhappy. Tina, for example, had had a very insecure relationship with her father. He had a tendency to 'come and go' as she put it, moving in and out of the family home. Her mother had coped with this by seeming not to mind whether he was there or not, masking her need of him with jokey insults. Tina had been Daddy's girl until she was about twelve, had enjoyed flirting with him and being the centre of attention.

Then her father finally moved out for good and seemed to make little effort to keep in touch. Tina had met him a few more times, had felt very angry with him for leaving but had never expressed any of it. She realised that over the years, she had 'replayed' her feelings against her father with her partners; she would go all out to attract them physically, and then push them away with jokes and teasing. Counselling helped Tina to realise that, in fact, much of what she felt about Chris was not about Chris at all, but about her father. By not being able to have an erection and make love with her, Chris was reminding Tina of her father's lack of interest in her, even though he didn't mean to reject her. And her teasing, though it protected her, was actually making things worse.

Realising that Tina's jokes were not really aimed at him helped Chris to get back some of his confidence. Yet he too had a past history that was creating difficulty. He had never been very confident with women; his longest relationship so far had been when, in his late teens, he had spent six months with a partner who had eventually left him, giving as the reason that he was 'no good in bed'. Since then, he had had a number of short-term relationships, and it was only when he met Tina that he had felt able to commit himself more fully. He said that he had felt safe with her, but that feeling of safety had quickly disappeared when she started to tease him.

What made the difference for Tina and Chris was that they were able to tell each other about those parts of their past lives that were most affecting them. Tina was able immediately to reassure Chris that, far from being no good in bed, he was a kind and arousing lover. Also she was able to begin to believe that, unlike her father, he was not going to walk out on her at a moment's notice.

Chris still needed to get his confidence back, so once the therapist felt sure that the couple were making headway with their feelings, he suggested that they begin to try some exercises at home between sessions. These 'sensate focus' exercises are the foundations of the kind of help that Relate offers for sexual problems; they help you 're-learn' how to make love in a way that encourages you to find out what feels best.

Chris and Tina were asked to take it in turns to touch each other, slowly and sensuously. The therapist told them that the aim was not to give Chris an erection, in fact quite the reverse; if he started to become erect, they should stop and allow his erection to go down before starting again. This would build Chris's belief that he could become erect, again and again. With the pressure off, Chris and Tina had great success with this exercise and within a few weeks, Chris was much more confident. The therapist suggested that they try allowing Chris to penetrate Tina.

This time, there was a problem. They came back reporting that when they had tried, Chris had lost his erection, and Tina had responded to the problem, as she had in the past, by mocking him. The therapist reminded them of what they had already learned: that the original issues were mostly in the past, and that they were able to respond positively to each other now. They went back to touching and stroking for a few more sessions, and the next time they tried penetration, had complete success.

Over the weeks, Chris built up trust that he could gain and maintain his erection. Like many men who have such problems, his basic difficulty was lack of confidence. Once he got his confidence back, the problem disappeared. Tina and Chris did some more general work on the way they related to each other, but soon left therapy, happy with their result.

SEXUAL MISUNDERSTANDINGS

Some sexual problems arise simply because you misunderstand things. Sex is such a taboo subject that you may well have got the wrong impression somewhere down the line. Particularly if you were taught the facts of life by your same-sex parent and same-sex friends, and have never really had a chance to check things out with people of the opposite sex (or with partners of the same sexual orientation if you are gay or lesbian), you can still have mistaken ideas that trip you up, and cause problems in bed. Here are some myths that are still alive today and which can contribute to all kinds of sexual difficulties.

Men should make the first move

This can cause a problem if he feels pressured to start sex, or if she wants to start sex and thinks she isn't allowed to.

The good news is that men sometimes like to be seduced because they often get tired of taking the lead. Many women love to make the first move and get very aroused by doing so.

Bigger is better as far as a penis is concerned

This can cause a problem if he thinks he has a small penis and so feels inferior; his partner thinks that with a big penis, there'd be more pleasure and so criticises him.

The good news is that most penises are about the same size when erect; a penis you see from across the room (that is, someone else's) always looks bigger than one you look down on (that is, your own); a big penis doesn't necessarily give more pleasure; a woman's vagina contracts and expands to fit the penis available; most partners say that size is less important than what a man does with what he has.

Good sex simply happens

This can cause a problem if sex isn't good for either or both of you and you think there's nothing you can do about it.

The good news is that really good sex can happen spontaneously, but more often is based on knowledge, understanding, and experiment over many years. If you practise, sex will improve.

Men are always up for it

This can cause a problem if he feels pressured always to have an erection, or if his partner feels rejected when he doesn't have one.

The good news is that neither men nor women always feel like it; he isn't a failure if he sometimes can't get it up; it doesn't mean that he doesn't love his partner if, occasionally, he doesn't want sex.

Good sex means simultaneous orgasms

This can cause a problem if you don't have simultaneous orgasms, or if either of you doesn't have orgasms at all.

The good news is that orgasms are great, but foreplay and cuddles can be more important to some people; simultaneous orgasms are a lot less common than many sex manuals would have you believe.

Trying different positions or variations means you're weird

This can cause a problem if you feel you can't experiment because you think you shouldn't; because without different positions, one or the other of you may not get the pleasure you are capable of.

<u>The good news is that</u> many people use unusual positions and really enjoy them; some positions are particularly useful to help partners last longer, come more quickly or have different kinds of orgasm.

?_____*Quiz*_____

Sexual knowledge

This is a quiz in two parts which you have to do together. Each of you should use first the part of the quiz about your partner's sexuality. Complete the sentences. Then you should fold the paper so that your answers are hidden and hand it to your partner. This time, of course, you will be using the second part of the quiz which is about your own sexuality; again fill in the sentences.

Part one

- I think you most like to be touched . . .
- I think one thing you would rather I did less of is . . .
- I think you most like it when I . . .
- I think one thing you want me to do more of is . . .
- I think one foolproof way to turn you on is . . .

Part two

- I most like to be touched . . .
- One thing I would rather you did less of is . . .
- I most like it when you . . .
- One thing I would rather you did more of is . . .
- One foolproof way to turn me on is . . .

When you have finished, unfold the papers and check. How far did each of your answers about your partner's sexuality actually tally with what he or she really thinks, feels and likes?

Don't feel bad if there are differences between you; it takes a long long time to really learn what another person likes sexually. Use this opportunity to talk about what you like, and to learn what really turns you on.

_____**?**

' ——————————— Talking point ——————————

Talking about sex

Often one of our biggest blocks to being relaxed about sex is that we can't really talk about it. We simply don't have words that we feel happy using. Our parents may have stopped us talking about sex; we may have been told off in school for using sexual words. So now, we may feel tense and embarrassed about using certain terms, or referring to certain parts of the body.

Relate sex therapists often encourage clients to become more relaxed around sex, not only by themselves being willing to talk about sex and discuss questions around it, but also by asking their client to build a 'sexual vocabulary'. This can help you to start to talk more easily in bed and out of it.

What words would you both be happy to use for each of these parts of the body? Make suggestions: they could be technical words, funny words, your own special words. Make sure that both of you are happy with the words you choose; if either of you isn't sure, keep going until you find a word that is right for you. (If you are a same-sex couple, ignore the words that refer to the other gender's body parts)

penis
testicles
breasts
nipples
clitoris
vagina
cervix
orgasm
erection
ejaculation

Now decide which words you are going to use for these acts of love-making. Again, keep talking until you find the words that are right for you. If you usually don't do any of these things, find words for them anyway.

man masturbating
woman masturbating
penetration
manual masturbation performed on man
oral masturbation performed on man
manual masturbation performed on woman's clitoris
manual masturbation performed on woman's vagina
oral masturbation performed on woman

NB: Just to be clear, the clitoris is the sensitive female sexual organ whose tip lies under its own 'hood' just in front of the vagina. The vagina is the passage that leads to the cervix. The cervix is the mouth of the womb. Orgasm is the series of pleasurable contractions in the penis or vagina at the height of love-making; it can also affect the whole of the rest of your body. Ejaculation is the release of fluid from the penis during orgasm.

UPDATING YOUR SKILLS

Particularly if you have been together for a while, you may be falling into some traps that are making sex together less than wonderful. It is quite usual to fall into these traps; many couples do, just because they don't realise what is happening. For when you first meet, you usually take things slowly; you will probably spend hours kissing, touching, fondling and learning exactly what each other needs.

Unfortunately, over time, almost every couple starts to change their approach. In some ways, this is good; you both stop being nervous about each other and relax into knowing each other's bodies. But as a side effect, you stop learning, stop experimenting, and start cutting corners. The sex act can sometimes be reduced to its bare bones, which is often seen as penetration. All the other bits – before, during and after – just get briefer and briefer. Soon, many of the parts of love-making that allowed both of you to become properly aroused and so really enjoy what is happening, start to get left out. The result can be that you don't make love as much, or that when you do, you find it boring or unarousing.

Sam and Donna came to Relate after they had been married for two years because Donna was now wanting sex less and less. They were very young – Donna was only just twenty – and obviously still very much in love. But the fact that she was 'going off' sex was worrying to both of them. She felt guilty about her lack of desire; Sam was desperately concerned that it might be his fault.

They first explored just what the problem was. The therapist very quickly realised that what Donna and Sam meant by 'going off it' was that Donna no longer wanted to be penetrated. She loved to be cuddled and caressed, but as she put it 'when we start doing it properly, I turn off.'

It turned out that in fact, this had always been the case. Donna was a virgin when she met Sam, but she had had a few boyfriends whom she had allowed to touch her. She really liked this, and sometimes she had an orgasm, though rarely and not very strongly. When she met Sam, she said that she had fallen in love for the first time. They had felt passionately about each other, had kissed and cuddled as before, and soon he was giving her orgasms by hand in the back of his car. They had slept together within two months of meeting; they had got engaged three months after that.

Donna had looked forward to making love, but hadn't been really disappointed when the first time was good emotionally but not physically. Compared to the passionate sessions in the back of Sam's car, actual penetration had not given her much pleasure at all, but she believed it would get better as they got more used to each other. However since then, she complained, it had if anything got worse. She didn't really get aroused during sex, and once they'd started having penetration, she only felt able occasionally to ask Sam to give her an orgasm by hand, as that 'doesn't give him much pleasure . . . it isn't the real thing.'

Sam said he enjoyed his sex life with Donna, and always had. He too had not had a wide range of experience; of his four previous partners, two had been one-night stands. He got a great deal of pleasure from making love with Donna, but was now worried that he wasn't giving pleasure in return. He had tried different positions, tried keeping going for as long as he could. What was he doing wrong?

The therapist was able to reassure Sam and Donna. She explained to them that most people, once they had slept together, tended to fall into the trap of moving straight to penetration. While this might be great for men who can usually enjoy penetration as soon as they have an erection, for women, who often need to build up slowly to being able to allow a penis into the vagina, foreplay is almost always essential.

The therapist also explained that it was not unusual for a woman to fail to reach an orgasm just through penetration. Certainly just 'keeping going for longer', as Sam had tried, is very rarely the answer. Usually, a woman needs extra touching of her clitoris with her partner's hand or her own, or she needs a position for intercourse that allows a male partner's penis to touch the clitoris. This is why women often climax with foreplay, but not with penetration – and why, when a couple start having intercourse, orgasms sometimes stop. This came as a great surprise to Donna and Sam, and Donna said that she was very relieved that she wasn't abnormal or strange.

The therapist first suggested that the couple talk more about sex, so that Donna could explain to Sam the sort of foreplay she really liked. The therapist suggested they develop between them a list of 'acceptable words' with which to talk about sex, so that they didn't get embarrassed and didn't turn each other off. After some giggling, Sam and Donna developed their list.

To help them practise giving each other more pleasure in more ways, the therapist then suggested that they do some sensuous exercises at home. These began with Donna exploring her own body, alone, really learning just what did and didn't turn her on. She was a little embarrassed at first to be touching herself, but over the weeks, reported to the therapist that she was now able to bring herself to orgasm, and that she knew far more than before about what she liked. After this, Sam was encouraged to join in, at first just touching her sensuously, then gradually following her instructions to bring her to orgasm by hand. (The therapist helped Donna and Sam to understand that orgasm through hand or mouth was just as much the 'real thing' as an orgasm through penetration.) In the final sessions, they moved to full intercourse, with Donna on top, so that it was easy for either of them to touch her clitoris and so bring her to orgasm while Sam was inside her.

The therapist reported that Sam and Donna were very happy with the outcome of their work. They were reassured that in fact their only problem had been lack of information. Neither of them was actually doing anything wrong, and their relationship wasn't in difficulties. They had been able to learn to communicate more about sex, swap notes about what they wanted, and experiment more. Donna now looked forward to intercourse, although one of the things that both she and Sam had learned was that penetration was just one of many options for enjoyable love-making.

! ———————————— *Task* ————————————

Mutual massage

A really wonderful thing you can do for each other is to give a back massage. Set aside a whole evening, and choose a comfortable room. Make sure it's well heated; the partner who is being massaged can get quite cold if the air isn't warm. Turn the lights down, play some soft, sensuous music, spread a firm mattress or quilt on the floor. Have ready some oil; baby oil will do.

Get undressed slowly, together. Then take it in turns to lie on your tummy and receive a massage.

If you are the one doing the massaging, relax. As long as you are loving in what you do, you will give your partner pleasure. Tip some of the oil into the palm of your hand, and warm it by rubbing your hands together. Then spread it on your partner's back. Stroke gently but firmly, avoiding the spine. Press gently into the muscles each side of the back, the muscles on the shoulders, the muscles of the neck. Use different sorts of movement: little, circular moves; strong moves full of pressure; light taps; feather touches; movements that keep pace with your partner's breathing. Keep massaging for up to a quarter of an hour, or until your energy runs out. Finish with several long, smooth strokes from the back of the neck to your partner's buttocks.

Then swap over.

!

__ DO YOU NEED TO TROUBLE-SHOOT?__

There are some sexual blocks which may need extra trouble-shooting, either by your taking particular action, or by your getting support from a sexual therapist. If you go to Relate for help, as an individual or as a couple, the therapist will, as mentioned before, check out how far your problems are being caused by difficulties in your relationship. He or she may also arrange ways for you to check that there are no physical causes of your problems. You may then be given some 'sensate focus' homework tasks, which, as described earlier, will help you as a couple to overcome the blocks you have. These tasks are always carefully chosen to suit you, and go hand-in-hand with discussing and exploring how you feel. Each week, you will report back on how things have gone, and the therapist will help you look at problems you are meeting, and work out why they are happening.

Here are four of the more usual blocks. For each, there is a brief outline of the kind of action that may be suggested to solve the problem. Of course, there are other sexual issues, such as recovering from sexual trauma, that will need different and more specific expertise. The appendix at the back of this book offers some suggestions for further help; and Relate therapists can also advise you on other problems that this book doesn't mention.

Erectile difficulty

There is probably no man in the world who hasn't, at some time, been unable to have an erection when he wants to. It isn't an unusual thing, but it can be very worrying. If a man has never been able to have an erection, then this is called 'primary' erectile difficulty, and will often be due to a physical cause; the therapist may refer on for medical treatment. Or, it could be that the man has had a traumatic experience, such as sexual abuse when young, which has taught him that it is very threatening to have an erection, so he has never had one. Then, the therapist will need to explore fully just what happened, and work with you to diminish the fear that is causing the problem.

Much more likely is that a man who has erectile difficulty used to be able to have erections but has now 'lost confidence' in his own ability; this is called 'secondary' erectile difficulty. Perhaps because he was tired, had been drinking, was upset or grieving over something, was embarrassed or under pressure, he was unable to perform. This worried him, particularly if his partner reacted badly. Next time he wanted to have an erection, the worry stopped him doing so, or made him lose his erection once it had arrived. Chris, whose story was told on pages 201–3, reacted in this way when his partner Tina teased him over his lack of erection.

In most cases of erectile difficulty, the therapist will suggest the sensate focus programme, with the emphasis on pleasure rather than performance. Almost, the couple should try not to create an erection, and if they do, they should let it die again before continuing. First touching non-genitally, then touching genitals; the aim is to enjoy themselves. By the time they have done several sessions of this, the man is often having spontaneous erections. If not, the therapist will do his or her best to explore the reasons why, which may be to do with past experiences, or with pressures built up in the current relationship. Then, once the man is starting to gain confidence in his erection, the couple can move on to penetration. Using these methods, problems of erectile difficulty are often quite straightforward to solve, and as an added bonus, both partners learn more about each other sensuously and sexually.

Vaginismus

Some women are unable to allow a penis inside their vagina; their muscles automatically contract, making penetration impossible. This isn't something they have conscious control over; they may long to have a sex life that includes penetration, but for some reason, their body says 'no'.

There are a wide range of reasons why this may have happened: sometimes it is due to an obviously upsetting sexual experience such as an insensitive internal examination, but just as often, the reasons are complex and unclear, a mixture of physical and emotional worries that simply leave the woman unable to respond positively to her partner's penis.

Vaginismus may seem a difficult problem, and can make both

of you feel guilty, fearful or angry. It may be necessary to explore what emotions you both feel, to look back at previous sexual experiences, in particular the ones the woman has had. Once any unhappiness has been diminished, and you are feeling more relaxed about things, then the therapist will suggest tasks that you can carry out to resolve the problem.

Relate therapists work with clients to help them feel more comfortable and relaxed in intimate siutations. They will suggest homework tasks that gradually and sensitively explore and resolve the problem.

These tasks may be for the woman to do on her own at first. As confidence is gained her partner may be involved. Therapists take care to work with clients at their own special pace towards a success-ful outcome.

Orgasmic difficulty

Most women who have difficulty reaching orgasm are simply suffer-ing from a misunderstanding. For as mentioned in Donna and Sam's story, many people believe that the thrusting action of the penis alone is enough for a woman to 'come'. In fact, in order for a woman to have an orgasm, she almost always needs some extra sort of stimulation on her clitoris. She could get this from her own or her partner's hand, her partner's mouth, or from a male partner's penis angled in such a way that the shaft touches her clitoris during intercourse.

Many ways of penetration just don't touch the clitoris, and because of this, much love-making that works for a man doesn't work for a woman. A couple may have to learn what does work, what positions or extra touch she needs in order to be fulfilled. Sometimes, in therapy, as soon as a couple realises this, they can often easily develop for themselves a sexual approach that works.

A couple may need extra help to 'learn' how to have an orgasm if the woman has never had one at all before, or if she finds it difficult to find the right approach with her partner. She may first have to explore her feelings about sex, in case they are making it difficult for her to really know what she needs. Sometimes women are brought up to be inhibited and guilty, and this of course makes learning how to orgasm a very difficult task.

The therapist will probably ask the woman first of all to explore on her own, touching her body all over, touching her genitals, learning what feels good and gives her pleasure. (We are often taught that touching yourself is 'wrong'; in fact, it is an ideal way to learn about how your body works and how you get aroused. You can then use these lessons to improve your love-making.) Progress to orgasm often follows, and once a woman has learned to orgasm by herself, the couple can then move on to using what she has learned to help her orgasm when they make love together.

Premature ejaculation

Premature ejaculation is one of the most common male sexual difficulties. It means that a man isn't aware of the signs his body sends him to signal an impending ejaculation, and so can't control its happening. This can be upsetting for the man, who can't keep going as long as he wants to, and for his partner, who may want him to carry on for longer. Premature ejaculation sometimes happens when a man hasn't made love very much, or for a while, and so isn't really able to judge correctly the signals his body is giving him. But it can also happen in a regular sexual relationship if, because of an unhappy experience or some kind of strong emotion, a man is effectively 'blocking off' his sexual signals and so can't feel them.

An example of this was the case of Sean and Anne. They came to Relate because Sean was suffering from premature ejaculation. They had met through work, at a conference held for sales managers from different parts of the country; Anne was from Yorkshire, and Sean from Wales. They fell for each other at once, and then had met up for weekends that became more and more regular. They married very quickly, and Anne had had a child within a year.

Two more babies followed in quick succession, and between the births, Anne had not felt much like making love. When they did have sex, it was quickly over, but as both of them were very physically affectionate people, the lack of sex in many ways didn't bother them. It was only when the last child started play-school, and they were able to take more time together, that the fact that Sean always ejaculated within seconds of penetration started to matter.

When Sean explored his sexual history with the help of the therapist, he admitted that he had always ejaculated quickly. Before marrying Anne, he had had only two very short-term relationships and in both of them had experienced premature ejaculation. In some ways, he admitted, he was almost glad that he came so quickly, because he didn't want to bother Anne with sex. He had known within hours of meeting her that he wanted to marry her, and was still very much in love with her.

Delving back further into his past, the therapist helped Sean to work out why he felt he shouldn't 'bother' Anne. Sean's family had been very inhibited around sex; it was never talked about at home, and Sean had got the impression that it was something to be avoided. When he met Anne, who was very physically affectionate, he had loved being cuddled and stroked, but was still not really at ease with the more intimate acts of sex.

When Sean talked through his feelings with Anne, she was very sympathetic. The therapist felt that they had a strong relationship that was fulfilling for them even though sex didn't happen very often. They talked openly, cuddled a lot, and had a partnership that was based around giving to each other and to their children. Did they want it to include good sex? To Sean's obvious surprise, Anne said immediately that she did. Now that they had more time, she wanted to rediscover the sexuality that she had had as a teenager, when she felt passionate all the time. She wanted to do this with Sean because she loved him. Having heard this, Sean agreed that they should try to improve their sex life.

Sean needed to explore his past and work through his very real inhibitions and doubts, and this he did over a period of time. As Sean felt happier about sex, the therapist suggested a programme of tasks which would not only help Sean to develop his sexuality, but would also teach him to be able to 'hold back'. At the moment, he simply wasn't able to tell when he was about to come. This was partly because up to now, he had in many ways wanted to get sex over and done with; he had blocked out any body signals that might have helped him to pull back from coming.

Sean and Anne worked together on the sexual tasks they were set. At first, she stimulated his penis, stopping occasionally so that he never quite reached the point of coming, and then letting his erection go down again. As well as simply stopping, Anne also learned to reduce Sean's erection by what is called the 'squeeze' technique, pressing with her thumb and two fingers around the ridge under the head of his penis. Through this repeated 'stop start' method, Sean gained enough experience of arousal without orgasm to be able to learn the first signals that he was about to come, and what he could do to hold himself back. The aim, by moving from manual stimulation through to intercourse, was to allow Sean to control his orgasm himself.

Alongside these very specific tasks, Sean and Anne practised slow touching, to give each other pleasure. They experimented with sensuous, different ways of making love and bringing each other to orgasm. They were able to build on their natural love of touching to overcome Sean's inhibitions and embarrassment. Their therapist says that they are doing well, and enjoying the work more and more!

16

CREATING THE GOOD TIMES

Many couples who come to Relate in order to rebuild their relationship want to bring back the good times, the times they spent together when they first met, the incredible excitement of first romance. In fact, that's impossible. You can never really fall in love again because now, you know each other. You have a history together; you know the reality of living with each other; you know the bads and the goods.

Nevertheless, you can successfully create some of the elements of the good times within your relationship as part of the overall changes you are making. For example, when you both met, you spent lots of time together, getting to know each other, but over the years probably your time together has faded. You can alter that, choosing to start spending time together again. When you first fell in love, you probably told each other how wonderful you were all the time, but now you probably don't bother to do that; you can start complimenting each other again, particularly now that you really appreciate each other's good points. And when you first committed yourselves to each other, you happily planned your future together; you can do that again, now, as a sign of your new commitment.

MAKING TIME

Once any basic conflicts have been recognised, one of the main things that Relate counsellors notice in most relationships is that couples don't spend enough time together. Or if they do, then it isn't good-quality time. With work, home, children, relatives, and hobbies, you may find that there is just no time left for you – and often, because you feel safe and secure in your partnership, you accept this until you hit problems.

If you can begin to make good-quality time for each other, you achieve a number of very positive things in the relationship. First, you give the message that you are important to each other, particularly if you are prepared to let go of other important things in order to be with each other. Second, you build a bond, because the more time you spend together, the more you get in tune with each other's ways of doing things, the more you see the world through each other's eyes. Finally, by touching down with each other regularly, you get to update each other on how you are changing, day to day. It is this updating which is so essential to being able to avoid conflict.

The story of Daniel and Julie shows clearly the problems that lack of time together can cause in the long-term. They didn't erupt into the counselling room rowing with each other, as some couples do when they come to Relate. On the contrary, Daniel and Julie seemed very polite to each other, but 'almost as if,' as the counsellor put it, 'they were acquaintances instead of husband and wife'. Their relationship had started happily; they had met through friends. Julie worked in an estate agent's office; Daniel was a computer programmer. They had seemed to have a great deal in common, got on well, both were very active. Sex was good, and they felt very comfortable with each other. Julie moved in to Daniel's house, and a year later they married.

Safe in each other's affection, they carried on living their lives more or less as they had done before they were together; even, as the counsellor put it, as they had 'before they met'. They each liked their jobs, and sometimes worked late. Daniel was a keen member of his local formation dance team, while Julie played squash. They met up with friends at the weekend, often separately, and often took activity holidays with these friends. They were both perfectly happy with this; both came from families where their parents were affectionate but not particularly dependent on each other.

Slowly, however, over time, their partnership seemed to fail. They weren't talking much, at least not on a deep level, and weren't making love much. When they were at home, which was rarely, they would share the housework, watch some television, eat and go to bed. They tended to confide their problems, which were mostly about work, to colleagues rather than to each other. And sooner or later, the inevitable happened. Daniel began an affair with his formation dance partner. They would drive out into the country to spend time together after their practice sessions, and soon Daniel was also taking lunch hours off work to be with his lover, Kate. He knew he didn't feel seriously about her, though the sex was good, but he liked the contact, the sense of closeness that he felt had completely disappeared from his marriage.

Things might have continued like this for ever, if Daniel and his lover hadn't been found out. Kate's husband caught them kissing in Daniel's car when he unexpectedly dropped in at the dance school practice session. There were strong words, and some pushing and shoving. Daniel realised that it was time everything was out in the open, went straight home and told Julie the truth. Several hours later, they had decided to go to Relate, and if they didn't work out, to split up.

With Daniel and Julie, unlike some couples, there was very little painful emotion to overcome. Their problem was almost that there was very little emotion at all. Julie said that she hadn't felt particularly betrayed by Daniel's affair, because 'I knew that there wasn't actually much of a relationship left to betray'. For his part, Daniel had known from the start that his fling with Kate was just that – a fling; he had, in fact, already thought of ending it several weeks ago. But the drama of discovery had made both Daniel and Julie stop and take stock. Did they still have a relationship left? So the counsellor began by exploring with them whether, if they could develop a positive future together, they would want it. They didn't know; but they were certain that they wanted to find out, and if not, they wanted to part.

The first task the counsellor set Julie and Daniel was a challenge. Could they find time, each week, to spend together? Looking at their diaries, it seemed at first glance that they couldn't. At this point, with some couples, counselling reaches a standstill. If they aren't prepared to give up other parts of their life to spend time with each other, then the relationship may not mean all that much to them. Daniel and Julie, however, at least wanted to give things a chance. They cancelled meetings with friends, stopped working late. They were each prepared to give up something important to them, prepared to pull back from other commitments and other relationships. By the third counselling session, they were spending two evenings a week and most of each weekend together.

During this time, the counsellor asked them to talk to each other, in depth. They used communication exercises to start to 'update' each other on what they had been thinking and feeling, particularly about what had happened to them over the past years they had been together, and particularly about why the affair had developed.

Next, the counsellor suggested that each of them deliberately start including the other in their lives. Daniel was to go to watch Julie play, and then go for a drink with her and her squash friends afterwards. She was to call for him at work, and take him to lunch. The counsellor stressed that the aim was not for them to do everything together: that would be just as damaging to their relationship as for them to do nothing together. The aim was to combine their lives more fully, so that each of them started to see the other's interests as being as important to them as their own.

Daniel and Julie had a head start in that they had originally fitted well as a couple; they had simply let that 'fit' be worn away. By spending more time together and using that time to get to know each other again, they were able to re-establish that 'fit'. Though they haven't yet finished in counselling, they are now confident that they have made a firm decision to stay together – and that they can put the time and the energy into making things work.

Daniel and Julie's story not only shows how a relationship can fossilise if it is not given the opportunity to grow through time spent together. It also shows how just a regular commitment of good-quality time can make an amazing amount of difference. This time has to be regular: daily or weekly, never less. It has to be a commitment: so that both of you know that it is a priority and that during that time your relationship comes first. And it has to be quality time together: not watching television or entertaining the family, but a real chance to be alone, touch, talk and get to know each other again.

!————————— *Task* —————————

Setting a date

Can you make time for each other? With your partner, make a plan of the week ahead, listing each day, with spaces marked for each hour. Then take some coloured pens. Mark in one colour every hour that one of you is out of the house – at work, taking the children to school, going to evening class. Then mark, in another colour, every hour that the other partner is out of the house. Mark in a third colour if, although you aren't out of the house, you won't have time for each other, perhaps because the children need to be cared for, or because you have visitors.

What time is left? Choose three half-hours, at three points in the week, that you can spend time together without worrying about other people.

If you can't find those half hours, look first at the times you've marked that you are at home but have child-care duties or visitors. Could you cancel the visitors? Could you find alternative child care?

If not, what else could one of you cancel so as to spend time with the other? Maybe the following week, the other partner could cancel something instead. These three half-hours are your 'investment time', time when you build the 'bank balance' of your relationship for the years to come. **!**

————————— CELEBRATING —————————

However well you are doing in life, as individuals or as a couple, if you don't remind yourselves and each other that you are doing well, then you will lose heart. Without celebration, the acknowledgment that you are doing well and have succeeded, you can easily get demotivated, stop trying to succeed, and in the end, start failing again.

There is a taboo against celebration. In our culture it's seen as 'big-headed' to be too proud of ourselves, to tell others of our achievements; but when people are told they have done well, they not only feel more secure in themselves, but they go on to do better. As well, they are more likely to be able to be genuinely happy for others who have succeeded. For all these reasons, it's a good idea to celebrate each other, and the relationship.

Start by reminding yourself what you like about your partner. Kindness, sense of humour, skill in coping when the children are misbehaving? What has your partner done to support you, over the years? Where has he or she been loyal, hard-working or considerate? Get into the habit of noticing your partner's good points rather than his or her bad ones.

As you do, start to tell your partner what you are noticing. It can be hard for people to accept praise; so don't be put out if your partner gets embarrassed or shrugs off the compliment. Particularly where you have both been having problems, a partner may find it difficult to accept what you are saying as genuine and well meant. But if you keep going, and keep genuinely telling him or her how happy you are and how well things are going when he or she is making you happy, in the end your partner will believe you, and will want to make you even happier.

Celebrating your partner may be slightly embarrassing, but it can be even harder to start celebrating yourself. This means allowing yourself to realise what's positive about who you are and what you've done. Perhaps write down each day one thing that you are proud of. Try to accept compliments when they are offered, by your partner or by other people. Give yourself treats occasionally, to reward yourself when you feel you have done particularly well.

Also celebrate your relationship. Relate counsellors sometimes suggest that clients each remember and mention in their counselling session three positive things that have happened between them during the past week. You could vary this idea by making a weekly date with your partner to tell each other what is going well, maybe over supper on Saturday night, or as you wake in the morning on Sunday.

It's also good to celebrate key stages in your partnership; this is why it is so good to celebrate anniversaries. At this point in your relationship, when you are coming back from the brink, try celebrating not twenty-five years together, but a day without a row, a week of being able to talk freely again, or the first time you make love after not doing so for three months. Perhaps celebrate by buying special food, opening a bottle of wine, buying each other a card or a present. If you get into the habit of doing this regularly, the good feeling will spread, and you'll be even more motivated to make the relationship work.

!——————————— *Task* ———————————

Congratulations!

In the next week, find, make or buy something for your partner to celebrate him or her. This present doesn't have to cost much; it could be a single flower or a card you drew yourself. It should be something that gives your partner a clear message about how well you think he or she is doing. !

!——————————— *Task* ———————————

Play truant

Being willing to enjoy yourselves is an essential part of any love relationship. If you don't, and everything becomes too serious, then you exhaust yourselves physically and emotionally. Your relationship becomes hard work. You can even be tempted outside the partnership to other relationships that offer you a chance to have fun; many affairs start simply because life is too serious at home. In fact, it is best to start to begin to have fun before you have ironed out all the conflicts. This will help dissolve the bad feeling, help you take everything much less seriously, help you both succeed with each other where, up to now, you have failed.

So sometime soon, play truant together from your joint responsibilities. If you always cook, go to the fish-and-chip shop. If you have work to do at home most nights, take just part of an evening off and watch a video together. If your responsibility is your children, meet each other in the lunch-hour when the kids are at school, and have a milk shake somewhere. Enjoy playing truant – you deserve it! !

PLANNING FOR THE FUTURE

When you met, you probably had goals that matched; over time, they may well have diverged and started to clash. Now, planning for the future reassures you both that you do have a life together, and so allows you to be more secure with each other. It gives you something to work for together. It will focus your attention on the future rather than the past, and so help to heal the wounds.

An example of how focusing on the future made all the difference for a couple is the story of Sarah and Gerald. Gerald had met Sarah on the rebound from his first marriage, which failed when his wife had left him for someone else. As soon as the divorce was through, he had set out, almost deliberately, to find another partner who would help him look after his daughter Hannah, who was five. He had felt that he mainly needed companionship and a mother for Hannah, and without really realising it, had rushed into marriage for many of the wrong reasons.

Sarah was charmed by Gerald, and thought Hannah was wonderful. She liked being part of a ready-made family, although she looked forward to having a child of their own. For their first few months they were incredibly happy, and for the next few months, they were very happy.

Slowly, however, it became clear that Gerald was still living in the past. Sarah was quite able to accept that he still met his ex-wife, Sally, when she came to pick Hannah up each week for their day together. She wasn't quite so happy when it became clear that Gerald kept trying to phone and see Sally regularly, and that he still had pictures of her in the house. Gerald defended this at first by saying that he didn't want Hannah to grow up without having a good relationship with her mother; but in the end, Sarah began to seriously doubt whether Gerald was emotionally connected to her. It seemed that in many ways, he was still married to Sally. She demanded that they come to Relate before everything fell apart.

In the counselling, the couple worked in several ways. Gerald, first of all, needed to come to terms with the fact that his relationship with Sally was over. This was quite difficult for him to do, but as it was clear that Sally had moved on to a new life and didn't want her relationship with Gerald any more, in the end, he accepted it. After this, he went through a period of grieving for the old relationship. Sarah, meanwhile, had had sessions on her own, and had come to the conclusion that she still did want to be married to Gerald, because she loved him, but that if he couldn't let go of the memories of Sally and commit himself fully to a relationship with her, then she would probably leave.

Faced with this very definite choice, Gerald started to look clearly at Sarah and his relationship with her. He realised, as he said, that 'without knowing it, I made a really good choice'. He had, by this time, accepted that his original motive in getting together with Sarah was not true attraction; he had simply chosen a woman, any woman, as a wife and mother. But in fact, he did like Sarah. More than that, she was important to him; she and he fitted together well. He had begun, without being aware of it, to love her.

With the counsellor's guidance, Sarah and Gerald next looked carefully at what their possible future together could be. They looked at the far future and imagined growing old together. They looked at the medium-term future, at building a home together, supporting each other through their different aims in life, at bringing up Hannah, at the possibility of starting their own family. Over the course of several weeks, as they built up a clear picture of their future, they grew more and more enthusiastic. They realised that they did fit together, that they could do together far more than they could do separately, and that the thought of a future together was an exciting one. When they left counselling, they had committed themselves to each other, almost for the first time.

Your relationship and the future

If you both feel that your relationship is beginning to come back on track, then take time together to look at future plans. You may want to start with very short-term things, such as your next holiday or how you will spend Christmas. Or, you may want to look at the far future, and then work backwards from that.

When you plan, be careful not to simply build up a fantasy of how things will be. Now is the time to let go of ideal futures of a perfect life. Concentrate instead on being realistic, looking at what will happen for you, as two different and imperfect human beings with some good and some bad in your lives. Each of you can outline what you want; the other should listen carefully and, of course, recognise that your ideas are probably not the same. When both of you have taken your turn, go into more detail about your ideas. Try to be clear about what you want and what you don't want, what you each have to say no to, and where you can easily compromise. Take good ideas from each other, realising how much more exciting and fulfilling your future will be if you combine possibilities rather than simply follow the path that one of you suggests.

From all your ideas, choose one particular plan that you are both happy about. Then look at how to make this plan happen. Put together a 'To Do' list, of things that you will need to achieve in order to move house, go on holiday, start up a new business. Decide whether to ask for help, perhaps from friends and family, perhaps from professionals. You could also do a time plan, showing you when things have to happen, marking in points where you need to check that these things have been done.

It's good, in fact, always to have at least one future project on the boil, to keep you both focused ahead. It may not be a big project. It could be putting some new plants in the garden, or having some friends round for a pizza next Saturday night. But if at any one time, you can look ahead positively even just a few days, then you will begin to build trust that you will eventually be able to look ahead positively for more than a few years.

PART 4
MAINTENANCE

17

BUILDING ON COMMITMENT

Once you've have begun to understand and change what is happening, things will start to improve. You will start to gain a sense of that deep commitment you are working towards. But to keep building this commitment, you also need to step back from the process, to make sure as you go that what you are doing will last for a lifetime. This part of the book looks at how to do that, not only in the short term, but also in the long term.

CHARTING YOUR PROGRESS

As you improve your relationship in all the ways described in this book, it's good to keep a check on what is happening and how things are going.

It's tempting to judge your progress on individual incidents – a hopeful conversation, a thrilling bout of love-making, a painful counselling session, a chapter of the book that really created a change – but this may not be wise. The process of working through relationship problems is not a predictable one, and sometimes it is difficult to tell whether you are doing well or doing badly; what seems like disaster can sometimes be good news. Because of this, perhaps the best way to gauge things is to look at the overall pattern of what is happening and interpret that; Relate counsellors speak of a number of typical patterns of progress that you can expect.

One possibility is that you start work on your relationship

optimistically. Within a few weeks or a few days, you are on the point of separating. From the very moment you try to improve things, they go downhill: you row more, you make love less, you seem to disagree on everything. Though this seems like the worst scenario, it is actually quite a promising one, because it means that you are both adjusting your ideas of each other or of what the relationship means. You may well be facing reality for the first time, and this is a painful thing to do. The best option here is to stick with it, and avoid panicking. When the dust has settled, you may well be stronger than ever.

Almost the reverse of this is when things seem to go too well. At first, you get immediate hope and insight; within days, you are talking deep into the night, writing each other love-notes, ringing each other at work twice a day. Within a few weeks you are tempted to ease back on the work you are doing because everything seems so much better. (This is what one Relate counsellor called 'third session euphoria', a phrase that is relevant whether or not you are in counselling.) In fact, your efforts have cleared up the surface problems, but not the ones underneath. You need to be prepared for more hard work before your relationship becomes stable.

Surprisingly, another piece of good news that may in fact be bad news is a sudden impulse to go for a formal or obvious sign of commitment, such as getting married or having a baby. It may be that you are ready for this, that the effort you have put into your relationship is really working. But more often, such impulses hide a fear that in fact, you are going to split up. You may think that if you marry or have a child, this will make it easier for you both to stay together, but it won't. The problems will still be there, and the new responsibility of marriage or parenthood can often just make those problems worse.

Less often, you suddenly find something that works. One of you may discover a key piece of information about the other, perhaps about an unhappy childhood; both of you may learn a new skill, such as how to recover after rows. Almost overnight, given this new piece of the jigsaw, you do change, the problems seem to disappear. This is wonderful, but be prepared for more work to have to be done: it is rare that everything gets cleared up in one go.

Or, you may work on your relationship regularly, but feel that very little is changing. If you are feeling like this, look back; you may well find that actually, things have changed, but in a series of small steps. Remember the night you sat and talked together for almost an hour after the children went to bed; the occasion you made love for the first time in ages; the point at which your father commented that you were both looking well and happy? This is a hopeful pattern. You are building slowly but steadily, on a solid foundation; the important thing is that you are changing.

One of the most frightening things that can happen as you improve your relationship is that you see-saw. When one of you is hopeful at the start of your work, the other is convinced you will split up. As the pessimist starts to gain hope, the optimist hits a crisis of confidence. It can seem as if you will never both feel the same.

This is a very typical pattern for couples whose relationships are troubled. Given time, work and guidance, it will often resolve itself happily, as is shown by the story of John and Ruth. Both were in their mid-twenties, and the reason they gave for coming to counselling was that they wanted to decide whether to have children. They believed that having a baby was so important that they didn't want to make the decision without support and guidance. They seemed to get on well as a couple and have a lot in common. In some ways, the counsellor was unsure why they felt that they needed her to help them explore the issue.

When they talked about it, John said that they had been clear before they got married that they wouldn't necessarily have children, 'but that when the time came, we would talk it all through'. Ruth agreed, and seemed happy with this summary of how they both felt. As session followed session, however, they seemed to be getting nowhere; John felt that he still wanted to wait; Ruth felt that they were running out of time. They would repeat the same arguments, over and over. The counsellor suggested that, just for a few sessions, they see her individually.

When they did, a very different picture emerged. Ruth was desperate to have a child. Ten years ago, she had fallen pregnant and had a termination. Although she had chosen to do it, losing the baby had upset her deeply, and she had always felt guilty. Now, faced with not ever having children, she was panicking. She really wanted a child, not only because she felt she would make a good mother, but to make up for the baby she had lost. She had told John what had happened but had never told him how much it had affected her, nor really expressed her deep need to have children.

At the next session, Ruth explained to John how she felt. Up until then, he had been calm and reasonable, but now he got very angry. He talked about how pressured he felt, and how he had believed that their marriage was about joint decisions, not emotional blackmail. He was withdrawing from counselling.

Ruth came to the next few sessions alone and in tears, convinced that her marriage was at an end. She continued to work not only on what she really wanted, but also on her feelings about John.

Much to the counsellor's surprise, a month later, John said that he wanted to begin counselling again. Given time, he had stepped back and started to see things more long-term, to want to work on the relationship. He started with a few individual sessions, and began to explore just why he felt so strongly against having a family. His parents had been divorced and he had mostly lived with his father. He had been brought up to be a very self-sufficient little boy, and this had made him react in two ways. First, he was filled with panic at the thought of having a child which would be dependent on him; second, he was very afraid that he would also divorce, and that his children would suffer just as he had. The safest thing, some part of him had decided, was not to have a family.

When John and Ruth were ready to work together again, they were both very different people from when they had first come to counselling. Both of them had much more understanding of the way they thought and felt about the issues; both of them were being much more honest with themselves and each other about what was happening. So when they once again began to negotiate, things were a great deal easier. They were each able to list out what their fears were, what they needed to know and do in order to be happy with their decision, and what the bottom line was if they couldn't come to a decision at all.

In fact, they began to move much closer together in their aims. As John gained more confidence in the relationship, he started to be more optimistic about the thought of starting a family. As Ruth began to realise that having a baby was not something she could do just to resolve her own past issues, she started to take account of the very real worries that John had. Their counsellor reports that they are both now completely committed to making a decision that is right for both of them.

! ——————————— *Task* ———————————

How far have you come?

One good way of charting your progress is to look at how far you've come since you first realised that there was a problem. You may want to look back at the time when you did a stock-take on your relationship (whether or not you used the relationship survey included in this book), and compare what you thought and felt then with how you think and feel now. These questions may guide you.

The problems: How far have your actual difficulties receded into the background? Issues between you, such as money or sex, won't disappear overnight, but they may have reduced.

How you handle the problems: Are you coping with these issues better than you were? Is there less blame, less nagging, less turning-away; more listening, more eye contact, more touching, more cuddles?

Your feelings: These can be a red herring, because your emotions can shift very quickly indeed. But if, in general, over the course of weeks rather than hours, you are feeling better about yourself, your partner and the relationship, you are making progress.

What the future can tell you: While couples in difficulty often check the past to see what is really happening, couples who are recovering from problems tend to look to the future. If you are finding it easier to think of the future positively, confident that it will be good, then this may well mean that things are getting better.

A final check: Counsellors report that clients whose partnerships are improving often also have lives that are improving. Are you looking better, feeling better, suffering less illness? Are you starting to tackle new projects: moving house, going to the gym, going for promotion? If you're not simply using these activities as a way of ignoring the problems, they may be a sign that the problems are disappearing. It's as if, now that your relationship is settled, some part of you knows that you can turn your attention to building a better life.

!

COPING WITH SET-BACKS

Whatever the general pattern of your progress, at some point you will hit a set-back. It can come at the start of your work, but often it comes after a period where things have gone particularly well. You both work hard, understand, communicate, regain the good feeling. You start to relax and think that the worst is over; maybe you are even tempted to stop working for improvement. Then the bomb drops. Or, you may hit a time of particular strain: one of you has to work double shifts, and all the old doubts come rushing back. Something happens from outside to rock the boat; your daughter gets reprimanded at school, and all of a sudden you are rowing as never before.

There are times when these set-backs should give you cause for worry. If you find yourself 'forgetting' to work on your relationship; if you somehow fail to do exercises that you have both agreed on; if, when in counselling, you miss or keep cancelling sessions, then look closely at what is happening. Doing these things doesn't mean to say that you are failing, that you are a 'bad person', or that you don't love your partner. They do mean that the ways you are trying to improve your relationship are not the right ones for you, or that, in the end, rebuilding your partnership may well not be what you really want. Try to be completely honest with yourself about exactly why you aren't still putting your relationship improvement above everything else.

But more often than not, these danger signs are not present, and what seem to be set-backs are simply part of the process of changing your relationship. Exploring the past will stir up your emotions; struggling to understand each other will make you both confused; developing your skills in communication or sexuality can be a strain. And particularly if your relationship is under external stress, such as that caused by a life stage or a life event, you can feel as if you are back to square one, when in fact you are actually doing well, just suffering a temporary set-back.

Here is the good news. Counsellors look on set-backs such as these as very positive. They are a chance, as one counsellor said, to 'put the fly back in the ointment and see what happens'. By facing up to a set-back, be it an old one or a new one, you learn to handle the fly in the ointment in a much better way. You learn to spot the signs of a looming problem, and know what to do. You learn to trust that you can get through set-backs on your own. You often get to explore your relationship problems more deeply than you did the first time round, and maybe make more progress. And you get to practise the skills that you have developed through counselling, in a real life 'test' of how far you have come.

Carl and Joanna came to counselling a year into their marriage because they were very disillusioned with each other. It was a second marriage for both of them; her teenage daughter still lived with them, but his children were both grown and living in other parts of the country.

Carl was still trying to run his second marriage in the same way as he had run his first. There, he had largely ruled the roost, making the major decisions but also taking most of the responsibility. In fact, it was this that had brought his previous relationship to grief: after twenty years, he had grown tired of shouldering every burden. When he met Joanna (who had sold him his new car), he had fallen in love with her because she was capable and self-sufficient.

They had started an affair which began as a fling at the firm's Christmas party, but had soon developed into something a lot more serious. Within months, Carl had told his wife that he was leaving, and there then followed a year of painful negotiations while he freed himself from his previous relationship and finally moved in with Joanna. Throughout this time, as Carl put it, Joanna was a 'tower of strength', supporting him when he needed it, steering clear when he needed space. He was absolutely sure that he had made the right choice of partner this time.

However, Joanna's self-sufficiency was just as strong when she was married to Carl as when she had simply been his lover, and this began to irritate him. He liked to organise things in his way, to be in control, and Joanna wasn't controllable. And, now that they were living together rather than meeting only at weekends, she began to feel very trapped by his way of doing things. He was fifteen years older, as he often reminded her, but she regarded herself as his equal and he didn't really like it.

When they came to counselling, Carl once more tried to take control. When the counsellor asked what the problem was, it was Carl who jumped in with the answer. When the counsellor suggested exercises, Carl suggested alternatives. But slowly, because of the love he felt for Joanna, Carl changed. He faced up to his need to control everything, and began to appreciate that this wasn't the best way to run his relationship with Joanna. In return, Joanna explored her need to be completely independent, which was a reaction to the pain she had felt when her first marriage broke up. Over the weeks, they each allowed the other to see how vulnerable they were, and made great progress.

Then one week, shortly before Christmas, they came into the session hardly speaking. Carl's daughter had visited for the weekend – and in Joanna's words, it was 'as if the clock had been turned back'. Carl had suddenly gone back to all his old behaviour, making arrangements without checking with Joanna, ordering her about the house. Joanna had objected, they had rowed and Carl's daughter had felt caught in the middle.

Joanna was panicking; she felt that all the progress they had made was just 'an act', and that all their work had been wasted. Carl too felt everything was slipping away. Both of them, it seemed to the counsellor, had forgotten not only how much they had changed since they began counselling, but also how to get back in touch with each other's needs by communicating calmly.

The counsellor was able to remind Joanna and Carl of these things, and they left the session feeling reassured. Over the next week, they worked hard to talk positively and keep communicating about what they needed and what they felt. A few weeks later, they were back on top again. During their first session of the New Year, they were able to celebrate a trouble-free holiday, despite the fact that Carl had been under stress at work, and that they had had all the children to stay. 'We could never have got through this without tearing each other's eyes out this time last year,' said Joanna.

‘ ============= Talking point =============

Survival pack

If you do hit set-backs, sit down and talk about them as soon as you can. The following three guidelines will help you to be positive, and to work out how to cope.

1 Find out why

Set-backs are a normal part of the process of rebuilding your relationship. They will be happening for a good reason: to alert you to a hidden problem, for example, or to show you that you haven't yet worked enough on a particular issue. Can you find out what that reason is?

2 Look back at what you have done right

Almost always, a set-back that really worries you happens after a period of relative calm. You can gain strength by remembering this calm, remembering how well you've done. If you can, list out the issues you've worked on and solved, and celebrate the progress you've made.

3 Remember what you have forgotten

Set-backs often occur because you have forgotten what you did last time that had an impact. So think back to what you understood; remember what you did that changed things. What worked last time will probably work this time, if you do it with confidence. ’

! ============= *Task* =============

Fall-back plans

Choose one set-back that you think you could have in the future. What might it be? What might happen? How might your relationship get into trouble again?

Now, together, think of three ways that you could both cope. This might be by trying to understand each other more fully. It might be by remembering to put into practice some of the skills you've learned in this book. It might be by getting outside support.

Plan ahead. Then if that set-back happens, you'll know exactly how to handle it. !

OTHER PEOPLE – HELP OR HINDRANCE?

Your progress in rebuilding your relationship may not only be down to you. Other people around you will always influence you, individually, and as a couple. When you first suffer problems, then as you decide to stay together, as you work to improve your relationship, your success or failure will always be affected by those around you; their reactions, their opinions and their hidden motives.

Insisting that everything is all right

First, even when faced with the most obvious evidence that you are having problems, family, friends and children may well deny that there is anything wrong. They will change the subject if you try to mention it; reassure you when you express worries and concerns. In some ways this is helpful; it means that they won't try to pressure you into taking action, leaving, staying or seeking counselling before you are ready. But it also means that you may find it difficult to ask these people for support to change things, because they will simply tell you that nothing needs changing, and try to undermine you if you aim for change.

Blaming one of you, supporting the other

Alternatively, family and friends may feel free to express their fears on behalf of one of you, and their anger towards the other. If you are the one being blamed, you may feel horrified at the strength of feeling against you. Such blame is obviously unhelpful. If you possibly can, avoid these people until you and your partner feel stronger in your relationship.

If you are the one who's not being blamed, this can feel very supportive, but it will also make it more difficult for you to become involved again in your relationship: you may join other people in blaming your partner or you may feel you are letting these people down if you start supporting your partner again. Remember that if you decide to give up on your relationship simply because of others' influence, you may never forgive yourself and you will certainly find it difficult ever to forgive them. Once again, it is probably most useful to your partnership to cut down on your contact with these people until you are strong enough to stand up to them if they query your decision.

Pressuring you to get help

Many counsellors reported that couples turned up for their first session saying, 'Mum told us we had to come', 'Dad said that counselling was the best thing for us'. This book aims to support you if you seek counselling, because it is almost always positively helpful when a relationship is in difficulty. But counselling is only helpful if you yourself choose it. If you go to counselling, or even buy this book only because someone else has told you to, you may resent having to do what you are told, and that may undermine the process. Of course, if you try counselling on someone else's advice and do find it useful, it will help. But 'force-fed counselling', however well-meaning the people who are force-feeding you, will rarely be successful.

Thinking that your relationship is theirs

People who have themselves been through relationship problems may try to support and advise you as if your difficulties are the same as theirs were. This not only means that the advice they offer may be inappropriate. Far more dangerously, it may mean that they have a hidden agenda. They may actually want you either to do what they did, or do what they really wished they had done: stayed with their partner, or split up. They want this because they want you to be happy, but they don't realise that every relationship is completely different from every other; and that what was right for them may not be what is right for you. And, in a nasty twist, if you do make your relationship work when other people were advising you to split up, then in the years to come they may undermine you, always reminding you of the crisis, always warning you that it could so easily happen again.

This is what happened for Dot and Tom. Dot was an electrical assembly supervisor, Tom was a centre lathe turner for the same firm. They had got to know each other gradually. It was over a year before Tom plucked up the courage to ask Dot out, and she accepted.

She learned that he loved his work, but it was clear from the start that he had very little self-confidence. Dot encouraged him to go to night school, and aim for promotion to supervisor. When he got it, no one was more pleased than Dot.

No one was less pleased, however, than Tom's mother Sheila. Dot had learned early on in their relationship that Tom lived with his mother, who was divorced from a husband who had left her for another woman. Herself coming from a close-knit family, whom she visited regularly, Dot found nothing odd in Tom's living at home, but as the two of them became more involved, she did get worried by the influence his mother seemed to have over him. At first, Tom wouldn't even stay overnight with Dot because his mother hated to be left alone, and when his promotion to supervisor meant he had to start working permanent nights, Sheila complained bitterly that he was neglecting her.

For a while, though, Dot and Tom seemed to be good for each other. She liked to support him; he gave her the love and attention she wanted. He reminded her strongly of her younger brother, whom she'd always got on well with. After a year together, and after a number of pitched battles with Sheila, Dot moved out of her flat, and they found a house together.

As they started to become more settled, however, things began to go wrong. Tom missed his mother, and felt guilty about having abandoned her just as his father had done. And as he and Dot started to lose the first excitement of romance, and come to terms with the nitty-gritty of living together, Tom started to miss the total mothering that life back home had offered him. Dot expected him to behave like an adult, to give as well as take. Tom began to visit Sheila regularly; Dot found out and they rowed, so then he went on visiting, but without telling Dot.

When they came to counselling, they were both weary and sad, but not completely at the end. Dot desperately wanted Tom to make the break and commit himself to her; she even suggested they move away from the area but this seemed to him to be a complete betrayal of his mother. They explored their family situations deeply during counselling, and seemed to be making headway.

Then one day, during a session, Tom revealed that each week he was telling Sheila what was happening in the counselling. She, unsurprisingly, kept telling him that it was all a waste of time, telling him not to carry out the exercises, telling him to leave Dot.

Dot was appalled. She felt utterly betrayed by Tom telling his mother things that, in her words 'I only wanted you and the counsellor to hear.' She announced, in the session, that she was leaving and stormed out.

Faced by the very real possibility that he could lose Dot, Tom suddenly made his choice. He truly seemed to commit himself to Dot for the first time. At the next session, they agreed that he should cut down his visits to Sheila, that they should always visit her together, that he shouldn't again discuss the counselling with her. Six months after beginning sessions, their relationship seemed to be stable, they had set a date for their wedding, and they agreed to take a break from counselling.

A year later, they were back, now married. They were still holding their partnership together, but now Dot was pregnant, Sheila had become even more hostile. Faced with the evidence that Tom and Dot were committed to each other, she had started to drag up from the past their previous crisis, reminding Tom, often within Dot's hearing, that they'd had to go to counselling so were they really a stable couple? Stressed by the fact that they were facing parenthood, Dot and Tom felt very pressured by this, and were back in counselling not so much because they felt their relationship was falling apart from within, as because they felt it was being threatened from the outside.

The counselling helped Dot and Tom not only to acknowledge how much love they felt for each other but also to face the fact that someone else was trying to force them apart. Tom was clear that his first loyalty was to Dot, and the counselling supported him to realise that, however guilty he felt about standing firm against Sheila, he had to do it. Tom and Dot left counselling feeling much stronger and more able to cope with the situation.

Seeing your relationship improvement as their problem
Strange as it may seem, some people see any improvement to your relationship as being a bad thing. Particularly if they have disliked one of you, or disapproved of your partnership, they may regard your relationship success as the worst news. In the same way, if they

have suffered a break-up themselves and you seem to have avoided it, they may be jealous.

Two special cases here are children and lovers. If your relationship problem has resulted in an affair, it is unlikely that the lover will welcome your getting back together and staying back together. It will be almost impossible for him or her to retain a place in the triangle if your relationship improves, so they may apply pressure, they may use blackmail, they may threaten to reveal everything. Because of this – and because relationship improvement is impossible if one of you is still dividing your time and energy between a partner and a lover – an affair will probably have to end if your partnership is to survive.

Children too may, in a curious way, resist you changing. They almost always want you to stay together and are happy that you have done. Even so, your conflicts may have given them rewards. They may have got 'goodies' for siding with each of you, benefits from playing you both off against each other, attention that they wouldn't have got from a completely happy couple. As you rebuild your relationship, you may have less time for your children; may provide a more united front when disciplining them; may even start – to their deep embarrassment – being romantic or sexual with each other again.

However your children react, there are certain things you can do to make it easier for them to support you. Give them as much information as you can about what is going on; not loading them down with your problems, but being clear that you are trying new things in order to get on better together. Second, don't use them as 'pseudo-counsellors'. However adult or mature they are, they aren't sufficiently separate from the situation to help you, or to escape unharmed if you ask them to cope with your problems.

Last, make it clear just how important your partnership is to you. If your children complain because you are leaving them with baby-sitters more often, spending more time talking to each other, or going away for a weekend without them, ask yourself this question. Would you prefer to have a partnership that will hopefully last for your lifetime, or children who will be satisfied for the next few years and will eventually leave you anyway when they find loving partners of their own?

‘ —————————Talking point ——————————

Friend or foe?

As you both start to realise that your relationship is going to survive, you can also work out who will support you in the future, and who won't.

List ten people who are part of your life: family, friends, work contacts. This could include your children, parents, boss or colleagues.

Alongside each person, each of you should mark whether, in your honest opinion, this person will support you to make the relationship work; may be ambivalent about whether you make the relationship work; or will clearly be against your making the relationship work.

The results may be hard to bear. You may find that you both agree that some people will undermine you. If so, you have to decide how to handle this: not see them for a while; see them only when you are together rather than separately; be open with them about how you want them to behave.

You may find that you disagree on who will support you and who won't. Talk this through until you have worked out, together, a way of handling these people that you are both happy with.

Where you discover people who will support you, ask yourselves how you can ask for this support, accept this support, and use this support.

,

—————LONG-TERM MAINTENANCE—————

There will almost certainly come a point where, if your relationship does improve, it is no longer in crisis nor even troubled. Perhaps you are both getting on so well that you feel you have fallen back in love again. More likely, you will simply have gained a quiet confidence in your partnership that convinces you that this is where you want to be for a long, long time to come. This is the point at which you need to develop long-term ways of making sure that your relationship is never again rocked so severely.

The most basic strategy here is to work out how to spot problems between you before they start. This doesn't mean to say that you should both be neurotic about your relationship, nor demand reassurance from each other every day. It does mean making sure that if one of you is even slightly disturbed by what is happening, you can say so. Some couples develop 'codes' to check out that they are both happy with the way things are going. 'Still love me?' is a classic way of checking out. One Relate client used to ask her partner, as they passed each other round the house 'Are we still bunnies?'; another knew that things were on an even keel when his partner hugged him every day as they awoke. If this 'code sign' is missing, or if when you offer it you get an uncertain response, then you can both sit down and face the challenges together.

Those challenges are likely to be of two kinds. First, it could be that without realising it, you have not actually solved all the problems that originally put your relationship into difficulty. Perhaps you sorted out the issues that were frustrating you, but never really did anything about the poor communication which allowed those issues to build up in the first place. Perhaps you solved the issues and started to communicate well, but left some underlying painful emotion unresolved. The fact is that you can remove the surface tension, but still not meet the basic needs of one or both of you, and if you don't, it is likely that you will continue to have difficulties some way down the line. So, if you think that your original problems are starting to creep back into the relationship, go back and take another look at what is happening. You may need to understand more, to communicate more, to learn more about coping with your emotions. It's not that you didn't sort things out the first time round; it is just that there is more to do.

The second kind of long-term challenge you may face is that something completely new happens in your life. Then this creates completely new problems between you. If you have lived happily for a while, and if your relationship has been working well for a while, then difficulties are more than likely to be coming from some kind of life change that is affecting you. Part 2 of this book, on Understanding, has already explored what can change, because of the different life stages you may pass through, and the different life events that may happen to you. These life changes can be immensely exciting and challenging and there is really no reason, given good communication between you, why they shouldn't make your partnership better rather than worse. But if you do start to suffer difficulties again, it is worthwhile checking what has recently been happening in your life. If you do know that a life stage or life event is approaching, it is also worthwhile planning ahead and making sure that you are fully prepared.

A couple who were able to use counselling to face a life stage that they both knew was near were Norman and Lynn. In their early forties, they felt that they had had a good marriage, but now the children were becoming independent, they were both anxious about the future.

Lynn was a working mum who liked her job in a travel agency, but she also enjoyed her children's company, and the day-to-day pleasure of supporting them and looking after them. She feared that life would be empty without them. Norman too, was dreading the day that his children would leave. He had loved bringing them up, and had to some extent held back in his job, turning down promotion so that he wouldn't have to travel and leave the family alone.

Although Norman and Lynn still got on well, they were aware that things weren't as good as they had been when the children had been younger. The early years of their marriage had been difficult. At one point, Lynn had left and lived with another man for a while, but had come back to Norman when she realised that she had made a mistake. Once they were settled again, and sure of their relationship, she had become pregnant, and that had put the seal on their commitment. They had been very happy together, and had thoroughly enjoyed the last twenty years. Both spoke of the children as being the glue that bound them together and both admitted being afraid that when this glue was gone, they would have problems. They realised that one of the things that they had been doing, as that time approached, was pulling back from each other in order to protect themselves in case something did go wrong. It was at that point that they came to counselling, as they put it 'to get in quick before we hit trouble'.

Their counsellor suggested that Norman and Lynn start now to rebuild their relationship in preparation for their youngest child leaving. Their family was quite old enough to look after themselves if Norman and Lynn started taking time for themselves, so they started spending days and weekends away. Given the time and the skill to talk things through, they discovered things about each other that they had never suspected: about their likes and dislikes, their work, their interests and their feelings. They needed to re-learn who they were, how best to support each other, how best to love each other. They are still in counselling, making sure that they have completely resolved all the many painful issues that they built up between them, but they are now planning confidently for the time when their youngest daughter finally leaves home next year.

Norman and Lynn were able to tackle their potential problems as they approached them. You may want to look back at the descriptions of life changes in Chapter 10 and make sure that you are prepared for them in advance. Many can be eased by practical action: organising your new life roles when you retire; finding out about medication to ease the symptoms of the menopause. In many cases, you can get outside help: child-care support when you have a baby; career counselling after a job loss. Talking through the possible problems of each life change as it approaches – and reminding yourselves of the possible rewards – will make it much more likely that you will be able to cope.

Whatever the kind of challenge you think you are facing, you can always go to Relate for support. Whether or not you've been working with a counsellor since your problems started, you can turn to one at any time along the way. Relate counsellors will not be offended if you go to them having previously tried to solve your difficulties alone; they will also be very happy to see you if you have started counselling, stopped because things are going well, and now need to return because you have hit a set-back. Counsellors will appreciate the work you have already done, and will help you to build on that work.

'—————————Talking point—————————

Cracking the code

Discuss together what codes you have in your relationship. How do you signal contentment or dissatisfaction to each other? How do you signal that you want to touch down and negotiate about a problem? These codes might be a word, a phrase, a non-verbal sign. If you don't feel you have any codes, then agree on at least one that aims to signal whether you are happy or not. Use this code regularly for a few days, so that you get into the habit.

,

_____ONWARDS AND UPWARDS_____

At some point along the road of your relationship, you may both want to make some sort of statement of how far you have come. You may wish to mark your deeper commitment in some visible way. Your reasons for doing this may be the same as the reasons couples have for having a formal marriage ceremony. You are celebrating your relationship. You are promising each other a future of commitment. You are also marking the start of a new phase in your lives.

What kind of statement of these things would be right for you? Relate counsellors told me of many such statements that their clients had made. You may want to plant a tree to symbolise your growing relationship. You may want to buy rings, a sign of your commitment to each other. You may want to put aside your old rings; one counsellor spoke of a couple who held a 'burial service' over a wedding band when replacing it with a new one.

You may extend your statement to other people. You may want a ceremony where you repeat your wedding vows, or new ones that are now more meaningful for you. You may do this in private, even in secret, or you may do it in front of your friends, family or children, asking them to witness your new life together, and support you through any future difficulties. If you aren't yet married, you may in fact want to take that step as a sign that you are now confident in your new partnership.

Whatever statement you do both make, and however relieved, delighted and thankful you are that you are able to make it, remember that it is only the beginning. For once you learn how to improve your relationship, you also learn that there need never be an end to that improvement. The more you understand about each other, the more you are able to understand. The more you change your relationship for the better, the more you make it possible to keep on changing. Now that you have realised you can gain a deep commitment to each other, you'll also realise that, as the years pass, there is every chance that you will be able to make that commitment even deeper.

!—————————————— *Task* ——————————————

Future vision

Do this exercise only if you both now feel that your relationship is moving forwards and that your real problems are behind you.

Imagine yourselves, together and happy, in ten years' time. Be realistic, but don't worry too much about job prospects or possible money problems in your life. Concentrate on your relationship.

Where will you be? Where might you be living? Where will your children be, if you have them or plan to have them? What will each of you look like? How will you spend each day? Will you be working? What will you do at weekends? How will you be relating to each other? How will other people see your relationship, from the outside?

What will be the best thing about still being together in a decade's time?
                                                                    !

FURTHER HELP

The address and telephone number of your local Relate centre will be found in the telephone directory. A telephone enquiry will provide information about the centre's counselling services, and can be used to arrange an initial appointment.

The organisation's headquarters is in Rugby: Relate National Marriage Guidance, Herbert Gray College, Little Church Street, Rugby, Warwickshire, CV21 3AP. Tel: (01788) 573241.

Headquarters' staff will provide information about Relate's involvement in the development of social policy, and will respond to issues raised by the media relating to family life. Intending clients should contact a local centre in order to gain access to counselling.

Relate's distinctive focus is the adult couple, recognising the benefits of this focus to the mental, physical and emotional health of adults and children involved. This focus recognises different cultural understandings of marriage and other couple relationships, and encompasses work with the adults together or on their own, at any time in the life or ending of their relationship, whether the couple wish to stay together or whether they wish to separate.

Other useful organisations

Age Concern offers information, practical advice and help for the elderly:
Age Concern (England), Astral House, 1,268 London Road, Norbury, London, SW16 4ER. Tel: (0181) 679 8000.
Age Concern Scotland, 113 Rose Street, Edinburgh, EH2 3DT. Tel: (0131) 220 3345.
Age Concern Wales, 4th Floor, 1 Cathedral Road, Cardiff, South Glamorgan, CF1 9SD. Tel: (01222) 371566.

The British Association for Counselling, 1 Regent Place, Rugby, Warwickshire. Tel: (01788) 550899. A central organisation which provides information about individuals and organisations who offer counselling.

British Pregnancy Advisory Service, Austy Manor, Wootton Wawen, Solihull, B95 6BX. Tel: (0345) 304030. Information, advice, counselling and practical help on all issues surrounding pregnancy, contraception, termination and fertility.

Marriage Concern, 1 Blythe Mews, Blythe Road, London W14 0NW. Tel: (0171) 371 1341. An advisory service offering support to couples where one or both partners are Catholic.

Compassionate Friends, 6 Denmark Street, Bristol, BS1 5DQ. Tel: (01272) 292778. A befriending service for those whose children have died.

Cruse, 126 Sheen Road, Richmond, Surrey TW9 1UR. Tel: (0181) 940 4818. Help, support and counselling for the bereaved.

Gingerbread, 16-17 Clerkenwell Close, London EC1R 0AA. Tel: (0171) 336 8183. A support organisation for single-parent families.

The Family Planning Information Service, 2-12 Pentonville Road, London N1 9FP. Tel: (0171) 837 4044. An organisation offering advice and support on all aspects of contraception, pregnancy and sexual health.

Focus (Forum for Occupational Counselling and Unemployment Services Ltd) Northside House, Mount Pleasant, Barnet, Hertfordshire, EN4 9EB. Tel: (0181) 441 9300. Support and counselling on all aspects of career issues, job search, job change, redundancy and retirement.

Irish Family Planning Association, Half Penny Court, 36–37 Lower Ormond Quay, Dublin. Tel: (0110) 353 1872/5033. Offers advice and support on family-planning issues.

Jewish Marriage Guidance Council, 23 Ravenshurst Avenue, London NW4 4EE. Tel: (0181) 203 6311. An advisory service offering support to couples where one or both partners are Jewish.

National Childbirth Trust, Oldham Terrace, Acton, London W3 6NH. Tel: (0181) 992 8637. Organisation offering support in pregnancy, child-bearing and child-rearing.

Parentline-OPUS (Organisation for Parents under Stress), Endway House, The Endway, Hadleigh, Essex, SS7 2AN. Tel: (01702) 554782. Offers support and befriending to parents stressed because of their children.

Parent Network, Room 2, Winchester House, 11 Cranmer Road, London SW9 6EJ. Tel: (0171) 735 1214. A course and support system for parents who wish to raise their children more effectively and cope with children's problems.

The Samaritans offer telephone and befriending help to people who feel desperate. Their local address and phone number will be in your telephone directory. Available 24 hours every day of the year.

SANDS (Stillbirth and Neonatal Death Society), 28 Portland Place, London, W1N 4DE. Tel: (0171) 436 5881. Support and advice for bereaved parents.

Books

The Courage to Heal by Ellen Bass and Laura Davis (Vermilion, 1991). A self-help book for women who have been sexually abused during childhood.

Divorce: The Things You Never Thought You'd Need to Know by Jill Black (Elliot Right Way, 1993). A practical guide to surviving divorce.

Divorce and Your Children by Anne Hooper (Robson Books, 1990). How to help your children survive your divorce.

Families and How to Survive Them by John Cleese and Robin Skynner (Vermilion, 1993). A light-hearted but extremely informative look at how our families make us who we are.

How to Make Love to the Same Person for the Rest of Your Life by Dagmar O'Connor (Virgin, 1993). A book to help you enhance your sex life within a committed partnership.

Living, Loving and Ageing by Wendy and Sally Greengross (Age Concern, 1989). A guide to help older people make the most of their sexual potential. Also available in a large-print edition.

Men and Sex by Bernard Zilbergeld, (HarperCollins, 1995). A direct, comprehensive book for men wanting to know more about sex and to be better lovers.

The Relate Guide to Better Relationships by Sarah Litvinoff (Vermilion, 1998). For couples starting their relationship or wanting to improve it.

The Relate Guide to Starting Again by Sarah Litvinoff (Vermilion, 1993). For couples who are divorcing or divorced.

The Relate Guide to Sex in Loving Relationships by Sarah Litvinoff (Vermilion, 1992). For couples who particularly want to improve their sex lives.

Step-parents and their Children by Stephen Collins (Souvenir, 1988). A guide to becoming a step-parent.

Sexual Happiness for Men and *Sexual Happiness for Women* by Maurice Yaffe and Elizabeth Fenwick (Dorling Kindersley, 1992). Comprehensive, quiz-format-type books covering most sexual issues.

Working Mother: A Practical Handbook by Sarah Litvinoff and Marianne Velmans (Pocket Books, 1993). For working mums in all situations.

Women's Pleasure, or How to Have an Orgasm as Often as You Want by Rachel Swift (Pan Books, 1994). A self-help book for women who want to have orgasms, or more and better ones.

INDEX